OTHER BOOKS BY WILLIE MORRIS

THE GHOSTS OF MEDGAR EVERS

RANDOM HOUSE NEW YORK

Willie Morris

THE GHOSTS OF MEDGAR EVERS

A Tale of Race, Murder, Mississippi, and Hollywood

Portions of this work were originally published in different form
in *George, New Choices,* and *The New York Times.*

Grateful acknowledgment is made to the following for permission
to reprint previously published material:

ADDISON WESLEY LONGMAN: Excerpts from pages 26, 56, 208, and
253 in *Of Long Memory: Mississippi and the Murder of Medgar
Evers* by Adam Nossiter. Copyright © 1994 by Adam Nossiter.
Reprinted by permission of Addison Wesley Longman.

WAYNE M. ROGERS: Excerpt from a letter by Wayne M. Rogers
about *The Ghosts of Mississippi,* which was published in the
Los Angeles Times. Reprinted by permission of Wayne M. Rogers.

Library of Congress Cataloging-in-Publication Data
Morris, Willie.
The ghosts of Medgar Evers: a tale of race, murder, Mississippi,
and Hollywood / by Willie Morris.
p.   cm.
Includes bibliographical references and index.
ISBN 0-679-45956-1
1. Ghosts of Mississippi (Motion picture)   2. Evers, Medgar Wiley,
1925–1963—Assassination.   3. Jackson (Miss.)—Race relations.
4. Mississippi—Race relations.   5. Beckwith, Byron De La.
I. Title.
PN1997.G447M67   1998   791.43'72—dc21   97-24077

Random House website address: www.randomhouse.com
Printed in the United States of America on acid-free paper
9 8 7 6 5 4 3 2
First Edition

Book design by J. K. Lambert

To three brave Mississippians:

Aaron Henry (1922–1997),
Bobby DeLaughter,
and, again, JoAnne

A friend loves at all times,
and kinsfolk are born to share adversity.

—Proverbs 17:17

As soon as I heard wheels I knowed who was coming. That was him and bound to be him. It was the right nigger heading in a new white car up his driveway towards his garage with the light shining, but stopping before he got there, maybe not to wake them. That was him. I knowed it when he put out the car lights and put his foot out and I knowed him standing dark against the light. I knowed him then like I know me now. I knowed him even by his still, listening back. . . .

He had to be the one. He stood right still and waited against the light, his back was fixed, fixed on me like a preacher's eyeballs when he's yelling, "Are you saved?" He's the one.

I'd already brought up my rifle, I'd already taken my sights. And I'd already got him . . .

—Eudora Welty, "Where Is the Voice Coming From?"

CONTENTS

THE GHOSTS OF MEDGAR EVERS

Chapter 1

GHOSTS

This is not a book about the *business* of moviemaking, or the inner workings of the modern corporate film studio, or the often fierce competition among high-powered executives, stars, and agents, or the sophisticated technology demanded in contemporary motion pictures. All these are important, of course, and as a layman and newcomer with no previous expertise in filmmaking I have tried to deal with them.

Rather, this book is about the individual people involved in a large endeavor in what everyone in the trade calls "the Industry," how they came together, the day-to-day realities, the eternal struggle in good movies between commerce and art, and how these things related to the essence of this particular film itself. It is about one peculiar place, Mississippi, set as it is in the larger American context, and race and commitment and justice, and how all these crystallized in a real-life drama: the interrelated complexities of the merging of these, and what these might suggest about the cosmos of Hollywood and the modern American society that it both shapes and reflects. My intention, then, was to follow from beginning to conclusion the filming of a movie about which I had some inside knowledge; to make a side-road dalliance into a subculture I knew little about, a dalliance that might interest readers much as, for instance, *Picture,* Lillian Ross's enthralling 1952 book on the filming of John Huston's *The Red Badge of Courage,* had, and in a different perspective Sidney Lumet's 1995 *Making Movies* and John Gregory Dunne's 1997 *Monster: Living Off the Big Screen.* All this would prove a personal diversion from the essentially solitary calling of the writer, for a Hollywood movie is a surpassingly communal enterprise, one that in a maverick kind of spirit I welcomed and know I will never encounter again.

Along the way, however, this book became about more than that—it became a chronicle of the hazards, pitfalls, and surprises involved these days in making a meaningful, dramatic, nondocumentary movie based on authentic and recent history, especially on such a volatile history set in such a volatile milieu and encompassing such a range of flesh-and-blood living people to be depicted with their own proudly personal and emotional investments, for these incipient stresses were always just beneath the surface of things.

Ghosts of Mississippi was perhaps fated to be embraced in the turmoils and vagaries of our times: a contemporary American culture, in William Styron's words, "dominated by hostility and suspicion, by doctrinaire attitudes in matters of gender and race, by an ugly spirit of partisanship and exclusion, and by an all-round failure of mutual generosity." The controversies and conflicts that would come later might in some measure have been foreseen, and indeed the elements of these were quietly present at the very start, but I myself was not nearly so prescient as to have augured their full dimensions. From one of the finest film directors of our day on down, there was an honest spirit of excitement that enveloped this film from its inception. I had seldom seen people so caught up in an undertaking. Everyone was trying so hard and was so happy, with little clue of what might be waiting. Would *Ghosts of Mississippi* satisfy its original promise? If so, why? If not, why not? If

Ghosts had subsequently swept the Oscars and been a box-office smash, this book would likely have turned into a valentine to moviemaking, to the drama and allure and power of it, but in movies as in life the best and most honorable intentions sometimes go awry. Making an ambitious movie with an eye to human things that matter is never a clear sail, and certain innocent decisions, not in the least devious, would come to have unforeseen results. In a most contemporary way *Ghosts of Mississippi* would become not only a movie, but an almost symbolic public document raising questions about who we are as Americans and Southerners in the late 1990s, who we are as whites and blacks, and what we expect or do not expect of ourselves. *Ghosts* would elicit responses, both petulant and admiring, across an unusual national spectrum.

Hollywood was the last place in the world I might have expected to raise certain questions and to learn certain truths about Mississippi and Mississippians and America and Americans. The filming of this movie would turn out to be as delicate and multilayered as the final Beckwith trial itself and all that had gone before, for *Ghosts* would represent nothing if not a stark reliving of an unquenchable past.

—

In 1994 I was drawn to an extraordinary story. That year in Jackson, Mississippi, I covered for a national magazine the third and final trial of the radical white supremacist Byron De La Beckwith for the June 12, 1963, assassination of the thirty-seven-year-old Mississippi civil rights leader Medgar Evers, shot in the back with a powerful deer rifle in the driveway of his house before his wife and three young children. I had interested a longtime comrade of mine, a prominent Hollywood and Broadway producer, in pursuing the intriguing tale of how the murderer, freed by two hung juries thirty years before—both all white and all male—was finally brought to justice by Mississippians. (Beckwith's lawyers would appeal the decision to the state supreme court.) Fred Zollo, the producer, had gone to Rob Reiner, the director; the film would come to fruition much more swiftly than the vast majority of big Hollywood movies.

—

To understand the world, William Faulkner once said, you have to understand a place like Mississippi. One loved a place, he wrote, not so much because of its virtues, but despite its faults. Faulkner understood Mississippi in his soul, and so did Medgar Evers. It is America's Ireland. Richard Ford observes that it, as with the larger South, has produced such a wealth of writers because it is so complicated it takes that many writers to interpret it.

One of Faulkner's most persistent themes, as Malcolm Cowley wrote about the great tortured labyrinth of his work, was "the belief in Isaac McCaslin's heart that the land itself has been cursed by slavery, and that the only way for him to escape the curse is to relinquish the land," and that the proponents of slavery and secession, in that dark curse, "built not on the rock of stern morality but on the shifting sands of opportunism and moral brigandage." Faulkner's work abounds in the truths and complexities and harkenings, the Dilseys and Beauchamps and Christmases, the severance the society inflicts on two seven-year-old boys who are comrades, one white and one black, and that to the character Roth Edmonds is the "day the old curse of his fathers, the old haughty ancestral pride based not on any value but an accident of geography, stemmed not from courage and honor but from wrong and shame descended to him"; and aging Ike McCaslin, in the last finger of the vanishing Mississippi Delta woods, tells Roth Edmonds's black mistress to go north and marry one of her own kind: "the instant when, without moving at all, she blazed silently down at him. 'Old man,' she said, 'have you lived so long and forgotten so much that you don't remember anything you ever knew or felt or even heard about love?' "

When you live in Mississippi you cannot escape race, because it is in its deepest convoluted being and in the very soil, which haunts you with its lineage. In his 1996 *Dixie Rising: How the South Is Shaping American Values, Politics, and Culture,* Peter Applebome, an Easterner with *The New York Times,* observed of race in the South "what Southerners tend to know instinctively and Yankees have never figured out. Race is so powerful that we usually can only see it in searing, vivid colors—'I Have a Dream' or *Mississippi Burning* . . . that there are moments when you remember that the shades of gray are so infinite and subtle, the dreams so elusive, that the bright lights are more likely to blind than to guide."

It is no accident that Mississippi elicits such rage and passion and fidelity in its sons and daughters of both races, in Faulkner and Evers, or that Northerners have forever been beguiled by what takes place here, for Mississippi has always been the crucible of the national guilt. All one has to do is read *Dark Journey,* Neil McMillen's history of Mississippi from the 1880s to the 1930s, with its unremitting accounts of cruelty, murder, and injustice, to have some sense of the tragedy of this soil. "As ye sow," the Book says, "so shall ye reap."

I am a sixth-generation Mississippian. I grew up in the time of "the troubles," as people sometimes refer to them here now, absorbing the turmoils and extremes of the Delta, my native ground. I went to college in Texas and in England, became an editor and writer, and observed Mississippi from a distance. I never met Medgar Evers and was living in New York at the time of his death. I wrote a book on the massive integration of the Mississippi public schools in 1970 and sensed the gradual softening of my home state's more virulent strains of racism. Federal legislation and court decisions were central to the salubrious changes that took place.

But in Mississippi the outcroppings of the past are forever with us. After years in the East, I returned here in 1980, to live and die in Dixie. There are, to draw on the Lillian Hellman title, abundant pentimentos here.

The confluence of past and present, the day-to-day mingling of the dark ghosts and the better angels of our nature, graphically evoked for me on the sets of the movie, was strange and often painful but emotionally redemptive at the same time. There has always been what historian David Sansing cites as "the *other* Mississippi," the Mississippi not of illiteracy but of literary tradition, not of ignominy but of nobility, not of nihilism and injustice but of charity and humanity. In both symbolism and substance, the merging of this real story and this real movie embodied for me something of the best of that indwelling vein.

The tumult of its elements and the tension of its paradoxes lay at the core of the town where I grew up, Yazoo City, sitting there on the precipice of the great Delta flatland where providence had set us down. Its rough-hewn democracy, complicated by all the visible textures of caste and class, encompassed harmless boyhood fun right along with all sorts of treacheries and tensions and deceits: murders and other lesser transgressions, rank hypocrisies, churchgoing sanctimonies, unrepentant avarice, and above all, I would someday grow to see, racial hatred and calculated repression.

The blacks who constituted nearly 60 percent of the town's population were largely quiet, or so it seemed. But every so often there were rumors of a mass uprising, and my father and the other white men would stock up on bullets and shotgun shells and lock all the doors and windows. It was planters' heaven then. The larger plantation owners, who were once going broke on ten-cent cotton, were now getting the Roosevelt relief money, funneling it to the workers in the off season, and then shutting it off when they needed the labor. They were churchgoers and whiskey drinkers all. One noticed the prolix restlessness of the young playboy planters who drove the newest Cadillacs or Lincolns or sports cars to the Peabody or the Moon Lake Casino or Bourbon Street or the roof of the Heidelberg in Jackson where they brought their own sourmash whiskey in brown paper bags and danced with the wives of other men. In 1934, the year of my birth, 44 percent of all Agricultural Adjustment Administration payments in excess of ten thousand dollars nationwide went to ten counties in the Mississippi Delta, as cited in the *Encyclopedia of Southern Culture*. "This largesse facilitated the mechanization and consolidation of agriculture, and as federal farm programs continued, the money kept rolling in." In 1967, four years after Medgar Evers's death, "Delta planter and U.S. Senator James Eastland received $167,000 in federal payments. The Delta's poor blacks were not nearly so fortunate, as a power structure dominated by lavishly subsidized planters declared war on the War on Poverty."

The impoverishment of the black people, in their hovels in town and their tenant shacks in the flatland, was wrenching and inscrutable, as Medgar himself would learn firsthand as an insurance salesman in the Delta in the early 1950s. And so too was that of the poor whites. We children of the middle class absorbed all this as mindlessly as we would the insects or the fireflies in driftless random, or the red water truck of the summertimes with our prancing in its wake. These childhood and teenage years were poised, fragilely and inevitably, before *Brown* v. *Board of Education.*

There are intense memories. In *North Toward Home,* published in the late 1960s, I described a scene of those years. On each side of the bayou running through the Delta side of town to the Yazoo River was a low concrete wall only inches from the street. On Saturdays the blacks sat in a long row on the top of the wall. White men in soiled T-shirts, with anxious, marginal countenances, would drive by in cars decorated with Rebel flags and open the doors and watch the black people topple backward off the wall like dominoes. "That really didn't happen, did it?" my Northern readers asked.

There are not many prospects in America so beautiful as a field of white cotton in the early fall; and if you stand in the right spot in late afternoon in the Delta, you catch the golden glow of autumn's setting sun, the verdant green of the trees along the rivers, the bright red mechanical cotton pickers, the panoply of white in the undulating gloaming. It makes you feel big and important in such a moment—at least those who never worked these fields—to know that the ancient Egyptians grew this same cotton, and that it has been with us since hieroglyphics. There are not many American places where you can *see* so far, thirty miles away, it seems, under the copious sweep of the horizons. You can stand up there in Kansas or Nebraska and do that, but there is nothing to see except more of Kansas and Nebraska. Yet, in this glutinous and devouring soil, cotton has forever pertained to blood and guilt, as it must have too with the Egyptians.

This incredible Delta land consumed and shaped me, irrevocably and forever, as a child—it was not in my mind then, only in my pores—and as a man and a writer I find it dwells in my being. I love it beyond all measure, and I fear it too, as I always did. It is the very power of this land itself that makes you both love and fear it. It is what I am, and always will be till I die.

Here is a summer tableau from my boyhood: My friends and I drive in a vintage Plymouth with dual exhausts through the Delta stretches of Yazoo County, along some of the same roads that Medgar Evers and Byron De La Beckwith would separately travel in the fifties and sixties. All about us is the warm, deep aroma of July. The asphalt road on which we are going is built a little higher than the land that encompasses it; there are the occasional BURMA SHAVE signs and, every other mile, it seems, a small concrete cross off the side where someone died in a car accident. Soon we pass an unpainted country store mere yards from a horseshoe lake; turtles bask in the sun on logs in the water, and on the gallery of the store a sign advertising its minnows, worms, and crickets: OUR WORMS CATCH FISH OR DIE TRYING. In the distance are the spooky old Indian mounds where we came as children in search of arrowheads and earthen fragments of pottery. In the flatness they are the only rises; they resemble miniature grassy hills.

Soon we find ourselves on one of the largest plantations of our neighborhood. It is three thousand continuous acres, we have always been told, beginning at a tortuous creek seething with crawfish and cottonmouths and stretching all the way to the most dramatic bend in the entire Yazoo River. All about us the plants show green and white in the rows; occasionally deeper green patches appear in the farther fields, which means they are experimenting with rice and irrigation. POSTED signs dot the dark soil. As we drive farther, the blacks are everywhere, ambling along the road, bent low before the cotton in the ancient ritual, ebony silhouettes in the sunshine. They stand and wave, as if the car itself is a magnet that ripples among the flesh. The tiny unpainted shacks pervade the landscape, often with a tree or two in front, a worn-out tire roped to it for a swing, a modest vegetable garden planted with corn and tomatoes, a slumping outhouse with a half-moon carved in the door, and a clothesline from which garments flutter in the breeze. After a time the shacks appear more frequently, in clusters along the road, with barefooted children in ragged clothes staring out at our approach, naked infants in the grassless yards, and hybrid dogs under the arching chinaberries. We go by the schoolhouse, a gaunt wooden structure set back from the road with a rusty sloping tin roof and, as if in afterthought, a whitewashed porch filled with derelict furniture. And then to the commissary, another unpainted and unadorned edifice, a dozen black men in front lifting sacks of flour from a truck and one of the enormous new mechanical pickers parked in back. A strange sense of doom seems to hover over the land itself.

"If it wasn't for the Negroes," I overheard a "moderate" white lawyer say in those Delta years, "people around here wouldn't have nothin' to talk about."

I remember pondering this; it was indeed the simple truth. Mainly they were *there*, they were *ours*, and they were blamed for everything wrong under the sun. "A servant of servants shall ye be unto his brethren." In the town, almost every house had its black maid, who for fifteen cents an hour left her own dwelling early in the morning and did not return until late afternoon—cooking, laundering, mopping, sweeping, as Medgar Evers's mother had done. They would take the dirty clothes home with them in straw baskets balanced on their heads, boiling them in iron washtubs, scrubbing them on washboards in their backyards, pressing them with irons heated over wood fires; their labors never ceased. Then almost every second house had its yard man, Jap or Redeye or

Shorty or Potluck or Shenandoah, who wore a sweaty bandanna and was given his own private Mason jar to drink tap water from. From the womb to the tomb, the blacks tended to the substantial whites of the town: their women raising the white infants, their men digging white graves, mowing the cemetery grass, clipping the hedges surrounding the very plots of the dead. In the proper season, the town blacks went out in trucks to the plantations to work from dawn to dusk. They lived in sprawling precincts with gravel or dirt roads and situated without rhyme or design, sometimes separate from the white sections, sometimes bordering and even mingling with them. If, through some precipitous act of nature, the blacks of our town suddenly vanished from the earth, we would have been strangely empty and bereft.

As a grown man I have thought often of those who labored so against the soil and who still live now in the town, or in Memphis or Chicago or Detroit or Gary or Los Angeles, but mostly in Chicago, to which they had drifted by the thousands from the Delta with their belongings in cardboard boxes and suitcases tied with cotton clothesline; others lie now in pine boxes under the very earth they once tended. It was mysterious and cruel and profoundly interior, that merging here in the Mississippi Delta of the great European and African sources; yet it was vital and even life-giving—as if we belonged together and yet did not, the barrier between us acute and invisible. It was very strange and hard.

One Sunday morning several years ago I found myself in a Shoney's in Clarksdale in the Delta having breakfast with my friend Alex Haley. As we sat in our booth, the word began to spread that he was there. First the black waitresses began coming up to talk with him and to ask him to sign his autograph on paper napkins, then one by one came the black workers from the kitchen. The news circulated quickly, and large numbers of black people began drifting in from Highway 61 outside. In a momentary lull my companion said, "I apologize for this. It's not me really. It's the effect *Roots* had on black people."

"On white people, too," I suggested. In minutes a number of white Deltans entered the establishment to seek a word with Alex Haley.

I have a white friend my age, Charles Henry, whose father once farmed in the upper Delta. His mother died when he was little, and his father was courting again, and for all purposes he was raised by an illiterate black muledriver named Shotgun, whom he loved. "The black people of the Delta didn't sail past the Statue of Liberty when *they* came to this country," my friend once said to me. "They made this place down here. They worked to death and got nothin', except just the ground itself, and it wasn't theirs either. I'd look out from my porch at night when I was a boy and see all the coal-oil lamps in their houses and wonder what they were thinking that night with their lamps blinking in the shadows. Now I know they were thinking of the same things I was."

—

Of this let there be no mistaking: It is the ghost of Medgar Evers, pervasive and implacable, that reigns over everything to follow in this narrative, even in deepest Hollywood. For that reason it is important for the reader to know precisely who he was, what he did, and why he was killed.

When I was later in New York City for the premiere of *Ghosts of Mississippi,* I would be approached by Richard Valeriani, the long-time NBC radio and television commentator, who wanted to know how close the film was to the actual facts. He had covered the civil rights leaders in the 1950s and 1960s, he said, and knew Medgar Evers well. "He was the best of them all," Valeriani said. "He was a very great man."

Medgar's family came from the area around Newton County, Mississippi, not far from where he himself was born and raised. His paternal grandparents were freed slaves and landowners. Over three hundred acres in nearby Scott County belonged to his paternal grandfather, Mike Evers, but whites later stole it from him

through legal chicanery. His paternal grandmother was part Cherokee; his maternal great-grandfather was white. His grandparents
were noted for being fiercely independent and for resisting the
white establishment. Medgar was named for his great-grandfather
Medgar Wright, who was half Indian and reputed to be an incorri-
gible slave. The derivation of the name Medgar is unknown, though
it was possibly a variation of Edgar.

Medgar Evers grew up on a small farm outside Decatur, Mississippi, with three sisters and two brothers. He and his older brother,
Charles, were close. Charles loved Medgar so much, he said, that
on cold winter nights when the wood fire had gone out, he would
get in bed first and warm up the sheets for him. Their father, who
could neither read nor write, was a proud man who had a reputation for taking no nonsense from mean whites. Their mother
worked as a domestic for white families in town and took in laundry, getting fifty cents a household for washing huge amounts of
clothes.

Charles was ten and Medgar eight when some white men killed
one of their father's friends, Willie Tingle, for supposedly looking
at a white woman or insulting her. They dragged him through the
streets of town behind a wagon and hung him up to a tree and shot
him. For a long time his bloody clothes were allowed to remain in
the field, and the Evers brothers had to pass them daily on their
long walk to school.

The school they attended was a one-room shack with a pot-
bellied stove in the middle of the floor. Rain came in through the
shingled roof. One hundred or so students, grades one through
eight, crowded into the one room, where they were taught by two
teachers. Mississippi winters can sometimes be bitterly cold, and
Charles remembered that before they got a decent fire going in the
stove, the children "would all be huddled up in their old coats the
white folks had worn out and given them. Some of the girls would
bring old blankets to keep their feet from freezing. Maybe we
would have a little spelling or a little reading, but we were too cold

to study very much. Even the teacher was cold." They went to school only from mid-October to mid-February. The school closed down the rest of the time so the young blacks could join their elders in the fields.

They had to walk several miles each way to school, and when the bus with the white kids came by the driver would veer to the side and make the black children jump off the road, a routine ritual for black kids in the South then. The white students would shout, "Let's see you run, niggers!" Charles and Medgar started stationing themselves behind bushes on both sides of the road and throwing rocks at the bus, catching it in a crossfire.

Charles remembered Medgar as a bookworm who was smarter than the rest of them and studied harder. He would sit on their back porch for hours at a time reading books. He was easygoing and popular. The two brothers developed an aversion to the white peddlers who came across the tracks and barged into the black shacks unannounced to persuade them to purchase Bibles, mail-order shoes, cheap mirrors, brushes, tonics, broken-down furniture. They had been seeing Tarzan films in what Charles described as their "little buzzard-roof movie." They watched closely while Tarzan dug his ditches and made his traps. Then they would go out and dig holes under the peddlers' trucks when they were parked somewhere and bury two-by-fours with big spikes jutting under the tires. Then they would watch from a distance as the peddlers backed over them.

Medgar was not atypical of the black American veterans from the South who fought for the country in World War II, for democratic values as they had been told, and then returned home to find that nothing had changed at all. In 1946 he, Charles, and three friends went to the county courthouse to try to register to vote. Hostile whites blocked the entrances, but they managed to reach the clerk's office, only to be turned away by armed white men. The ironies in this were most abundant, and the litany of them in Mississippi during and shortly after the war as I learned of them much later was heartrending. One of the worst I heard of, for example, occurred in a small town in the Delta during the war; a decorated black veteran still nursing an arm wound was not allowed to enter a restaurant where several Nazi prisoners and their security guard from a nearby POW camp were eating inside. Medgar knew of such instances, and they had to have moved something in his soul.

To fully understand Medgar, one has to have some appreciation of the raw rampant fear among blacks in Mississippi in the years of his NAACP stewardship. (It was the blacks who were afraid then. It is the whites who are afraid now.) For them Mississippi was essentially a police state, which used every method at its disposal to keep the Negro down. Until Medgar came along there was no real outlet for these immeasurable grievances. Many blacks were also uncomfortable with him, with the basic activisim he was engaging in, and these included some of his neighbors living in the first middle-class black subdivision in Jackson, who were apprehensive that his endeavors might bring white retribution down on their neighborhood. Hired black informers reported on his activities to white authorities.

Yet in the early 1990s before the third and conclusive Beckwith trial, in many quarters Medgar seemed to exist in collective memory mainly as *the* martyr figure—mythic, remote, and piously memorialized, rooted forever in that chaotic long-ago day so far removed from our blander equivocating times and, although the first victim of the notable 1960s assassinations, by far the least known among Americans of the civil rights movement's conspicuous leaders and spokesmen. He was representative surely of the finest of the older struggle, but in the popular society he was not particularly well defined in a human way, or adequately noted beyond the ritualistic deferences. Many were not especially aware of his personal character and goals, of the honor inherent in the deepest springs of his life, of the rudimentary *guts* of what his lonely efforts entailed. Where did this great gritty courage come from? What were its sources? To comprehend this is to comprehend the dominion of the ghost itself.

In his early efforts, at a time before sit-ins, before Freedom Riders, before Rosa Parks, before Martin Luther King, Jr., in a place of abandoned repression, he had only his wife, Myrlie, and a handful of others wholly behind him. King had his Montgomery congregation and his father's in Atlanta, a much larger web of support, and later, of course, a national forum. Implicit in these circumstances are questions of greatness that transcend race but are even more unimaginable because Medgar was black, in Mississippi, in the first half of the twentieth century, and basically alone. Beckwith did not just kill a man whose hard life had instilled a quiet fanaticism; he killed a man almost fated for martyrdom, a man whose ability to rise every morning and take on the entrenched and cruelly arrogant mores as he did was little short of incredible.

"There are no pictures of him at the head of a great, epoch-making march," Adam Nossiter observed:

His image is preserved in a few dozen grainy group shots with other speakers on a podium, meeting NAACP officials at the airport or, sleeves rolled up, taking notes in the field. There are few newsreels of him. One of the better known, a dark and jerky sequence of under thirty seconds in which he urges blacks to boycott stores on Capitol Street, conveys nothing of the heroic qualities imputed to him after his death.

It is the images of his death that are better known, the memorial march in Jackson and the ensuing riot during which defiant young blacks shouted to the armed police, "Shoot us! Shoot us!" It is the family's grief, the Arlington burial, the widow and the children being solaced in the Oval Office by John F. Kennedy. For the first time the murder of a civil rights activist had a national impact. Bob Dylan wrote a song in tribute to him, "Only a Pawn in Their Game."

By innumerable accounts of those who knew him, Medgar was a fine, decent, efficient, highly likeable family man who could not ignore the compulsions of his heart. Much of his work was dutiful and routine: trying to get people to join the NAACP, to pay their dues. In this and more dramatic quests he spent a great deal of time traveling the highways and back roads of the state. He believed in a truly integrated society. "He was a man who'd been through a great deal and in no way was a hater," a close friend and associate said of him. "He was just not a hater." In meetings with white leaders late in his life he was invariably courteous and restrained, but his emotions ran deep. He once cried openly during a talk at an NAACP meeting while describing some particularly brutal wrong, and in his last weeks people recalled him as weary to the point of collapse.

He challenged the whole white power structure, and he did so across a broad spectrum, becoming by far the most visible and aggressive civil rights activist in the state. The white supremacists were aware of him, and for good reason:

• He investigated racial murders and beatings: the killing of the fourteen-year-old Chicago child Emmett Till near the town of Money; of the Reverend George Lee, the NAACP leader in Belzoni, who was felled in a downtown neighborhood with shotgun blasts to his face, with no arrests ever made, the police claiming the shotgun buckshot pellets were dental fillings; of a farmer named Lamar Smith, murdered outside the courthouse in Brookhaven. In the perilous work of examining these and other crimes, Evers often disguised himself as a sharecropper. He developed contacts among writers for the national media and kept them informed of his discoveries, and they trusted him.

• He was constantly on the road trying to get blacks to register to vote. Both Lee and Smith had been murdered for their efforts in this regard, and countless others had been beaten and driven away. By various extralegal tactics blacks were almost totally excluded from the voting rolls. (Lyndon Johnson's Voting Rights Act would not be passed until 1965. Not until two years later would Mississippians elect their first black legislator since Reconstruction. "The first time I ever voted, I voted for myself," the legislator said.)

Of all the multiple challenges to the indigenous system Medgar chose to live and work within, this may have been the most ultimately disrupting to the established white hegemony, and to the violent underlings it encouraged and condoned, because this challenge went to its wellsprings.

• As early as 1953 he was roaming the Delta photographing the horrible conditions of the black schools. (Earlier he himself had been denied admission to the University of Mississippi Law School.) After *Brown* v. *Board of Education* in 1954 he strenuously advocated public-school integration and encouraged local petitions among blacks to that end, including one in my hometown of Yazoo City that culminated in disaster.

• He espoused equal access to public facilities and, near the end of his life, organized economic boycotts, mass demonstrations, and lunch-counter sit-ins. Even his more modest pursuits suggested something of the daily life of Mississippi blacks then: to be able to try on hats in stores, to use public swimming pools and libraries, to have school-crossing personnel at the black schools, to be addressed as Mr., Mrs., and Miss.

• His most towering accomplishment, however, as Adam Nossiter has eloquently noted, was "his simple presence, his standing up for the idea of racial justice, in a time and place where it was extremely dangerous to do so. He kept that idea alive in Mississippi publicly, at a time when no one else did. When other civil rights leaders came into the state in 1961, they were not carrying their message into virgin territory."

For this he was beaten while trying to integrate a bus, threatened by a mob while attempting to get an NAACP member out of jail, attacked by police outside a courtroom, and routinely trailed and harassed by cops, and he received voluminous hate mail and telephone calls and had his home firebombed. Ed King, a veteran white civil rights activist, commented after the two 1964 trials that the issue before the court was not Byron De La Beckwith's guilt or innocence "but whether Medgar Evers was guilty enough in his agitation to deserve the death sentence which Beckwith, for all white Mississippi, had carried out." (I do not believe for a moment, of course, that the killer was acting for all white Mississippians, although he probably *thought* he was.)

Among the stresses and complaints in which *Ghosts of Mississippi* would eventually be caught up was that Medgar himself was not featured more prominently. But that lay in the future.

———

The basic crisis in America is racism. Future reactions to *Ghosts* would demonstrate to me that more than ever, perhaps, we are unable to think clearly and rationally about racial matters. The O. J. Simpson case of the mid-1990s, with all it symbolized, would divide the nation like nothing since Vietnam. The church burnings in the South would be frequent reminders of how close we sometimes remained to the older nihilism. With a 30 percent black underclass and hardening attitudes on both sides, the chasm would often seem unbridgeable. These would be times of immense pessimism. John Hope Franklin vividly reminds us that we have struggled with these tragic issues for 350 years on this continent. The heroic black pastor Gardner Taylor would ask if the suffering of blacks in this country had gone in vain. Would there ever be a resolution of race, so "woven into the fabric of American life?" Can we only ameliorate it, make it more manageable? He quoted a remark made about racism in America during a conversation he had had years before with Albert Einstein, who saw it as "a quality of primitivism in humanity, and the best we can do is keep it under control." One can only hope this will not be all.

As with many white Southerners of my generation, I believe passionately in the importance of race relations. "The South is the image of Huckleberry Finn and Jim," William R. Ferris has observed, "black and white figures dependent on each other for survival." I understand how profoundly the American and African experience, and especially the Southern-American and African experience, intertwine. If Henry Louis Gates, Jr., is correct in identifying slavery as "an economic form masked by race," then until the 1960s in places like Mississippi a neoslavery was still similarly masked by the canon of racial inferiority.

Racism would be the theme of *Ghosts of Mississippi*. The movie would be about Mississippi but also about contemporary America. The story of our country is the story of people of many races and origins trying to live together, most of all whites and blacks. Mississippi's white-black nexus is the most intense of anywhere in the nation. The state is a veritable morass of paranoia about the subject, further complicated by the fact that everybody here knows about everybody and everything. The obsession with what outsiders think of the place is a principal aspect of the Mississippi psyche. Many white Mississippians believe the rest of the country thinks them racist and wants to use the state as a whipping boy, and that others have never tried to understand the state and are always manipulating it. This kind of paranoia is unique to Mississippi.* Mississippians believe they have changed but will never be taken seriously. The other Americans, they feel, are not sensitive to the fact that they themselves are not dealing well with race, that the rest of the nation smugly tells itself, "We're not as bad as Mis-

---

* This obsession would likely have been sharpened among those Mississippians who read the November 1972 issue of the magazine *Lifestyle* ranking all the fifty states "from civilized to barbaric." As cited by William Manchester in his *The Glory and the Dream: A Narrative History of America 1932–1972,* the magazine updated a famous 1931 series by H. L. Mencken and Charles Angoff in the old *American Mercury.* The 1972 criteria, as *American Mercury*'s had, took into account "wealth, literacy, entries in *Who's Who in America,* symphony orchestras, crime, voter registration, infant mortality, transportation, and availability of medical attention." In the 1972 study, as in the 1931 one, Mississippi was last in the country, just below Alabama. In 1972 "the average Mississippian had less than nine years schooling. Over a third of the people were poor, as the Department of Commerce *Statistical Abstract of the United States* defines poverty. One in four households lacked plumbing and 29 percent telephones; only 24 percent read a daily newspaper and only 3 percent a news magazine."

sissippi." A woman of long and honored acquaintance who happened to be governor of Texas asked me not long ago, "How can you live there?"

In a sizeable spread under the title "South Toward Home" in 1997, *Newsweek* reported that the reverse migration of middle-class blacks back to the South was up 92 percent over the 1980s and that "a net tide of 2.7 million—more than half of the great post-1940 migration—will have headed South between 1975 and 2010." A veteran columnist recently wrote, "There is a weird pulling power about this state. Many people I have known have left and come back. I don't know what it is. It is a very strange place, Mississippi." A professional pollster retained by the Jackson *Clarion-Ledger*, the state's most widely read newspaper, reported that he had never seen anything like it. "I've never been anywhere," he said, "where people identified themselves more with their state."

Mississippians are nothing if not ornery and proud. In the autumn of 1997 the head football coach for the Ole Miss Rebels, Tommy Tuberville, issued a statement pleading with students not to wave Confederate flags at football games on the grounds that the flag is a visual reminder of a divisive past. (The university's enrollment is 12 percent black and about half the football team is black.) The coach argued that the flag tarnishes the school's image and has damaged his efforts to recruit black athletes. "I was hired to win football games," he said, "and other schools are using the Rebel flag against us." Some outstanding black prospects will not even visit the campus because of the school's reputation, he warned. In a football-crazed culture like this state's, one would have thought the coach's urgent appeals might be heeded. Nothing is simple as that. At Ole Miss's next game, the homecoming game against Vanderbilt, the student section was a sea of more Confederate flags than ever. And in the game after that, television cameras caught a similar flaunting for a national audience. This was hardly limited to students, many of them graduates of the "seg" academies. Alumni joined in, too. A prominent and lengthy piece in *The Washington Post* reported that men wore vests and ties adorned with the flag. One woman wore a Rebel flag skirt and her eleven-year-old daughter a flag-decorated blouse. Others attacked the football coach as an uncomprehending outsider from that den of Yankee radicalism, Arkansas.*

From my own experience I believe the nation is beginning to look more like the South, yet that personal race relations are better in the South than in the North. When I was in Los Angeles later to view the filming of the movie, a native remarked to me that in the wake of the Rodney King and O. J. Simpson cases and other matters the relationship between the whites and blacks in the City of the Queen of the Angels was not unlike that between the Arabs and Jews in the Middle East—there was practically no common ground as they faced each other across a nearly catastrophic divide.

Although it has been exceedingly flawed and complicated, much progress has been made in Mississippi since Medgar Evers's death. By the 1990s blacks, who numbered 36 percent of the approximately 2,690,000 population of Mississippi, the highest percentage of any state, comprised one third of its registered voters, and there were more than six hundred black elected officials, also more than in any other state. "The case against Byron De La Beckwith," one journalist wrote, "was brought back not because of any one event, but by a confluence of many events in a slow tide of change." As blacks mustered political strength, a younger generation of whites accepted integration, in part out of repulsion toward everything the Beckwiths had once stood for.

One of these younger whites was an assistant district attorney named Bobby DeLaughter, who would handle the new investigation into Byron De La Beckwith. "The growth I've had," he would say, "is symbolic of the growth people of our age have had." De-Laughter was a child when Medgar Evers was killed, and he remembered little of it. (Years later, when he and District Attorney Ed Peters were examining prospective jurors for the 1994 trial,

*The student-body senate later condemned the flag-waving by an overwhelming majority.

they discovered that almost none of the blacks had ever heard of Medgar Evers. One black member of that jury pool was actually employed by the local NAACP office.)

Yet the state overall remains staunchly conservative. Just before he signed the Voting Rights Act in 1965, Lyndon Johnson said to his White House assistant, Bill Moyers: "This will turn over the South to the Republicans in your lifetime." Mississippi remains close to the bottom in everything—education, economics, social programs—and it continues to elect people who keep it that way. Its public schoolteachers are among the worst paid in the Union; if a Mississippi schoolteacher crossed the state line into Tennessee he would automatically make $6,000 more a year. In many ways the old George Wallace constituency of a generation ago is the undergirding of today's GOP dominance, yet more urbane and business-oriented. Kirk Fordice, Mississippi's arch-rightist, neo-Dixiecrat Republican governor, "the exemplar," Peter Applebome of the *Times* wrote, "of the meaner-than-cat-shit, tough-nosed-businessman-turned-politician school of Southern Republicans," recently became its first governor in history elected to two consecutive terms. Once, around his campaign headquarters, he introduced Ronald Smothers, a black reporter, as "the spook from *The New York Times.*" Soon after taking office he announced he would call out the National Guard to fight against court-ordered equalization of appropriations for the state's white and black universities. At a National Governors' Conference, he declared the United States officially "a Christian nation." He would appoint in 1996 four conservative Republican white males to new vacancies on the Board of Higher Education, which supervises its eight public universities including three predominantly black ones, only to be rebuffed by the state senate. When in 1997 the U.S. Commission on Civil Rights held one of its infrequent hearings in Mississippi—it subsequently described public-school education in Mississippi, particularly the Delta, as bleak, inadequate, and racially polarized—the governor did not even bother to send his education aide to the meetings. Later that year, when he routinely vetoed a landmark Adequate Education Act, which would have established a long-overdue program of equity funding for schoolchildren in property-poor districts, Bill Minor, dean of Southern journalists and recipient of the first John Chancellor Award for Excellence in Journalism for his fifty years covering Mississippi politics, wrote: "That the remarkable legislative construction of the bill was treated so cavalierly by Fordice is so reprehensible it proved beyond a doubt his unfitness to govern. He is vying for the dishonor of being Mississippi's worst governor in my memory. And there have been bad governors."

For the outsider to comprehend the social climate out of which Myrlie Evers and Bobby DeLaughter gradually succeeded in their reinvestigation of Medgar Evers's assassination, a highly elusive and beleaguered quest, he should be apprised that approximately 65 to 70 percent of the white populace of present-day Mississippi endorsed the stands and statements of this public leader. This in itself should place the reinvestigation and subsequent conviction in a certain real and direct human framework.

As we approach the new century, it is the juxtapositions of Mississippi, emotional and in remembrance, that still drive us crazy. I cite Maryanne Vollers on the conclusion of the 1994 Beckwith trial because her words so faithfully reflect my own:

After the courtroom doors swung shut, the reporters and news crews caught their flights to Atlanta and New York, and another edition of the *Clarion-Ledger* was put to bed, what remained was still Mississippi, haunted ground: a place at war with its own history and destined to repeat its past, like a soul being reborn again and again until it gets it right.

Chapter 2

RENDEZVOUS IN THE RUINS

I was driving through the languid village of Port Gibson, Mississippi, on a very warm late afternoon of April 1996. An outsider might judge it a town time had forsaken. It is stunningly lovely, with old churches and a synagogue and sedate antebellum mansions on lanes lined with immense trees draped in Spanish moss. On his march toward Vicksburg, Ulysses S. Grant found the town "too beautiful to burn." It has a graveyard with long rows of Confederate dead and an ancient Presbyterian church, its steeple surmounted by a huge iron hand with the index finger pointing to heaven. The fine old houses belong to the white upper class, who surely on this day were inside for the air conditioning; I failed to see a single white person on the streets or sidewalks. Groups of black children were everywhere, playing and riding their bicycles. Elderly black women in straw hats strolled along the main street, which is also Old Highway 61—the Freedom Highway, the Blues Highway, one of the most distinctive of American thoroughfares. It begins on Tulane Avenue in New Orleans, traverses the Louisiana plantation country, goes through Natchez, Port Gibson, Vicksburg, and the Mississippi Delta, crosses the river at Memphis into Arkansas, and moves on through the Missouri boot, New Madrid and Ste. Genevieve, St. Louis, Mark Twain's Hannibal, Keokuk, Dubuque, a sliver of Wisconsin, on into Minneapolis and St. Paul, along Lake Superior to Duluth, and eventually all the way to Thunder Bay, Canada.

It was 5:00 P.M. on a weekday that appeared Sabbath-like; few businesses were open, not even the liquor store. This town had always magnetized me; my great-grandmother, grandniece of the first territorial governor of Mississippi, had been born and raised here and as a child was the only witness to the murder of her father, my great-great grandfather, by his business partner. The town cemetery had many of my blood people.

In its hot springtime indolence the whole neighborhood seemed oblivious to the unusual happenings taking place ten miles or so down the serpentine country road, west and toward the great river.

To me there is no more haunted, complex terrain in America than the countryside between Port Gibson and the river. In this spooky, seductive earth, the southwest corner of Mississippi, resides the colonial, territorial, Confederate, and American history of this beguiling and tortured state. Before the Civil War, this region was the richest per capita in the United States, all of it undergirded by slavery. The grand plantation houses, many of them now crumbling or derelict, were the apex of this culture. The woods are dark and profuse with creeping vines, snakes, and the ubiquitous Spanish moss. The hills and entangled embankments are precipitous, the older roadways deep tunnels of green, and the river is never far away. The land is full of ghosts.

Not far from here is the ghost town of Grand Gulf, where the river began to cut into the bluffs years ago, and where Confederate trenches, caves, and breastworks are still visible. Nearby is Rodney, once a thriving venue, likewise long abandoned when the river changed its course, with its contours of collapsed buildings and churches encroached upon everywhere by the lush woodlands. A few miles northwest is Bruinsburg, deserted today and surrounded by cypress woods along two forks of Bayou Pierre, where Grant and Sherman landed forty thousand men from the Louisiana side of the river in 1863, that war's closest equivalent to the Normandy beachhead. Thirty miles south is Natchez with its dozens of columned antebellum houses and the site of the old slave barracks and auction block. This is the hometown of Richard Wright, and one day a few years ago his daughter Julia, who lived in Paris and had never been to the South, and some other Wright relatives and I visited a few of the locales of his childhood as described in his autobiography *Black Boy,* including the ramshackle, forlorn one-room school he had attended out from town, not unlike Medgar Evers's in the 1930s and 1940s in Decatur, Mississippi. Both greatly reminded me of the descriptions of the little bare-bones black schools in Tennessee that W.E.B. Du Bois wrote about in such striking and searing detail as a young teacher many decades ago.

A little south and west of Port Gibson is Alcorn State University, founded in 1871 as Alcorn Agricultural and Mechanical College on the grounds of a religious finishing school for the sons of rich white cotton planters before the Civil War, the first black land-grant institution and the first state-supported institution for the higher education of blacks in the nation. Several times in 1994 my wife, JoAnne, and I drove down the Natchez Trace from Jackson to Alcorn to watch Steve (Air II) McNair, the fabled quarterback of the Alcorn Braves, candidate for the Heisman Trophy. He was a poor black kid from a small Mississippi town. His father left when he was young, and his mother brought up the family by working in a factory. He and his brothers used a cow pasture for their football field. The stadium seats 22,000 and, like the bosky campus itself, seems chiseled from the very earth. Except for the National Football League scouts and some of the journalists and photographers, we were the only white people in the stadium. We were there the day Steve broke the all-time National Collegiate Athletic Association total-offensive record for all college divisions; after the play that surpassed that auspicious milestone, he called time out, trotted to the sidelines, and gave his mother the football. When he later signed with the Houston Oilers for $28 million, the first thing he did was build her a new house.

The Alcorn campus is eight miles east of the river in bucolic, undulating terrain. Towering magnolias and live oaks festooned with moss cover the grounds; the students sit in their shade reading books. The buildings have the patina of time: aged brick walls, tall white columns, iron stairways. Many of the black schoolteachers in Mississippi were educated here.

There is another distinction to this school. Medgar Evers returned from infantry combat in France after World War II to attend college here. He was a running back for the football team, editor of the yearbook, and a student leader. Here he met and courted his future wife, Myrlie. And it is because of him and of her that I am making this journey on this day, to the Windsor Ruins a few miles north of the Alcorn campus.

In this whole vicinity the Windsor Ruins are the most striking landmark of all—twenty-two enormous columns with huge cast-iron Corinthian capitals at the top of each, which give the outline of an old destroyed plantation mansion, considered in its day the grandest in Mississippi, built before the Civil War by slave labor, enduring symbol now of the state's lost cotton kingdom. As a riverboat captain, Mark Twain used these towers to chart his course. Once you have seen these ruins you will never forget them. One of Eudora Welty's most indelible images in her early days as a photographer is set here. We would have picnics here before going on to the Alcorn football games, and from this spot we could hear the strains of the college band wafting toward us from the faraway distance. As a hospital during the Civil War this domicile ran red with blood. Vines now cling to the fluted columns. The encompassing soil is equally formidable, the brooding whispery forests all around.

Just out of Port Gibson, a temporary sign on the side of the road said: WINDSOR RUINS CLOSED TODAY. Hollywood had taken them over.

—

From childhood I had always been fascinated with film, yet I had never been involved in helping create one. A number of years ago Disney made a movie of a children's book of mine, filmed in Natchez, and the director asked me down to observe some of the shooting. Watching the Hollywood actors playing me as a boy, and my youthful chums, and my long-departed mother, father, grandmother, grandfather, and great aunts, was déjà vu of the most singular kind, and exceedingly strange.

But *Ghosts of Mississippi* was different. This story touched implicitly upon every significant facet of my Mississippi upbringing, my roots in the South, my wanderings as an editor and writer, the things I considered important as an American. In time all this would embrace for me in living dimensions two extremes of the American dream: racism in modern America and the magical illusions of Hollywood; racism, which alone prevented Evers and other blacks of the era from succeeding—in fact, prevented him from living at all—and Hollywood, whose dexterity and chimera can anoint *anyone* with success. The unadorned realities of race, which I know in my deepest heart, juxtaposed and intermingling with the politics, mechanics, and glamour of moviemaking.

A week or so before the shooting began, the Jackson *Clarion-Ledger* ran a banner headline on its front page: TIME, LUCK, PASSION PLAY KEY ROLES IN MAKING MISSISSIPPI FILM REALITY.

How this production came to be reads almost like a movie script itself: blind luck, good timing, strong passions, emotional conflict, and the kind of coincidence that Hollywood has trafficked in for a century.

This is the story of a confluence of energies, of heinous crime and government manipulation, of an unlikely hero, of an actor-turned-director who grew up wanting to make a movie about the civil rights movement.

It's a mystery story, a love story, a civil rights story, a story of restoration and redemption: of the soul and of a state.

The original title on the Lewis Colick script was *Free at Last*. Then for a time it went to being untitled. Next, when it was first announced that a substantial part of the movie would be filmed in the state, it was tentatively called *Ghosts of Mississippi*, then it was feared this title would cause problems during the Mississippi filming. It reverted to being untitled again, so that for the longest time the movie had no name. It was simply the Untitled Mississippi Project—UMP for short. The director announced a one-thousand-dollar prize among the crew for the best title. There would be six weeks' filming in Mississippi, followed by two months in Los Angeles, with national release aimed for just before Christmas.

The prologue of the movie would be about Medgar Evers's life and death, and about the two 1964 trials of Byron De La Beckwith. Then, leaping forward from 1964 to 1989, the bulk of the plot would portray the contemporary story of the young white assistant district attorney Bobby DeLaughter and his interminable search, against staggering odds and eventually at great personal and professional cost, for both old and new evidence, and his growing bond of trust and cooperation with Evers's widow, Myrlie, in that arduous quest. The trial and the investigative work that led to it culminated one of the most unusual episodes of criminal prosecution in American history. It is a tale about ghosts; the final title, indeed, would be *Ghosts of Mississippi*. (This also had been the title of Maryanne Vollers's 1995 book about the trial, but the movie would not be based on that book.) "The story of Mr. Evers and Mr. Beckwith is almost too profound to be real," Rick Bragg would write in *The New York Times* after a couple of days on the Mississippi sets, "as if it were pulled straight from Eudora Welty's short stories instead of being the inspiration for one of them." As the months progressed, this uncanny blending of the "real" and the re-created "unreal," between the authentic fact and the filmed fact, between the shadow and the act, would make it exceedingly difficult for me to distinguish the two: layer upon layer of ironies, of painful and public personal memories, surreal to me in their unfolding.

———

It is late afternoon as I drive out now from Port Gibson, and the shadows are lengthening. The cicadas are singing in the trees, and the first fireflies of springtime are drifting out. There is a faint smoky haze in the atmosphere. The land itself hums with April's bursting. Some minutes down the winding roadway from Port Gibson as a curve opens up to the ruins is a big congregation of eighteen-wheelers, highway-patrol vehicles, cars and site vans, and beyond these a base camp that resembles a circus: more eighteen-wheelers, several trailers, and dozens of cars and vans situated around a huge red-and-white tent filled with long tables and dozens of chairs. Along a blocked dirt road are distant shouts: "Lockup!" "Quietly!" "Rolling!" Farther up the path is a sudden stunning sight: the ruins themselves, and hundreds of people scurrying about.

The whole vicinity is a luminous burst of light—lights everywhere in the middle of the woods. To the side is a big rig, several vans and smaller trucks, a Lincoln Town Car for the star, Alec Baldwin, steel trunks filled with esoteric equipment, portable generators, a great welter of cable, nets, sandbags, grip stands, opaque boards, trucks loaded with ladders, tools, tripods, reflectors, ropes. Between the massive columns of the ruins, a camera arches upward and dollies back. Paraphernalia dangles from the belts of these bustling people; many of them carry walkie-talkies and wear headsets. Everyone seems to be rushing somewhere. Almost everyone has on a stainless steel necklace with a laminated card attached. The cards display a blown-up Mississippi road map tinted red in the background, with MISSISSIPPI PROJECT CAST AND CREW written across it. Muscular figures bearing tattoos shout, "Coming through! Watch your feet!" They are carrying boxes, two-by-fours, axes, saws, crates, odd items of all descriptions. Many are wearing bandannas, which they often take off to wipe away the sweat. These, I learn, are the grips, the equivalent of stagehands, and they seem heedless to the filming itself, even to the anarchy they themselves are helping create. They move forward to whatever destination with an almost rank and churlish resolve. Testifying to the nomadic existence not only of these grips but also of the gaffers, the electricians, the carpenters, the set dressers, all of them, is the variety of logos on their T-shirts: of earlier movies— THE AMERICAN PRESIDENT, HYDROFLEX, FREE WILLY, WITNESS, THE PAPER—and American place names and sports teams and watering spots—NEBRASKA CORNHUSKERS, MINNESOTA GOLDEN GOPHERS, FIGHTING ILLINI, YUMA CRIMINALS, FREMONT DRAG STRIP, CHICAGO BULLS, CHICO STATE ATHLETICS, STEAMERS BAR AND GRILL HYANNIS, CAPE HATTERAS N.C., WELCOME TO CAPE COD.

The sense of frantic motion is notable: what appears to be chaos, tension, and confusion interspersed with swift moments of utter stillness and quiet, then noise and movement again. For the maiden visitor, such as I, to an important Hollywood set, the mood appears enigmatic, almost demented. On this evening I feel like an intruder in an ant colony, the worker ants everywhere hurrying along, each with a task to do, the security men who enforce lockup being the guardian ants of the colony, protecting the accesses to the heart of the compound, and in the middle of this ceaseless motion the monarch, stationary in front of the monitor, the center of attention, everyone scurrying around this personage desiring only to please: the director.

Rob Reiner and a few others sit behind two monitor screens one atop the other, one in color, the second in black and white. He looks much as he did as Meathead in the television series *All in the Family,* with a little less hair now, a little more gray, a large, bearish figure with gray too in his beard. He is discussing the angle of the next shot. A young assistant walks over to him: "Ten minutes for lighting."

A woman approaches. With her is a black man dressed in a suit from the 1960s with a fedora on his head. "Here's the man with the hat for tomorrow. What do you think?"

Reiner looks the man over. "Good," he says, then shakes the man's hand. "I like your hat."

For various logistical reasons movies are never shot in sequence. The scenes being done tonight are Numbers 83 and 83A of an ultimate 164. It is the third day of shooting of a projected 61 days.

The scenes at the Windsor Ruins tonight, like so many of the others to come, will elicit for me that bizarre chemistry where real life and this movie converged. Everyone would soon be enveloped by this odd, enticing, dreamlike ambiance—"a distillation of reality," Truman Capote had said about the movie of his book *In Cold Blood.*

It is 1990. Assistant District Attorney Bobby DeLaughter, with the help of two detectives named Charlie Crisco and Lloyd "Benny" Bennett, are immersed in their complicated investigation into the new and old evidence pertaining to Byron De La Beckwith and the Evers assassination. After considerable difficulty they have finally tracked down a former Ku Klux Klansman and later FBI informant named Delmar Dennis. As an informer, he had been instrumental in the probe that led to federal conspiracy convictions of eight Klansmen in the murders of civil rights activists Michael Schwerner, Andrew Goodman, and James Chaney in Neshoba County, Mississippi, in 1964. DeLaughter had come across an obscure book published in 1975 called *Klandestine*, which quoted Dennis having heard Beckwith, speaking before a Klan meeting in 1965, admit that he had murdered Evers: "Killing that nigger gave me no more inner discomfort than our wives endure when they give birth to our children." DeLaughter had arranged a secret meeting in the woods with Dennis to try to persuade him, in the event of a third Beckwith trial, to testify. Four actors are involved in tonight's scenes: Alec Baldwin as Bobby DeLaughter, William H. Macy as Charlie Crisco, Benny Bennett as himself, and an actor from Georgia named Jim Harley as Delmar Dennis.

There is a warm burgeoning sunset now, and a full moon grows brighter by the moment, hovering over the ruins and casting the surrounding pine trees and the Corinthian columns in wispy shadows. Around the ruins, in between the columns that will be seen in the shots, small trees, still in their black plastic pots, lean against one another. The production designer has reproduced two other columns in the middle of the ruins as if they had fallen there; they are made of fiberglass painted to look like molded brick and plaster. The actors will sit on these. Off to the side a machine simulates fog by shooting compressed air through crystal oil. Two crew members wander about creating dust particles. They are shaking large plastic garbage bags with small holes punched in them. From the bags tiny bits of what appears to be lint cascade downward; they are lifted upward by artificial air currents.

Behind his monitors the director resumes his analysis of the angle for the next shot. I watch the images on Reiner's screens; they are somehow much clearer than the images seen by the naked eye, as if the video monitors themselves encapsulate people and things more fully than our own vision. The zooming lens of the camera collects the smallest particles of dust flying through the sunset glow surrounding Alec Baldwin and the others. The camera absorbs everything.

In this eerie counterpoise between twilight and dark, the rich, profuse smells of Deep South springtime all about, I reflect on the great house that once stood here, and the long-ago beings who once dwelled here, the stirrings of old twilight conversations, of mute possessions and fears and loves in the gone charters of time: the mint juleps and elaborate parties, the betrothals and weddings and funerals, the echoes of steamboat horns from the river down the way (Mark Twain's?), their black slaves, the coming of that war. I recall my Emily Dickinson:

> *This quiet dust was gentlemen and ladies*
> *And lads and girls,*
> *And laughter and ability and sighing,*
> *And frocks and curls.*

What in heaven's name would they have thought if some ethereal visage had arrived to tell them that one day many years from then a Hollywood movie about civil rights would be filmed right here on their ruined grounds? Would they have inquired: "What's Hollywood? What's civil rights? What's a movie?"

———

The cop who plays himself, Benny Bennett, will tell me tonight's scene is so emotionally authentic to the true-life rendezvous that it is like investigating the case all over again. It was his most pointed memory of the actual investigation and one of its most crucial development. Bennett was carrying a 9-millimeter and a .38 revolver on that day in 1990: "I felt Delmar Dennis probably had a sniper in the woods. *I* would've if I'd have been in his position because his life had been threatened and we very well could've not been who we said we were." Long after the real meeting, Bennett would still believe Dennis had an accomplice stationed somewhere out of sight. Also, on authority of the real DeLaughter, Crisco, and Bennett, the man playing Dennis bears a striking resemblance to the real Dennis. He is sitting in a tall canvas folding chair as scenes are set up. He is menacing and commands attention: a huge frame, a shaven head, and most strikingly as I subsequently chat with him about his role, two different-colored eyes, one blue, one brown, just like a cat of mine named Spit McGee.

The crew now begins to prepare for the filming of the arrival of the assistant D.A. and the detectives looking for the former Klansman. The lighting experts are changing the gels, I am advised, since the scene happens around dusk. Quiet once more descends upon this populated place in the forest. There is a muted solicitude on the set now as the technical experts confer among themselves. People walk on tiptoes.

After the fifth or sixth take of the actors' entrance into the ruins, Reiner shouts: "Cut! That's it! Wonderful! Print it!" The crew starts to move the tracks on which the camera rolls and readies to shoot the scene again from a different angle. An assistant director shouts, "Second team!" The canvas chairs with flaps for notebooks and refreshments in which the director and the upper management have been sitting are carried to another spot, as are the cumbersome monitors. "Video Village on the move!" someone yells. The actors retire beyond the set to have their faces repowdered as their stand-ins, who are indeed the "second team" and are used to minimize the need for the real actors to loiter about, stand in their places while the director of photography and cameramen judge distance and light, using tape measures and light meters, sometimes framing the tableau before them with their hands in rectangular frieze. Reiner does this also, narrowing his eyes like a hunter squinting out from the brush. Everyone defers to the autonomy of the camera, even these wizards of light who make sure the camera will work its magic for them. I am beginning to comprehend it is the live camera, mesmerizing and totalitarian, that is truly the hurricane's eye, and everyone from director to grip dwells in its encompassing responsibility and thrall.

Between almost every take I notice a tall, distinguished-looking man carrying a clipboard, the screenplay, and other booklets and documents conferring head-to-head with Alec Baldwin, in subdued tones as if he is reciting something. He is, I will learn, doing just that. He is the dialect coach, who rehearses Baldwin and the other non-Mississippian cast members in the Mississippi accent. He goes over the lines with the star; Baldwin nods his head as he listens. Then another take is ready.

"Quiet, everybody!" "Lockup!" "Rolling!" "And—action!" Out of the shadows steps Delmar Dennis.

DENNIS
One of you Bobby DeLaughter?

BOBBY
Yes, sir. And this is Charlie Crisco and Benny Bennett.

DENNIS

I like to come out here sometimes and think. It's a
good place to talk.

BOBBY

It's not wanting for privacy.

Time slips by as the scene is shot again and again from additional angles. Just before the filming of every take an assistant
cameraman lifts a slate before the camera with the scene number
and take number. This one reads SCENE 85—TAKE 8. Then the
stick strikes the slate with a noisy *clap*. Everyone has seen this, in
movies, on TV, and it actually happens. The sharp clap of the slate
permits the synchronizing of video and audio. The camera operator nods to the director. *"Action!"*

Now the crew readies for shots in which the three actors appearing as before are surprised by some threatening movement
and noise behind them as Reiner shouts the cue: *"Birds!"* There are
no birds yet, but the men swing around to the right as if startled,
raise their hands slightly, and Benny Bennett withdraws and bran-
dishes his 9-millimeter automatic. This scene is shot interminably
from various angles.

Everyone pauses for yet another setup in which boxes of quail
are to be released from behind vines and flowers by a man with the
designation "quail wrangler." The quail in the finished movie, I am
told, will look like crows. Since this set will also require numerous
takes, dozens of quail have been brought in. The lights have all
been set to shine on one particular corner of the ruins. A tall ladder rests behind the column and the staged growth. From this
height, the wrangler will release four to seven birds at a time. This
requires frequent takes. Director Reiner is dissatisfied by the modest height to which the quails rise before flying away. Before one
such take he orders the wrangler to release not one but two boxes
of the birds. This too proves uninspiring. "So much for the two-box
theory," he declares, with the disappointment one has when holi-

day fireworks are set off and the display is less than anticipated. The director, however, finally gets a take that pleases him. A technician explains to me that the "crows" will be impressive on video, sufficiently so to efficaciously frighten the assistant D.A. and the two cops. One surmises that in future years the quail population in these woods will have increased stupendously, and that this will mystify the local people because they will not know why, but one or two of their number will years hence learn the reason, and then the history of the Windsor quail will enter the oral tradition.

The final scene of the night is shot, one in which Bobby De-Laughter has a tense conversation with Delmar Dennis. It is a long and substantial scene: three pages in the script and all dialogue, twelve exchanges altogether. Alec Baldwin is having trouble with his lines. He is angry with himself. "Take your time," Reiner says. Between the frequent takes and cuts Baldwin retreats beyond the lights and repeats these lines out loud to himself. Once again there is take after take.

BOBBY

Murder is murder, and it's still my job to bring the sonuvabitch who did it to justice. It's still *your* job to help me.

DENNIS (*raising his voice*)

I did my job. I testified against the Klan. They shot out my windows and blew up my car. They hunted and harassed me for twenty-five years. Don't that get me even for the wrong I've done?

BOBBY

We never get even for the wrong we've done.

DENNIS *is thrown by this answer.* BOBBY *and the others start to leave.*

DENNIS

If I do this thing . . . you gotta promise me protection.

It is 3:00 A.M., and at last Reiner gets what he wants. "Cut!" he shouts. "Good for you?" he asks the camera operator. The cameraman says yes. "Print!"

At this juncture the search, as does the movie itself, has a long path to follow, full of false leads and discoveries and crazy side roads, secrets and histrionics and doubtings.

Chapter 3

JUSTICE DELAYED

M y son David Rae Morris is a photographer based in New
Orleans. He knew a great deal about Medgar Evers and
had met his brother Charles and attended several of the Medgar
Evers Homecoming Festivals that Charles had organized in Fay-
ette, Mississippi. In February of 1994 he was assigned by his New
York agency to cover Beckwith's third trial in Jackson. I was under
deadline on a book and had not intended to watch any of the proceedings until its closing stages. On the first day David Rae telephoned from the Hinds County Courthouse. "You better get on
down here, Daddy," he said. "This is really something."

This was very good advice. It was one of the most dramatic events
I have ever witnessed as a writer, fraught with passion and consequence. In every measure this trial brought the contorted history of
the contemporary South full circle. In the final days of that uncommon reckoning Mississippi was enveloped by uncomfortable
memories, by the adumbrations of a past it wished to forget. Beckwith's 1994 conviction by a Mississippi jury and his sentencing to
life in prison could possibly open a new era in which unresolved
racial murders of a generation ago might come to justice.

Observing the former fertilizer salesman in all his squalid arro-
gance as he sat in the defendant's chair, restless and wiry and of singularly average countenance, a Confederate-flag pin in the lapel of
his cardinal-red sports coat and matching cuff links, ostentatiously
removing his hearing aid when the testimony was not to his satis-
faction, grinning occasionally at the spectators, I was overcome
with my own memories from a Mississippi boyhood of the zealous,
apprehensive men in my hometown whom the loftier and more re-
fined citizens allowed to have their way with the Negro. In town
after town in Mississippi the establishment men of the White Citizens Council—bankers, lawyers, preachers, planters, merchants,
doctors, dentists—organized economic boycotts and reprisals
against blacks who espoused school integration and the franchise,
and they tacitly encouraged physical intimidation. The council
became the most politically powerful organization in the state.
Hodding Carter, Jr., called it "the Ku Klux Klan with a clipped mustache"; Medgar Evers, "the uptown KKK."

In 1956, when I was home on spring break from my senior year
in college, I attended the organizational meeting of my town's
chapter of the White Citizens Council. I will never forget it. I returned to Austin and wrote a column on it for *The Daily Texan*. The
local NAACP had submitted a petition signed by fifty-three Negro
parents seeking an immediate end to school segregation—this two
years after *Brown* v. *Board of Education*. Although I did not know
it at the time, indeed was not familiar with him, the force behind
the petition was the state NAACP's Medgar Evers.

The most prominent white men in town had called the meeting
to deal with this challenge. The auditorium that night was packed.
In the audience were scores of men and women I had known and
admired since childhood. "Let's get them *niggers!*" people were
yelling. The chairman explained that this was the charter meeting
of a new group that would "protect our way of life." The audience
shouted its support while the chairman listed the steps to be taken.
White employers would immediately fire any of the signers of the
petition who worked for them. Those petitioners who rented

houses would be evicted by their landlords. White grocers would refuse to sell groceries to any of them. Negro grocers who had signed the petition would no longer get any groceries from the wholesale firms. And on down the list. Then the man with the unlikely name of Few Ball who lived across the street from the house where I grew up asked to be recognized. "I agree with everything that's been said and with everything we're trying to do," he said. "But, gentlemen, I work for a corporation, and all this is *unconstitutional*, it's against the Consti—"

His words were abruptly drowned out by the roar from the crowd. *"Sit down, Few!"* people shouted, and there were boos and catcalls. My neighbor smiled sheepishly, shrugged, and sat down. I was tempted to stand up and support my older neighbor, because this was my hometown, too, but I did not do so. Maybe I was as scared as everyone else and had to go five hundred miles away to write about it.

The strategy worked. All of the signers were fired, and many of them started leaving town.

The afternoon I was returning to college I went to say good-bye to a girl I had known since childhood. She was on her front porch sobbing. I asked what was wrong. Her parents had just fired Henry, the man who had mowed their lawn for as long as she could remember. "It's *wrong*," she cried. "Henry didn't even know he was signing that ol' thing. And we up and *fired* him for it."

Seven years later, in 1963, the statewide White Citizens Council unequivocally supported Beckwith in the Evers case and raised the money for his legal fees.

—

Beckwith had pretensions to Mississippi Delta aristocracy and made frequent reminders that his grandmother had been a friend of Jefferson Davis's wife. He called himself Byron De La Beckwith VI. I recalled the phrase from the title of Hannah Arendt's study of Adolf Eichmann: "the banality of evil." She had also described Eichman as a "clown" during the 1961 Jerusalem trial. Adam Nossiter, covering the trial for *The Atlanta Journal Constitution*, found Beckwith not very convincing as the symbol of 1960s white extremism. "In this he resembled nothing so much as those Nazi war criminals who have proven unsatisfactory, small and pathetic, when brought to judgment. . . . History had magnified the assassination of Evers into a mythic event, so that it was now difficult to connect it to a mere mortal, much less a pathetic one like Beckwith. . . . While Beckwith was in some way absent, Evers was a martyr-symbol, larger than life."

During recesses his son, Byron De La Beckwith VII, who physically resembled his father and wore an identical Confederate-flag pin in his lapel, conferred with him frequently at the defense table, and so did the little boy, Byron De La Beckwith VIII, who attacked certain people in the courtroom as "sorry Jews." It was as if the whole aura of the destructive 1960s in this state had come back to haunt and make jest of us, as if none of us mattered. Hate was in the atmosphere again. Hatred pervaded the whole courtroom. Seated behind Beckwith in the courtroom pews were supporters who included aging Klansmen, hate-mail publishers, and home-grown Mississippi neo-Nazis, many of whom called him by his nickname, "*De*Lay," the accent always emphatic on the first syllable. During these recesses he was constantly with his eighty-three-year-old wife, Thelma, whom he married in 1982. (His first marriage, a violent and brutish one, was amply recounted by Reed Massengill, nephew of that wife, in his book *Portrait of a Racist.* Massengill would be a prosecution witness in the 1994 trial.) Thelma wore a blond wig to the proceedings and told reporters it was Lee Harvey Oswald who really shot Evers.

—

"We both knew the end was near," Myrlie Evers said, remembering perpetually her late husband's work and murder. "You don't challenge a system like that without knowing the price to be paid. We lived with threats on a daily basis, and both of us knew in the last three weeks that it wasn't going to be long. He told me to take good care of our children."

On June 12, 1963, President John F. Kennedy delivered on national television and radio the strongest civil rights speech he ever gave, indeed the most unequivocal to that point by any American president. Evers and some of his colleagues watched it in their office in Jackson and then worked late into the night. He drove home shortly after midnight and turned his Oldsmobile into his driveway. He got out of the car. He was carrying a number of T-shirts saying: JIM CROW MUST GO! He was struck in the back by Beckwith's bullet. As the blood streamed down the driveway, he crawled nearly forty feet to the back door. His wife and three children rushed to him from inside the house and held him as he lay dying. "Daddy, what's happened to you?" one of the children cried. Detectives at the scene were stunned by the prodigious amounts of blood on the driveway and the pieces of flesh on the car, as if, in the words of one of them, "someone had butchered a hog." His last words were "Turn me loose." He was buried four days later in Arlington National Cemetery. Beckwith was swiftly charged with the shooting. His fingerprint was on the scope of the rifle, but he claimed the gun had been stolen and that he was ninety-six miles away, in Greenwood up in the Delta, at the time of the murder.

We were not far from the crest of the tumultuous 1960s when the very fabric of American society would seem ripped asunder by forces beyond its control. The assassination of Evers would be followed by John F. Kennedy's, then Malcolm X's, then Martin Luther King's, then Robert Kennedy's.

Mississippi today, where much of *Ghosts* was to be filmed, is far from the perfect place, but neither is it what it was in 1963. Blacks were largely excluded then from the vote, schools and public facilities were assiduously segregated, and for various reasons there was no real freedom of expression. The historian James Silver, driven from Ole Miss for his views, called his subsequent book *Mississippi: The Closed Society.* Racial violence was rampant. Whites addressed black adults as "boy" or "girl." Such day-to-day meannesses ranged from the mundane to the ritualized. Proper white kids such as I were dutifully instructed on all sides in what was called "the Mississippi way of life." Race was the thread that ran through everything. Margaret Walker Alexander, the black novelist and poet who knew the Evers family and still lives a few houses away from the dwelling where he was murdered, once told me that when she and her husband built their house in 1956 no white contractor would erect a residence for Negroes in Jackson with more than two bedrooms; it was the most decent neighborhood for blacks in the city then, and the street was not paved until the late 1960s.

Reinhold Niebuhr, speaking for much of the American sentiment of the early 1960s, would indict Mississippi as a place in which "the instruments of justice are tools of *in*justice" and where "there are no limits to inhumanity, cruelty, and sheer caprice once communal and social restraints are no longer in force. Mississippi standards can sink so low that only the legal and moral pressure of the larger community can redeem them—just as only the pressure of the British Commonwealth can save Northern Rhodesia from becoming another South Africa." And Hodding Carter III, the Greenville, Mississippi, editor, noted that the brutality, bombings, and terror "can be accurately attributed to the silence of good men, bowed by a system which in the name of self-preservation dictated public toleration of the excesses of the vicious and the ignorant." This history evoked for me as a Southerner the lines of Yeats:

> *Mere anarchy is loosed upon the world,*
> *The blood-dimmed tide is loosed, and everywhere*
> *The ceremony of innocence is drowned;*
> *The best lack all conviction, while the worst*
> *Are full of passionate intensity.*

In 1964 the three civil rights workers in Neshoba County—Michael Schwerner, Andrew Goodman, and James Chaney—disappeared. In one of the many tapes of Lyndon Johnson's Oval Office telephone conversations released in February 1997, one hears Senator James O. Eastland of Mississippi telling Johnson that their disappearance was nothing but a hoax, that the three of them were probably in Chicago celebrating what they had done. This suggests much about the mentality of the state's political leadership then.

In the 1964 trials Beckwith was represented by politically connected lawyers, and former governor Ross Barnett openly shook his hand in the courtroom during a recess. To show his contempt for the court, the defendant would nod and wink with the deputies. When he returned to Greenwood after the second hung jury, he was greeted with WELCOME HOME signs.

It is essential to what ensued years later that neither the first nor second trials ended in actual acquittal. The vote in the first trial was six for acquittal, six for conviction; in the second eight to four. In many Mississippi quarters these came as a surprise: Ten white males in two trials had voted to convict a fellow white man of killing a Negro. The prosecution concluded it would not seek a third trial without significant new evidence, and what would that be? The case under technicalities of the law would remain open but dormant. Almost everyone considered it dead, as indeed for all purposes it was. But there is no statute of limitations on murder. Bobby DeLaughter always praised the ten unknown white jurors who had the tenacity in that day's racial climate to find a Klan hero guilty of the murder of a black man. Had they not held to their decision, the assassin would have been free forever.

Beckwith went his own way, unregenerately remaining the stalwart apostle of white supremacy he always was, a prisoner to his own rampant disaffections. In the long years he was free he publicly, on television and elsewhere, called blacks "apes," "beasts of the fields," and "like bollweevils to cotton. . . . Some of these weevils are puny little runts and can't create the volume of damage that others can. Some are powerful, becoming mad monsters snapping and snarling and biting the cotton. They must be destroyed, with their wretched remains buried, lest the pure white cotton bolls be destroyed." Of Evers he said: "He's dead, isn't he? That's one nigger who's not gonna come back." Later he told a reporter, "We need to reestablish a Confederate state of America as a white Christian republic. We don't need any dark-skinned, yellow-skinned, or blue-skinned mongrels running it."

In the summer after the second 1964 trial he officially joined the White Knights of the Ku Klux Klan, a violent, extremist cadre even by Klan standards. He became an intimate associate of the Imperial Wizard of this secret group, manned by illiterate, nihilistic, ferocious thugs: Sam Bowers, who had been the mastermind behind the brutal Neshoba County murders and who had been accused of organizing the statewide reign of executions and bombings in the 1960s, a fanatic with respectable establishment antecedents who was known to salute his German shepherd with the Heil, Hitler sign. Beckwith and his White Knight associates began to take on a strident anti-Semitic tone; the Jews, all of them Communists, would ultimately destroy the white Christian race, using the blacks as their foot soldiers. Beckwith lobbied at political meetings and through voluminous correspondence to have fluoride removed from the Jewish-controlled public water supply. Jews used Christians for human sacrifice, with their Negro allies as the kidnappers. The Holocaust was a massive hoax. They advocated dropping bombs on Israel. In these years the assassin of Medgar Evers was more cocky and self-assured than ever. He considered himself impregnable.

In 1973, on an FBI tip, he was arrested as he drove from Jackson to New Orleans. He had a powerful time bomb in his car and a city map marked with the address of an Anti-Defamation League leader in New Orleans, along with an arsenal of pistols, rifles, ammunition, hatchets, hammers, and knives. He was convicted in a Louisiana court by a five-member jury, whom he described as "five nigger bitches," and served three years in solitary confinement in Angola Prison. Then he moved to Signal Mountain, Tennessee, and more or less dropped out of sight for a while.

—

After the passage of twenty-six years, the chance to try the case again involved a confluence of elements some of which were more histrionic and bizarre than any imaginative fiction. A principal turning point was the revelation in 1989 by a young reporter named Jerry Mitchell of the Jackson *Clarion-Ledger* of possible jury-tampering in the earlier trials. The reporter's sources led him to secret documents of a defunct organization called the State Sovereignty Commission, a sort of boondocks Gestapo drawing state funds to spy on civil rights activists, integrationists, intellectuals, and just about anyone else who was considered "different."

Beginning in 1990 Assistant D.A. DeLaughter began his research into the languished case. All the previous pieces of evidence had vanished entirely. Even the official transcripts of the trials were missing. One of the items of evidence that had been lost was the murder weapon itself. DeLaughter eventually found it under circumstances that defy belief. The original autopsy report was also missing, and the exhumation of Evers's body for new forensic analysis was essential. Some aspects of the lengthy search had burlesque overtones, as when DeLaughter and Clara Mayfield, a flamboyant administrative assistant in the D.A.'s office, went out to a huge, lugubrious warehouse lacking electricity to search unsuccessfully through hundreds upon hundreds of musty old boxes for missing records. They were wary of rats. Often DeLaughter held a flashlight in his mouth while rummaging with both hands through the boxes. He thought to himself: They didn't teach *this* in law school.

Feelings were mixed over this unexpected new investigation. "Country-club Mississippi," Beckwith himself declared, "is tired of this crap the Jews, niggers, and Orientals are stirring up." Many whites opposed a new trial because of court costs, of unfairness to an old man, of meaningless political window dressing, and, more than anything else, of the inevitable public airing again of the state's appalling past. Besides, the whole affair was a waste of time because there would never be a conviction in Mississippi. Even a few aging, battle-scarred white liberals considered the probe a diversion to draw sentiment away from the state's real contemporary failings. Yet for those who favored a third trial, whites and blacks alike, the symbolic aspect was paramount. "It was an act of cleansing," Maryanne Vollers observed, "of rubbing out the relics of a shameful era. Although . . . sending Beckwith to prison wasn't going to solve the problems of racism, crime, or poverty, at least it was something that could be accomplished. It made some people more hopeful." It was this emotion that carried to the ultimate climax.

—

We were in the city that calls itself the Crossroads of the South, which Sherman had burned down in 1863, almost precisely one hundred years before Evers's death. The 1994 trial was a warp of time for me, a vista unto itself of the passing of eras in the South and America, moving ineluctably from past to present and back again in montage. Witnesses who were young at the 1960s trials came back now in advanced middle age with gray hair and wrinkled countenances. There were literal ghosts too—"dead" witnesses—their word-for-word testimony of thirty years before read from the yellowed transcripts by various individuals appointed to that eerie task.

In the spacious hallway outside the courtroom was a pentimento. The door to a rest room was painted brown, with the word WOMEN near the top. But if one looked quite closely, barely visible beneath the newer brown façade were the words WHITE WOMEN. (One of the architects on the restoration of the courthouse in the 1980s told me that they purposely left this label faintly visible as a reminder of the racist past.) In this setting during the recesses the interracial crowds gathered, white and black deputy sheriffs, white and black TV anchorpeople, white and black reporters from around the state and the nation, all this presided over by a popular white sheriff with a reputation as an integrationist who was an Equity actor and performed roles in Tennessee Williams and Beth Henley

dramas at the city theater. Security was so stringent that everyone
had to walk through metal detectors and sometimes undergo frisks
and searches, and in the courtroom itself the great mélange of
spectators were subject to watchful stares from armed deputies and
district attorney's personnel, including Benny Bennett and Charlie
Crisco, Bobby DeLaughter's investigators in the case, with their
concealed .38s.

With Medgar's widow throughout the trial were two of her children, Darrell and Reena, just as they had been the night of the
murder thirty-one years before. Darrell, who was the same age his
father had been at the time of his death and bore a striking resemblance to him, said he had come to the trial so Beckwith could "see
the face of the man he shot. All Beckwith saw was his back." Many
local and national NAACP associates were at the trial with Myrlie
also. Conspicuously absent, as he had been for the 1964 trials, was
her brother-in-law Charles Evers. There was bad blood between
them, going back to his years in Chicago as a bootlegger and gambler. But Charles adored the memory of his brother. He had not
come to the 1964 trials, nor to the 1994 one, he said, because he
was afraid he would go up to Beckwith and kill him, "snap his
scrawny neck like a chicken's."

In the early part of the proceedings there were not many young
people in attendance, and there were professions of disinterest
from some of them in the newspapers that all this had happened a
very long time ago, but as the trial went on, more and more young
whites and blacks showed up. The crowds grew so large that spectators were allowed in the balcony that had previously been reserved for the press corps. I was sitting with Curtis Wilkie of *The
Boston Globe*, Ron Smothers of *The New York Times*, Adam Nossiter of *The Atlanta Journal-Constitution*, Maryanne Vollers of
Time, Jerry Mitchell of the *Clarion-Ledger*, and John Emmerich of
the *Greenwood Commonwealth* as we observed this volatile tableau
around us: venerable Kluxers, black college students, innocent and
curious schoolkids of both races, all sitting together there in quer-
ulous juxtaposition.

To me one of the most affecting sights was the large number of elderly gray-haired black men who hobbled up the stairs and stood in clusters during the recess discussing facets of the trial. "Medgar died to free black folks *and* white folks," one of them was over-heard telling a reporter from Pennsylvania. "He freed white folks, too." A retired local detective observed to an associate, "We solved this for you thirty years ago, but you couldn't get him convicted."

In the 1964 trials Beckwith's defense had produced three alibi witnesses, policemen in the defendant's hometown of Greenwood ninety-six miles away, a constabulary notorious even in that Deep South generation for its brawny racism, who testified that they had seen him in a service station pumping gas less than an hour after Evers was shot: "Approximately 1:03 A.M.," one of them said. Of the three, one was now dead, another seriously ill, but the third was back, and he was an apparition for me in the waning after-noon's sunlight that streamed in through the courtroom windows. Retired now, he was a caricature of the older troubled times: the obese, slow, small-town Southern cop, and in a rush for me he too brought back those years. D.A. Ed Peters kept him on the stand for more than two hours in cross-examination, drawing on humor and sarcasm to demolish every detail of his alibi story.

Then, suddenly, the final witness of that afternoon approached the stand. When I saw him, I had a stabbing intimation of recog-nition, another flesh-and-blood specter. I had not seen him in more than forty years, had not so much as thought about him, but in an instant I knew the stocky, aging figure was John Book, whom I had grown up with, played ball and dated girls with, and now here was my own past being summoned for me—all because of Byron De La Beckwith. His brief testimony was anticlimactic to those hoary recognitions: He had been Beckwith's boss in the fertilizer company and testified that his employee talked segregation con-siderably more than he did the fertilizer business and that he had a bruise over his eye that could have been caused by the recoil of a rifle.

The courtroom itself was the same one in which the 1964 trials were held, a distinctive chamber from the 1930s with teak paneling, high ceilings from which hung big chandeliers, and large carved American eagles adorning the walls, brushed with the patina of vanished human sins and foibles and the slow quirky paths of requital. The presiding judge, a neighbor of mine in Jackson named Breland Hilburn, had a natty beard, unheard of in these precincts in 1964.

Whenever the defendant left the room during recesses to fetch a cup of coffee or water, which was frequently, a sizeable white deputy wearing a service revolver casually got up and followed him. Sketch artists for the networks worked on the first row of the press balcony, and in silent intervals one could hear the faint muffled sound of their pencils, and in eventful moments you could observe the whole assembled national press corps leaning forward with hands cupped to their ears against the imperfect acoustics. They thought me flippant when I told them I myself had been tried at age sixteen in this very courtroom in the high summer of 1951 for embezzlement of state funds, but indeed I had, for as the elected state treasurer of the annual Boys' State, an exercise sponsored by the American Legion to teach us about government, I was indicted on such counts as part of a mock trial. I had been acquitted of all charges, but now, more than forty years later, I was suffused once more with time and remembrance.

But it was the jury itself, of course, that dominated all else, and they were absorbing. They were working-class people, consisting of two white women, two white men, four black women, and four black men. They were a young group with one exception: an elderly black man, balding and wearing glasses, who sat each day on the second row at the far right in the jury box. He was a preacher, we would learn, and also would be the foreman. They were country people from up in Panola County, a half-Delta, half-hills locale only a few miles from Lafayette County, Faulkner's fictional Yoknapatawpha. They had been empaneled from there rather than Jackson because of the pretrial publicity in the capital city and brought down by chartered bus. Every time they entered the courtroom and walked to the box there was a hush and rustle throughout the chamber, as if something grave and portentous might be transpiring. There was much pressure on them.

Much of the evidence against the defendant had been used in the earlier trials. Beckwith's fingerprint was on the rifle, which had been found in honeysuckle vines in the vacant lot across the street from the Evers house; when the Enfield rifle was passed among the jury two black jurors visibly cringed. The cabdriver of whom Beckwith had asked directions to the Evers house came forward again. A car matching the description of his white Plymouth Valiant, with mud all over it, a long radio antenna, and a fraternal emblem, was seen in the neighborhood three days earlier. Another witness, a middle-aged woman who in 1963 was a twenty-two-year-old carhop at Joe's Drive-In near the Evers house, had seen the same Valiant parked there that night and a man fitting Beckwith's description leaving it to use the rest room. The car was still there at midnight.

Perhaps more than anything else, it was Beckwith's own words that ultimately snared him. "When he thought he had beat the system thirty years ago," the assistant D.A. told the jury, "he couldn't keep his mouth shut with people he thought were impressed with him." The six star witnesses for the prosecution, including Delmar Dennis and another Ku Klux Klan informant, testified that he boasted to them over the decades about killing Evers. One of the most incriminating witnesses was a fifty-one-year-old woman who was dining with a companion in a restaurant near Greenwood in 1966. Beckwith and a friend were the only other customers in the establishment. She testified:

> I was introduced to him as "Byron De La Beckwith, the man who killed Medgar Evers." He stuck out his hand, smiling and nodding like this.
> I told him he was a murderer and I would not shake his hand.

He became very angry. He said he had not killed a man but a "damn chicken-stealing dog and you know what you have to do with a dog that has tasted blood."

The most effective of these witnesses was a former Louisiana prison guard assigned to Beckwith in a state-prison hospital ward in 1979, when the defendant was serving his three-year sentence for possessing unregistered explosives. The former guard had been watching the CNN coverage of the trial in Chicago and recognized Beckwith. He telephoned the prosecutors in Jackson and flew in for his testimony. Beckwith had taken a liking to him, he said, and told him he had killed "that uppity nigger Medgar Evers" and that his influential friends in Mississippi had protected him from being punished. When a black nurse in the prison hospital objected, he told her, "If I can get rid of an uppity nigger like Medgar Evers, I won't have any problem with a no-count nigger like you."

Rumors abounded that he would testify in his own behalf and that his lawyers were trying to dissuade him, possibly with good reason. In both 1964 trials he had taken the stand and testified with much swagger and bravado, acknowledging among other things his many letters to publications, such as the one he wrote to the National Rifle Association in 1963: "For the next fifteen years, we here in Mississippi are going to have to do a lot of shooting to protect our wives and children from a lot of bad niggers." The district attorney this time, Ed Peters, had a substantial reputation for his vivid cross-examinations, for his artistry in cornering a victim in his own words, as he had the former Greenwood policeman. Subsequently the defendant took the Fifth Amendment, to the keen relief of his counsel and the disappointment of Peters and DeLaughter. "Coward to the end," Myrlie Evers whispered to a friend.

Holding the murder weapon and facing the jury, DeLaughter in his closing argument declared "for the sake of a civilized society, that justice in this case is what you ladies and gentlemen say it is.

You twelve *are* Mississippi. What is Mississippi justice for the defendant's hate-inspired assassination, assassination of a man who just desired to be free and equal? . . . Is it ever too late to do the right thing?"

It had taken fifteen days of testimony, and at lunchtime just before a colossal Dixie thunderstorm, one of the most horrendous I ever saw, the jury began its deliberations. People had earlier heard animated shouting from inside the deliberation room. The stormy darkness came without a decision; the judge advised the jurors to get a good night's rest and come back the next morning and start again. There were apprehensions of yet another hung jury.

As the foreman later divulged, he asked the members of the jury to stand in a circle in the deliberation room the next morning to hold hands and pray that they might make the right decision. They had been deliberating for little more than an hour when with a surprising quickness they reached their verdict. People from all over the city, including Myrlie Evers and her children, rushed to get back before the courtroom doors were closed. The chamber was tense and silent as the judge asked the jurors to stand facing him in single rank in front of the bench. The old black preacher said, "Guilty as charged."

Within seconds, as the word got out, cheers echoed through the courthouse corridors and out onto the front lawn, where a mixed racial audience stood. Bobby DeLaughter later likened this rippling response to "a stadium wave at a football game." Beckwith, looking at the backs of the jurors, was unemotional. "He's not guilty!" his wife, Thelma, shouted. "And ya'll know he's not. The Jews did it." In the courtroom and in the hallways outside, there were more exultant cries. In seconds the defendant was ushered away between two black deputy sheriffs. In a press conference shortly after this, Myrlie Evers, flanked by her son Darrell and daughter Reena, fought back her tears. She raised her hand and shouted, "Yeah, Medgar!" Then, ruefully: "My God. I don't have to say 'accused assassin' anymore. Now I can say *convicted* assassin.

Medgar's life was not in vain, and perhaps he did more in death than he could have in life. Somehow I think he is still among us."

Like many others, David Rae Morris, the New Orleans photographer who got his father in on this trial, had not anticipated such a quick verdict that morning, and he missed it by five minutes. Despite that, he reminisced, "I'll always remember the week and a half I spent in the balcony of that courtroom, and the history that took place there. It was better than anything anyone could conjure up on television or even on the court channel because it *was* history."

Bail was denied. "He's been out on bond for thirty years," one of the prosecutors said. The Jackson *Clarion-Ledger,* the state's ranking newspaper, which in my boyhood had been perhaps the most virulently racist paper in America, known by black people as the *Klan-Ledger,* editorialized: "Now Medgar Evers can rest in peace and the state of Mississippi can again celebrate the ideals of freedom for which Evers died." It went on to demand the reopening of other investigations into the unsolved civil rights crimes in the state of that generation ago: "The foundations of our justice system cannot allow these cases of conscience to go unresolved."

Those festering transgressions foremost included the murders of the three civil rights activists in Neshoba County in the summer of 1964, which inspired the movie *Mississippi Burning.* Eight Klansmen, including KKK Imperial Wizard Sam Bowers, were imprisoned on federal conspiracy charges; none served more than six years. The state refused to press charges.

In 1966 Vernon Dahmer, an NAACP leader, died after a firebomb attack on his home in Forrest County. Thirteen people were charged, and four were convicted of murder. Two cases resulted in mistrials, and the others were dropped. The man accused of organizing the plot, the same Imperial Wizard Bowers who was Beckwith's superior and confidant in the Klan, was tried twice for murder and arson; all-white juries refused to convict him.

In 1959 in Poplarville, hometown of the late Senator Theodore G. Bilbo, a black truck driver named Charles Parker, accused of raping a white woman, was abducted from the jail by a lynch mob, who chained and shot him and threw his body in the Pearl River. Charges were never brought. Crimes such as these had remained a lingering disgrace for most Southerners.

——

On the night of the verdict William Faulkner's niece, Dean Faulkner Wells, telephoned me from up in Oxford: "Hooraw for Mississippi!" she said. "We got the ol' SOB!"

The night after the verdict was announced, JoAnne and I took Fred Zollo out to the Evers house. The tremendous rainstorm had now run its course. It was a dark windless midnight when we drove to the neighborhood, about the same hour as the killing in 1963. We proceeded to the thoroughfare that in those days was called Delta Drive, now Medgar Evers Boulevard. We passed what had been Joe's Drive-In, now a late-hour beer establishment with a black clientele, where Beckwith's muddy white Valiant with its long whiplike antenna and its sword-and-cross Shriners emblem dangling from the rearview mirror had been sighted by the young carhop that night. We traced the route he had walked some two hundred feet, to what then was the overgrown vacant lot where he surreptitiously waited in the clump of honeysuckle under the sweet gum tree. We crossed the street, then called Guynes Street, and tarried before the house itself. All the windows were boarded up. No one was about, and the neighboring dwellings were shadowy and still. We stood at the driveway where the victim had gotten out of his car carrying the JIM CROW MUST GO! T-shirts, then the bullet from the deer rifle ripped into his back. This was the door through which his wife and children rushed to him as they shouted, "Daddy, get up!" This was where he tried to crawl toward his wife's arms. This was the concrete over which his blood flowed. In the preternatural quiet I pondered anew how the passing of time itself had been the fabric and sinew of these recent events, witnesses who were young then grown into the fullness of their years, memory itself ripened and culminating. Medgar Evers, who as a young man had attained martyrdom that would soon heighten with the making of a Hollywood movie, would have been seventy years old at the time of the final verdict; his children now were his age then. Everyone, myself among them, was older.

Beckwith was older too, but just as many of the others had perhaps changed and matured, it was he who seemed the historical artifact. Dodgeful and unrepentant, he was taken away to spend the rest of his life behind bars, fading emblem of a destructive epoch. He would not be sent to the notorious State Penitentiary at Parchman because the authorities knew someone would kill him there. He would remain in the Hinds County jail. Others would still hold his views, but they were in a small minority here now, and never again would the acts of someone like him be so collectively condoned, or so shielded by official deceit. Or so I pray.

Chapter 4

MYRLIE AND BOBBY
AND TWO TOUGH COPS

A central thread of the real-life story was the relationship between two people, the widow and the lawyer. At the beginning, it was an uneasy relationship of doubting and ambivalence, but gradually it became one of collaboration, friendship, and affection. One of the future criticisms of the film was that Myrlie was not an equally major character.

—

Myrlie was seventeen, bashful and innocent, when she first met Medgar in 1947. He was eight years her senior. She was leaning on a lamppost on the Alcorn campus when she heard noises behind her—football players. One of them approached her, she recalled years later, and "looked me up and down." She said to him, "I don't talk to strangers." Later he told her, "You are going to be the mother of my children."

The early years of their marriage were difficult. She was the product of a protective middle-class black family in Vicksburg, and she loved music and the piano. At first she was alarmed by her husband's perilous, exhausting work with the NAACP. She craved more privacy and security for her family, but with time she grew to believe in his dedication; they would become in every sense collaborators.

As attractive, college-educated, family-oriented blacks, Myrlie and Medgar could easily have closed their eyes to the realities of 1950s and 1960s Mississippi and let others lead the struggle; or they could have joined the continuing exodus of Southern blacks to the North and the West. Yet they loved Mississippi and felt its promise. Neither of them set out to become historical figures, but they chose to stay and to lead the fight. "It may sound funny," Medgar once told a reporter from *Ebony*, "but I love the South. I don't choose to live anywhere else. There's land here, where a man can raise cattle, and I'm going to do that someday. There are lakes where a man can sink a hook and fight bass. There is room here for my children to play, and grow, and become good citizens—if the white man will let them." When the NAACP offered to send him to California for his own safety, he said, "I belong here." Shortly after his house was firebombed he told a reporter, "I may be going to heaven or hell. But I'll be going from Jackson."

In her 1967 memoir *For Us, the Living* (the title taken from Abraham Lincoln's Gettysburg Address), Myrlie recounts how her husband was constantly torn between love and anguish for Mississippi. His first job after college, obtained for him by the company's secretary, Aaron Henry, an active leader in the NAACP (who later would serve for many years as its state president and also be elected to the legislature from his Delta district), was selling insurance to black sharecroppers in the Delta, who lived in virtual peonage to the planters. Myrlie supplemented the family income as a typist. She writes of how Medgar would return home at night

bursting with stories of adults with nothing to eat; of sanitary conditions no self-respecting farmer would permit in his pigpen. He painted word pictures of shacks without windows or doors, with roofs that leaked and floors rotting underfoot. For a while he had ignored the worst of these shacks, sure that no one could live in them. But then he was sent to one and began to visit them all. "They are all of them full, Myrlie!" he would exclaim as he drove me by a cluster of the worst of them on a Sunday afternoon. "Every one of them! People live in there. Human beings. People like you and me."

In his initial bitterness and rage, Evers flirted briefly with radical approaches, then decided to work for reform within the democratic system. When he moved to Jackson in 1955 to become the NAACP field secretary, frightened and dispossessed people called on him about everything, and he comforted them with a furious desperation. It was during this time that he began traveling the dark roads of the Delta at night investigating the killings and other brutalities in his sharecropper's disguise.

He was in many ways a highly conventional man. When Medgar and Myrlie opened the NAACP office in Jackson, they were its only staff. Yet he insisted that if they were to work together they must conduct themselves in the office strictly as employer and employee, not only because of the appropriate forms but to avoid any charge that he was taking more money out of the organization for his wife. This behavior included never discussing personal problems in the office and addressing each other as Mr. and Mrs. Evers. She found this kind of formality difficult for eight hours a day. One afternoon when no one was around she went into his office and sat on his lap. He pushed her off. "Oh, Medgar," she said. "Who's going to know? Even if someone walked in, it isn't important. We *are* married." And he would remind her again that the NAACP was paying for them to work and conduct a dignified office, and that was what they would do.

As the years passed, eventually his name was prominent on the "death lists." By the spring of 1963 both he and Myrlie knew the end was near. They also believed that his murderer, whoever it was to be, would never be convicted, not in Mississippi. He was destined to become such a great American martyr not only because he died in his prime, but because, like Martin Luther King after him, he learned to live and work with the mounting inevitability of being killed and refused to turn away. He and his wife taught their children how to fling themselves onto the floor of their house on Guynes Street in Jackson at a strange noise, to train their ears to the sound of a passing car or the bark of their dog. "To three-year-old Van, it was all a game," she recalled, "and he dropped to the floor with complete abandon. Darrell, eleven, and Reena, ten, were serious about it; they listened carefully and practiced conscientiously. In the midst of the lesson, Darrell asked what they should do if Van forgot to fall. Medgar told him to pull Van down with him."

When he first confided to Myrlie his real fear, he said that if anything should happen to him, she must promise to take good care of the children.

> I pretended to take offense and reminded him that I, too, had played some part in their being here, that they were my children, too. And then I noticed tears in his eyes, and I said, "Oh, Medgar!" and we both broke down and cried together. We clung to each other as though it were our only hope, and in my heart I felt that time was running out. There was no anger, no bitterness, not even a sense of having been robbed of what other people took for granted. There was just a bottomless depth of hopelessness, of hurt, of despair.

In a 1967 review of *For Us, the Living* Southern journalist Ralph McGill wrote: "The story of young Medgar Evers—a young David determined to do open battle with the Goliath of evil, injustice, and discrimination—is one of the most heroic stories of our time."

He was shot only four hours after President Kennedy's civil rights address. Kennedy and his brother Robert had been slow in coming around on civil rights, in no small measure so as not to turn Southern senators and congressmen against the president's legislative programs. But developing events in the South had profoundly affected them. Kennedy's speech on that night pulled no punches. The movie *Ghosts of Mississippi* would open with an aerial shot of Beckwith in his white Valiant driving south through the Delta toward Jackson. From the car radio one hears Kennedy's voice: *"The heart of the question is whether all Americans are to be afforded equal rights and equal opportunities, whether we are going to treat our fellow Americans as we want to be treated."*

In the next scene Myrlie and her three children are shown watching the television in their house: *". . . if, in short, he cannot enjoy the full and free life which all of us want. . . ."* And then from the radio in Medgar's car: *"Those who do nothing are inviting shame as well as violence. Those who act boldly are recognizing right as well as reality."*

A week later Medgar was buried with full military honors in Arlington. I remember as yesterday, as a magazine editor in New York, absorbing the television images and the photographs in *Life* magazine of Kennedy's receiving the widow and three children in the Oval Office after the burial. To this day these scenes tear at one's heart—made all the more poignant by our knowledge that the president himself would be shot down by an assassin's bullet less than six months later.

Andrew Young, a civil rights activist in Georgia at the time, remembered in his book *An Easy Burden* the effects of the Evers assassination:

His murder brought home to us our own vulnerability. Our tendency had been to ignore danger, even in the midst of potentially violent confrontations. Medgar's murder was one of many in the South that made us aware of how deeply the progress we had made had disturbed the racist psyche. We were now in uncharted psychological territory: never before had whites seen blacks as determined, as defiant as they were in 1963; never had blacks themselves been so willing to throw off the accumulated mental shackles of the days of slavery and postslavery. Blacks were staging smaller-scale campaigns across the South, and it appeared as if the white supremacists were launching a coordinated counterassault. An increase in the violence against blacks in the South during that spring and summer of 1963 seemed like desperate, blind attempts to murder our new spirit and resurrect the Old South by the same means it had been so long sustained— through acts of terrorism.

In the days after Medgar's death, Myrlie stood at the bedroom window watching her son Darrell playing baseball with some other boys. He hit the ball, then stood there momentarily and threw the bat away. "His whole body shook and he broke into sobs and he ran from the street around the house to the back yard and the plum tree. I ran to meet him, and he cried as though his heart would break standing there under the tree that Medgar had planted. It was the first time he had cried."

For more than three decades Myrlie carried on a solitary, hopeless crusade to keep the Beckwith case alive. As I got to know her after the 1994 trial, I saw a person shaped by tragedy and sadness, as if she had been stripped of the foolishness most of us have in ourselves. I also saw a very strong, determined woman of sixty-two, whose trust one had to earn.

She had taken her children and moved to California. For five years she served as a commissioner on the Los Angeles Board of Public Works, the first woman to have done so. She married Walter Williams, a longshoreman, union organizer, and civil rights activist, and they eventually moved to Oregon, but over the years she kept her contacts in Mississippi. In February 1994, at the third and final trial, she and two of her children came from the West Coast to be there every day. Once more she would testify, just as she had at the two trials of 1964.

"At times I didn't know if I could make it," she would say. There were two points of closure for her in February '94. One was the day she went to the D.A.'s office in the courthouse and for the first time saw photographs of Medgar taken at the hospital after the shooting. "In one photo," she said, "Medgar's already expired, but his eyes are still open. He was on a stainless steel table. I put my fingers over his eyes, mentally closing them. Emotionally it was very important to me." Then came the guilty verdict. "And this was a point of closure for my children as well. It was as though every demon escaped out of every pore."

One night a few weeks after Beckwith's conviction, Myrlie had dinner in Jackson with me and my wife, JoAnne, who was Myrlie's editor at the University Press of Mississippi, which was reissuing *For Us, the Living*. Myrlie spoke of her husband, Walter, who was very ill in their home in Oregon. "There were always the three of us," she said, "Medgar, Walter, and myself." She talked about her son Van, a photographer in Los Angeles, who never wanted to return to Mississippi. But *she* might come back here to live when she retired, she said, because this had always been her home.

In New York City several months later, she was elected chair of the board of the NAACP, which had been racked by scandal and deficit. Six hours after she returned to Oregon, Walter died.

——

I had been enormously impressed by Bobby DeLaughter during the trial but did not get to know him until after it was over; he would become one of my closest friends. I telephoned him for the first time the day after the verdict. He was letting off the pressures of the trial at his cabin in the woods, drinking beer and watching old Westerns on his VCR. He and his wife lived in a rambling isolated wood-frame structure several miles out from Jackson with kids, a vegetable garden, country dogs, and a bottle tree, whose colored bottles stuck on the branches of a cedar stripped of foliage would suck in evil spirits, called "haints" according to Southern black tradition. DeLaughter's wife, Peggy, was responsible for the bottle tree. The first white person she had known with such a tree was a man in Clinton, Mississippi. "I vowed that I too would have a bottle tree like that someday, and when we moved to the cabin I had just the place for one in the garden. I was mesmerized by the sun shining through the colored glass and hearing the soft

Southern breezes blowing whistles against the mouths of the bottles. My spirits would lift, and I would feel relaxed and safe as a child."

Bobby grew up in a conservative white middle-class family in Jackson and was in the third grade when Medgar Evers was killed. He had never heard of Medgar then and would not for a long time. When he was fourteen years old he came to the same Hinds County courtroom of the past and future Beckwith trials on a field trip with his ninth-grade classmates and sat in the balcony watching a trial in which Bill Waller, who had handled the case against Beckwith in 1964, was the defense attorney and Russel Moore, Bobby's future father-in-law, was the presiding judge. "I was hooked on the law right there," he said.

He was a sophomore in high school when the massive integration of the public schools arrived. JoAnne's younger brother, Dr. Jay Shirley, was a teenager in the Boy Scouts when he got to know Bobby DeLaughter in the 1970s. This was in the Scouts' highest organization, the Order of the Arrow, and at Camp Kickapoo outside of Jackson, Bobby was an Order of the Arrow leader in his early twenties. Bobby, Jay remembered, was responsible for the campfire ceremonies based on Native American traditions. "He and a few others sang and chanted for us the traditional Indian songs while playing a large Indian drum. My warmest memories as a kid were of Bobby and others as my mentors, advisors, and leaders."

Bobby eventually went to Ole Miss and graduated from law school there. He married a girl from Jackson named Dixie, daughter of the circuit judge Russel Moore, who was a prominent racist. After he took on the dormant Beckwith case, he and Dixie quarreled over that and many other things. When they divorced he assumed custody of their three children. He later married a nurse, Peggy Lloyd, both sensitive and down-to-earth, who supported him unequivocally. "I don't believe I could have made it through this without her," he says.

He is an introverted, complicated man and, as with Myrlie

Evers, only reveals himself to people he really trusts. He is modestly self-confident and brave. He is deeply religious but does not advertise it. "I've never been much of a party person," he once said to me. "I've voted for Republicans and Democrats alike ever since I could vote. The one thing I've always been is a conservative. That surprises some people who viewed the reprosecution of Beckwith as a civil rights case or a liberal cause. I've been fighting that label ever since 1989—with my family, the public, the media, and later Hollywood. Beckwith is a cowardly, back-shooting, common thug with a pedigree, and his despicable crime was a monkey on Mississippi's back for a long time. It was from the depths of my conservatism, under God's guidance, that I drew strength enough to keep going. That's the reason I kept going back to the crime scene and visualizing what happened there."

He is the long-distance runner. "He runs real deep," a lawyer who worked with him for a long time said. "He's got a very deep, quiet conviction about things." Noting his "almost black-and-white sense of right and wrong," Adam Nossiter wrote: "The law, with its precise codification of this distinction, was natural territory for him to inhabit. It was important to believe in the justice of his cause. Once he did so, he was able to exercise the fierce tenacity others see as his defining characteristic." Yet beneath the often stoic façade there are intensely strong emotions, and also a strain of irrepressible humor, buttressed by a gift for telling stories. He is loyal to those who are close to him. He is a good judge of character because he *has* character; I always want to know what he thinks about things. Personal traits like these were indispensable for the person who reinvestigated and reprosecuted Medgar Evers's assassin; without Bobby DeLaughter, Beckwith would never have been convicted.

Despite the dire scarcity of evidence and the lack of enthusiasm in the state for a new trial, Bobby had grown increasingly committed. At first, he did not get much support from his superior, District Attorney Peters, an old-guard Mississippian who had put more murderers on death row at Parchman Prison than anyone in the state's history. Peters, silver-haired and flamboyant, had declared in 1987 that Beckwith was unprosecutable, particularly on the Sixth Amendment of the U.S. Constitution pertaining to "speedy trial." "Anyone having taken the first class in law school ought to know that," he said. For years he had had a dubious reputation among Jackson blacks. A controversial and enigmatic figure in Mississippi, he oversaw a D.A.'s office with a legal staff two and three times smaller than other Southern cities relatively the size of Jackson. The work was enormous, and a futile, meaningless case like the Beckwith one might detract from other, more pressing matters.

But Peters ran a laissez-faire office. He liked and trusted Bobby and eventually fully backed him, allowing him, Charlie Crisco, and Benny Bennett the time and leeway they needed to accumulate the evidence. He would play a critical, brilliant role in the jury selection and the trial itself with his talent on cross-examination and summation. His heart would ultimately be unreservedly with this conviction. "Ed Peters, as far as I'm concerned," Charles Evers later said, "was one of the greatest supporters we had. He could easily have stopped DeLaughter by saying don't do it. He did what a district attorney is supposed to do—be cautious and make sure they don't make mistakes."

It had dawned on Bobby that he himself was the same age, thirty-seven, as Medgar had been at his death, and that both of them had three children, two boys and a girl, of almost the same age. "What if my kids had had to go through what Darrell, Van, and Reena went through?" he asked himself. "What would their lives be like?" Bobby had political ambitions, to be a judge. The evil of Beckwith's deed began to obsess him. "This was something that ought to offend every decent human being, no matter what your race," he said.

He began receiving a lot of hate mail and anonymous telephone calls. For weeks every Saturday at 6:00 A.M. he was awakened by a call from Thelma Beckwith in Tennessee haranguing him about the investigation. Two or three times during the investigation, consumed with uncertainty over what he was doing and fear for his family, he drove to the Evers house alone at night and wept as he imagined what had happened there. He promised himself in such moments that he would see the case through, no matter what.

Many months later he would be watching the filming of the murder itself at the real Evers house in Jackson. His office had provided the movie people with photographs of the 1963 crime scene and of Medgar and Myrlie's cars parked in the driveway that night. It was the scene that had haunted him for years; he was used to seeing it all in black and white. During the filming he was sitting behind Rob Reiner's monitor. After the first take of Medgar being shot in the back, all he could do was sit there and stare at the monitor. Reiner turned to Bobby and asked him what he thought. "If feeling heartsick and angry all over again is a sign that this is a good shot," he answered, "then it's a good shot."

———

The most salubrious effect of reporter Jerry Mitchell's 1989 newspaper pieces was that in a roundabout way they were responsible for Myrlie and Bobby first meeting, for the initial halting beginnings of their partnership. After Mitchell's highly publicized allegations of jury-tampering by the State Sovereignty Commission in the second 1964 trial, Myrlie came to Jackson from the West Coast to push for a new one. Morris Dees of the Southern Poverty Law Center in Montgomery was representing her, and there was a cool initial confrontation in D.A. Peters's office. Since Peters had put his assistant D.A. in charge of taking at least a cursory look into what they had, Bobby was at this conference. Myrlie and Dees were shocked and disbelieving that all the old evidence had vanished.

Bobby was impressed from the start with Medgar's widow. Myrlie, despite her grave suspicions, would eventually sense something in the reserved assistant D.A., scion of the white Mississippi lineage though he was. He would remind her a little of Medgar, and indeed there were similarities: Both of them were workaholics, smart, brave, and stubborn, with a love of family and native soil. As the search for evidence proceeded, Bobby telephoned Myrlie every week on the West Coast to bring her up to date. There was precious little to report at first. She gave him leads to pursue in the black community and finally presented him with something invaluable: the only extant copies of the authorized transcripts of the 1964 trials, which she had protected all those years.

To Bobby two of the most compelling moments of the search were the discovery of the murder weapon and the exhumation of Medgar's body. A courthouse old-timer told him that local officials in those days were sometimes given trial evidence as "souvenirs." Bobby suddenly recalled that his former father-in-law, the late Judge Russel Moore, who was a gun collector, had years ago showed him a rifle that he said had been a piece of evidence in an old civil rights case. At his ex–mother-in-law's house he and Mrs. Moore found a bolt-action rifle stored on the shelf of a bedroom closet. On a small scrap of paper he had written the serial number of the missing weapon from the 1963 police files. Bobby remembers feeling a funny chill as he stood under a light and read the numbers on the metal under the telescopic sight and compared them with those on the scrap of paper: 1052682.

The 1963 autopsy report remained one of the many items still missing. At first Myrlie was shocked by Bobby's suggestion of an exhumation, but she relented when her son Van offered to go to Arlington National Cemetery as the family's representative. Bobby had sought out the most admired and famous forensic pathologist in the country, Dr. Michael Baden of New York, who had examined President Kennedy's and Martin Luther King Jr.'s autopsy reports for congressional investigations almost twenty years before. The testimony of a man with Baden's reputation on a new autopsy that might link whatever bullet fragments remained in the body to the rifle, Bobby felt, would be effective at a new trial. The case interested Baden, who had admired Medgar Evers, and he offered his services to Hinds County free of charge. The corpse was exhumed early one morning in June 1991. Bobby was there along with Charlie Crisco and Van Evers, now thirty years old. The casket was put in a hearse for the long drive to Albany, New York, where Baden had his laboratory. Van Evers sat next to the casket all the way, with Bobby and Crisco following. At rest stops he tearfully telephoned his mother.

In the autopsy lab the next morning Bobby left Van in the outside corridor and promised him that if the remains they found in the coffin were not too horrible, he would come out and get him. When Baden and the others opened the coffin, there was a collective gasp. After nearly thirty years, Medgar's body appeared perfectly preserved. Even his suit was clean and dry. Baden told the others that he had never seen anything like this in his entire career. He, Crisco, and Baden left the room to allow Van to be with his father. Van was very touched, Crisco recalled: "It was like his going to the funeral home as if his father had died yesterday." Myrlie later said she saw God's hand in this, to allow Van to see his father as he once was. Crisco had a video camera and taped the entire autopsy. Baden found tiny bullet fragments still in the body's chest, and they matched the rifle, yet another extraordinary piece of evidence the members of the 1994 jury would be able to hold in their hands, along with the rifle itself. Months later Bobby told me that the transfer of the coffin from Washington to the autopsy lab was so secretive that shortly before it was opened a young assistant of Baden's, who had only known that the proceedings had something to do with Mississippi, took Bobby aside and in all seriousness asked, "Is this Elvis Presley?"

—

Tortuous though the process was, important evidence was gradually brought together. An officer cleaning out the police evidence room came across an old canister of camera negatives from the 1963 crime scene. The fingerprint files and much of the original police report were found. A number of the witnesses from thirty years before were finally located. Significantly, several of the people who had heard Beckwith himself admit to the crime over the years were sought out and agreed to testify. "Let me say this," Myrlie Evers declared after the trial, "Bobby DeLaughter deserves all the credit that can be given to him for persevering in this case. He took a severe beating in terms of his reputation, job, and first wife leaving. Without him there would have been no one to prosecute that case."

Some weeks after the trial, Bobby ran for a newly established judgeship overseeing Hinds County and fourteen adjoining ones. His opponent was a conservative old-line white lawyer-politician. The responses to Bobby during his campaign ranged from receiving warm congratulatory handshakes to having his campaign literature thrown back in his face. His opponent used the "Beckwith card" at every chance. Myrlie Evers flew in at her own expense to help Bobby campaign in black precincts on the last weekend before the election. I accompanied them as she introduced him to black churches and organizations and radio audiences as a courageous man who prosecuted her husband's killer. The following Tuesday friends and family joined Bobby and Peggy in the motel room that served as his campaign headquarters. The returns were swift and decisive. He was beaten badly. He took it hard. We stood together on the motel balcony overlooking the lights of the capital city and talked for a long time about our native ground. When I went home that night, as promised I telephoned Myrlie in Oregon to give her the results. "Oh, God!" she said. "How is he?"

"He was hoping it would be just another legal case," actor Alec Baldwin said after he had gotten to know the man he was playing in the movie. "He's kind of this classic American. He just believes that the right thing is going to happen. But he suffered."

Shortly after that, Bobby gave me a copy of his closing argument to the jury. In his cover letter he wrote, "You are a brother Mississippian who shares the same vision for our state as I, and who grieves when we find ourselves in a crossfire of its mysterious forces." Then he quoted from Proverbs 17:17: "A friend loves at all times, and kinsfolk are born to share adversity."

Several months later Bobby switched from the Democratic to the Republican party. After his defeat in the judicial elections a law went into effect making these elections nonpartisan, but in his unsuccessful campaign he had run as a Democrat "based on advice that I'd automatically lose any black voting base if I didn't do so," he said, "and because I was of the belief that voters still considered Democrats to be just as conservative as Republicans. I was wrong on both counts. Black voters do not blindly put a mark by the candidate's name with the 'D,' nor do they blindly follow political recommendations of their ministers. Giving credence to either one of these previous beliefs that I was taught is, I came to learn, an insult to black voters. To the extent that I was labeled under the Democratic banner, it was as the bleeding-heart liberal that went after 'that old man' just to get in good with the blacks but was otherwise 'soft' on crime. Nothing could've been farther from the truth, but I learned then that in politics perception *is* reality. By the summer of 1995, before the nonjudicial elections that year heated up, I joined the party that I felt best coincided with my values: the GOP, the party of Lincoln. If I'm going to be labeled, I at least want it to be a label that fits."

———

Enter now Charlie Crisco and Benny Bennett, two very tough cops. I got to know them both in Jackson and in L.A. during the movie filming; they reminded me a little of the homicide cops I once hung out with at P. J. Clarke's in New York years ago, Deep Dixie versions. I had grown up years ago in Mississippi with guys like Crisco and Benny, played ball with them, gotten along well with them.

Charlie and Benny had known more than anyone's share of murder, gore, blood, and mayhem, and they were more than wary of the casual deceits and the larger treacheries as well. Neither ever talked much about such graphics, but one knew this was always close to their minds. Later, in the early stages of *Ghosts of Mississippi,* they had not yet seen the art-house smash *Fargo,* and its lead male actor, William H. Macy, who would play Crisco in *Ghosts.* "It's full of wild humor and bloody violence," someone on the set told them. "Then that's right down our alley," Crisco said.

For four and a half years they were Bobby's investigators in the Beckwith case. Given the nature of this case, the difficulties inherent in it, the criticism of it from all quarters, it was important that the three of them have a good working relationship. They became friends. Bobby had never carried a gun and refused to do so even after Crisco offered him one. They had worked together before. Crisco was assigned to Bobby in 1989, but before that he had been a homicide detective for the Jackson police for twenty years. He cracked some big cases, including the one of a notorious local serial killer. He also had a special aversion to cop-killers, whom he had tracked down too. He was the head detective on the first death-penalty case that Bobby tried.

Charlie was forty-one when he came to the D.A.'s office. He had grown up in Jackson and had been a star baseball player in high school, in college for a year, then in the semipros; he was such a good ballplayer that he was something of a hero to Jackson kids. He had been a teenager when Medgar Evers was murdered and pretty much a product of the segregated society then, as were Benny and Bobby. He was a lance corporal in the Marines in the 1960s; like Bennett he was an expert marksman and went armed everywhere. He was thin, wiry, with an abundance of quick nervous energy. Wily, attentive, suspicious, he had a challenging steel-trap gaze. Charlie had had four wives and suffered from an acid homicide detective's stomach, for which he drank Pepto-Bismol. His eyes put holes through you. He looked you over and stared you down, like the homicide cop played by Steve McQueen in *Bullitt.* And when Bullitt's girlfriend asked him what he had been up to at work that day, he said: "It's not for you, baby."

"You're living in a sewer, Frank," she said to him.

"That's half of where it is."

That was Charlie. Wherever he was he jumped a little at every noise: "What was *that?*" Once in Jackson JoAnne and I arranged to meet Crisco and Bennett at the Elite Cafe on East Capitol for dinner. We arrived early and took two seats at a table for four with our backs to the rear of the room facing forward. When the two of them arrived they had us move to the two other chairs. "You know better than that," Crisco said. "We *never* sit with our backs to the door."

Charlie was an avid golfer and had been known to carry a .38 in his golf bag. It took him a long time to come around to you. Once he decided you were worthy, he warmed up to you. He and Bennett played jokes on each other. Once Bennett brought a grocery sack with a possum inside, left it on the porch of Crisco's house, rang the doorbell, and ran away. Crisco opened the door, looked into the sack, and the possum bit him on the finger. Years later, in late 1996, when Benny and Crisco were on a New York radio talk show promoting the movie, Crisco introduced Benny as "Marvin," and the host called the new movie star by that name throughout the interview. "It took me twenty years to get even," Crisco said.

They likewise played hoaxes on others. In the mid-1970s the two of them worked as partners on special-assignment detail. One particular assignment was a "rolling stake-out" in which they and others were watching a whole neighborhood in Jackson. In this neighborhood on West Capitol a huge, sprawling cemetery happened to be located. Some months earlier Crisco and Benny had bought a Frankenstein mask, gruesome, realistic molded rubber that fit over the head, and had gotten some laughs and scares out of it. Their detail on West Capitol consisted of fourteen cops supervised by a lieutenant. One lethargic night Crisco and Benny cooked up an idea, and with the approval and assistance of the lieutenant, the entire unit met at about midnight in the cemetery. Everyone was in on the plot except two inexperienced young cops who were to be the victims of the prank. In the cemetery the lieutenant explained the supposed situation: "I just talked to a man who lives across the street from this cemetery. A pack of dogs have drug some bones into his front yard. The man believed the bones to be human. I looked at the bones and they're indeed human bones. That's why we're meeting here in the middle of the night. I think the dogs dug up a grave and took the bones to the complainant's yard. We're gonna fan out and find the grave." Crisco was lying behind a large granite gravestone far down the way wearing the Frankenstein mask. At the appropriate time, when the two unsuspecting cops approached, he was to rise up slowly with a flashlight under his chin. The trick went as planned, with Benny leading the two in Crisco's direction. As they neared, he slowly rose from behind the gravestone, uttered a low, guttural moan, and illuminated the monster face with the flashlight. The two victims were frightened witless. They both went for their pistols, then one of them turned and ran. The other had his weapon out and was pointing it at Crisco. Fortunately Benny was standing next to the young cop. While the dozen others were laughing, Crisco was ducking behind the gravestone. Benny grabbed the young cop's hand, deflected the pistol upward, and shouted that it was all a joke. "But I wasn't laughing anymore," Crisco remembered.

Benny Bennett was thirty-nine when he joined DeLaughter's search. He had been with the D.A. for two years. He was born and raised in Jackson. His father had been a detective on the Jackson police force for thirty-three years. As a Jackson cop himself for twenty years, Benny had worked undercover on various projects, including infiltrating what little remained of the Klan. He was six feet two inches and weighed about 250 pounds; if Bobby was the black Lab and Crisco the fox terrier, Benny was the Great Dane of the trio. Even off duty he carried at least one gun and two knives, with one knife attached to the bottom of a gold chain around his neck and concealed under his shirt. He had a long handlebar mustache and dressed in jeans and denim vests. He wore his hair long and had two gold rings and a silver skull-ring on his fingers. When I first introduced him to Rob Reiner, Benny was wearing a sports jacket, shirt and tie, and snakeskin boots.

Benny had been infiltrating a motorcycle gang in an effort to catch some drug pushers. He heard that a substantial sale was to take place late one night in front of the Eudora Welty Public Library. Benny was there, and when the transaction occurred he moved in to make an arrest. The seller resisted, so Benny picked him up and threw him through the plate-glass window. When the case came to court, Benny was called to testify. The opposing lawyer made the fatal mistake of asking a question to which he did not know the answer: "Mr. Bennett, what on earth could you have been thinking when you threw the defendant through the window?"

"I was thinking how honored I was, sir."

"Honored?"

"Yes, sir, I felt honored I was the person responsible for that low-life piece of scum you represent being inside a library for the first time."

Benny always said "Yes, sir" and "Yes, ma'am," and it took me a long time to get him to call me by my first name. In addition to being a good marksman, he was adept in the defensive arts. Whether he was driving a car, walking down the street, or sitting in a restaurant, in Jackson or L.A., he seemed to see 360 degrees around him. He was always looking. He operated, one surmised, from a perspective most people know little about; he saw a world they did not see. JoAnne said being with Benny was like being with Superman; no harm could possibly come when he was around. Yet, withal, he was in his heart rather gentle and loveable, his fealty to those around him combatitively tenacious. As a Mississippian who had not traveled much, he was likewise open to new experiences, as later descriptions of his Hollywood sojourn will testify.

While he was with the Jackson police before joining Bobby and Crisco, Benny guarded visiting dignitaries and VIP's, including presidents, presidents-elect, Oliver North, and even Elvis. He first met Myrlie Evers when D.A. Peters and Bobby asked him to pick her up at her sister-in-law's house and bring her to the D.A.'s office. "I was almost expecting an Angela Davis–type person, you know," he remembered, "but she was a real nice lady, very warm and cordial and easy to talk to. We talked all the way to the office, just general chitchat about L.A. She's got a great sense of humor, and she's pretty." From then on she was to him "Miz Evers."

He recalled an incident later that day in the courthouse. "I'm a fancier of all sorts of weapons. Somebody had given me a large butterfly knife a few days previous, and I was walking around in the hallway practicing opening and closing it. I rounded the corner just as I flipped the knife open and who was there coming down the hall but Miz Evers." She looked at him and grinned and said, "I'd heard things were getting bad in Jackson, but I didn't realize they were getting *this* bad." "I like Miz Evers," Benny said.

Their work reinvestigating the Beckwith case was not without repercussions for Crisco and Bennett. Neither of the detectives were what might be called inside-the-Beltway liberals, but there were certain elements of indigenous matters, as when Crisco heard people say, "We got enough crime, why we got to be chasing around trying to bring *this* back up?" Once a man on the golf course came up to him. "He wanted to know what the hell we were doing dragging this shit back up," he remembered. "I replied there was no statute of limitations on murder and that any son of a bitch waiting in ambush and shooting a man in the back in front of his family, you're damned right I'd like to see his ass convicted."

Benny felt similarly. "I can't imagine if I'd seen my father murdered before my eyes. The idea of seeing him murdered, I just . . . I've watched friends die. On the police force here in Jackson. Yes, sir. It's a terrible, terrible feeling. You know a man was murdered and it robbed his wife and kids. Nobody deserves that, black, white, red, yellow, just nobody deserves that. Bobby did his job and did it good. Medgar Evers's spirit was at rest, his family at rest, and if Bobby hadn't done it, it wouldn't have been done at all." As for criticism he received about helping Bobby on the case, Benny said, "Can't none of 'em whup *my* ass."

There must have been thousands of other guys around the country like Charlie and Benny: decent, smart, and unsung, and never once portrayed as real flesh-and-blood people in the movies as the two of them were being. I think they realized that, and in an odd yet touching way took their responsibilities regarding the film seriously, because of those unrecognized others.

There was a moment during the jury selection in 1994 when Benny saw Myrlie sitting in the back of the courtroom. "I just felt sorry for her," he recalled. "I felt like she was all alone and she needed somebody to talk to." So he walked over to her, and they had a pleasant conversation. He had not known then that she had had suspicions on the night of the murder that a Jackson policeman had shot her husband. "It had never crossed my mind to tell her my daddy was there," he said. "You know, Miz Evers," he said to her in the courtroom, "my daddy was one of the detectives who came to your house when your husband was shot."

She looked at him and said, "Oh, Benny. Do you know that I must have hated your father?"

Benny replied, "In your position I would've felt the same way."

Charlie Crisco had a similar moment on the Saturday morning the jury was expected to enter the Jackson courtroom with the verdict. Like Benny, who was serving as bodyguard to Judge Breland Hilburn, he was involved in security and was standing in front of the jury box. He saw Myrlie sitting near the front of the courtroom. She was holding on to Reena and Darrell. "They were all together there," he remembered, "and you could tell she was emotionally exhausted, drained all the way." Their eyes met across the chamber. "I gave her a thumbs-up. She saw me and kind of cracked a smile. It may have helped a little."

During the investigation and even the trial, Crisco later said to me, at no time was he fully aware of the historical importance of what was happening. "I'd handled so many homicide cases. I take them as they come, one step at a time." At the trial itself he was in charge of dozens of details, including getting the witnesses in from all over the country and setting up tight security for them on a whole floor of the Holiday Inn. "There was just so much going on," he said, "you didn't have time to sit back and say, 'Now, this is gonna be a part of history.' " Only a little while after the verdict, when Dr. Baden sent him a clipping from the front page of *The New York Times*, did he at last realize how really big were the events of which he had been a part.

Chapter 5

FIRST WAVES

The first wave and initial point man into Jackson for the movie consisted of Fred Zollo himself. A celebrated and prolific theatrical producer of more than fifty plays in New York and London, including *On Golden Pond* and *Talk Radio,* he had also produced the films *Mississippi Burning* directed by Alan Parker, *The Paper* directed by Ron Howard, and *Quiz Show* directed by Robert Redford; both *Mississippi Burning* and *Quiz Show* had been nominated for Oscars. I had gotten to know Zollo several years before when he was doing *Mississippi Burning* in Jackson, and we had stayed in touch ever since. He had taken a hard rap in Mississippi and elsewhere for *Burning,* which was fictional yet loosely based on the 1964 Neshoba County murders and was assailed by a veritable popular front of critics ranging from black activists to white liberals and conservatives. The film was so controversial that *Time* gave it its cover and Ted Koppel devoted an entire *Nightline* to it. Older white Mississippians deplored these events being brought up again. Blacks did not appreciate being depicted as so passive, or that the two white FBI agents were the heroes.

The first time I saw the movie was at a theater filled to capacity, about half black and half white, and at the moment when Gene Hackman as the homegrown FBI man set out to get the Kluxers, a young black seated behind me shouted at the screen, "Kick ass, Gene!" I liked much of the movie and consider it metaphorically truthful. One of the many odd twists of the DeLaughter investigation was that Bobby and the others found out about Delmar Dennis's statement that he had heard Beckwith boast about killing Evers in the obscure volume *Klandestine* through Zollo's own Mississippi lawyer, Jack Ables. Ables had turned up the twenty-year-old book while representing Zollo and Orion Pictures in a nuisance suit filed against *Mississippi Burning* by Lawrence Rainey, the sheriff of Neshoba County at the time of the '64 killings. Zollo went so far as to say that the Mississippi grand jury would never have indicted Beckwith again had it not been for *Mississippi Burning*. "It's the power," he said, "of a motion picture. Oddly enough, when some of the critics said we rewrote history with *Mississippi Burning*, we *did*—in the bigger sense. The movie was essential to the retrial and successful reprosecution of Byron De La Beckwith. Jerry Mitchell started poking around in the files of the Sovereignty Commission because he was charged up by the movie. No movie, no Jerry Mitchell, no Jack Ables, no *Klandestine*, no Delmar Dennis. And Beckwith is still living up in Tennessee a free man." Jerry Mitchell himself acknowledged that *Mississippi Burning* helped goad him and the *Clarion-Ledger* to start looking into the racially motivated crimes of the 1960s.

Even though *Ghosts of Mississippi*, unlike *Mississippi Burning*, would be essentially a true story, the precedent of the latter's tempestuous reception only eight years before would cast warning clouds into the future. In some quarters the two films would inevitably be linked, to detrimental effect.

Zollo is a tall, slender figure of forty-four with a golfer's putting slouch and sleepy Mediterranean eyes. He grew up in Boston and attended college in the East, where he was a first baseman who got only one hit his sophomore year, and that a broken-bat single (I thought he was dissembling about this until I checked the records). He later got a degree at the London School of Economics. He married Barbara Broccoli, who was in the movie business in Los Angeles. Her father was the legendary Albert "Cubby" Broccoli, who originated and continued the long line of lucrative James Bond movies; before Cubby died in 1996, he turned over control of the James Bond movie franchise to Barbara and her stepbrother. Cubby's father had invented broccoli in Calabria, Italy, by a process of cross-breeding cauliflower and rabe, and an uncle had brought the first seeds to the United States in the 1870s.

Zollo had developed an affection for Mississippi. He knew countless people here: golfers, businessmen, aging black civil rights activists, lawyers, politicians, cops, writers, artists, journalists, restaurateurs, bartenders, and not a few fakirs, reprobates, and charlatans. I always had the hunch that he *needed* something in Mississippi, not so much professionally, though that too, but personally, as if it provided him something elusive yet real, something not obtainable in the affluent and heady neighborhoods of Manhattan or Beverly Hills. He once flew in to Jackson just to attend the dedication of the new main post office to Medgar. Later, when the film was moving apace, he would say, "When I'm in Los Angeles and I hear people say stuff about Mississippi, I tell them quickly, 'They haven't had race riots in a long time down there.' I tell them Mississippi is better than L.A. At least people there are trying. L.A. just had the worst race riots in history not long ago. Racial tension there is so thick you can slice it with a knife. Same with Boston, where I'm from. Go to a Celtics game, and the only blacks you see there are on the basketball court. Same at Fenway Park. Blacks don't feel welcome there. They know they'll be stared at. The way I look at it, race relations is the number-one issue facing our country today. We can do more than make a solid movie about Medgar Evers. We can make a movie that helps heal. As Bobby DeLaughter said, it's never too late to do the right thing."

Zollo often advocated that Jackson and Mississippi had a potential to become important sites for moviemaking because of their benign climate, diverse and colorful locales, and adequate airport, much like Wilmington, North Carolina, a city one third the size of Jackson but with major studios, a theme park, and hotel, all of which brought untold millions into the Old Catawba economy. But some of Mississippi's conservative pols remained wary of liberal celluloid outsiders, no matter how much the nation's poorest, most biracial commonwealth might need the income.

—

Certain things germinate in inscrutable ways. It was 2:30 A.M. on a Sunday morning of February 1994, the jury verdict in the Beckwith trial having been announced on early Saturday, and I heard a loud succession of knocks on the back door of my house in Jackson. When I opened it I confronted a raucous group: Zollo, the painter Bill Dunlap, and three or four other acquaintances. Zollo had flown in from New York for a couple of days of relaxation, and he and his companions had just closed down the bar at Hal & Mal's. The bartender himself, "Shoeless" Jack Stevens, descendant of a prominent Jackson family, collector of vintage minutiae, actor, bon vivant, closed down the bar and showed up a few minutes later because he thought our household might need some help, which it turned out it did; Shoeless Jack would call this night "Ground Zero" for the movie, and two years or so hence he himself would be signed on as a set dresser, responsible for accumulating 1950s and 1960s Mississippi artifacts.

Once settled in front of the fireplace, this boisterous mélange started singing songs, including "Amazing Grace," "As Time Goes By," and "Home on the Range." JoAnne, who was trying to sleep, came out of the bedroom to quiet them all down, then petulantly returned to her fitful slumber.

Zollo wanted to know more about the Beckwith trial, which they had been discussing at the bar. History had just been made in the Hinds County Courthouse, he was told. He needed to make a movie out of this. We talked until dawn about what had transpired in the Evers-Beckwith story. "Send me a memo," Zollo said to me. When he and the others mercifully departed, the driver of the interlopers' automobile ran over my backyard fence and landed in a ditch. AAA had to be summoned. Repairs to the fence would cost five hundred dollars.

Indulge me the memo:

February 28, 1994
Jackson

Dear Fred,

Here is my Beckwith piece. And here are some of my thoughts, as you requested and as we talked about, on why I think this would make a remarkable movie. In very random and eclectic order, and brief:

—The visual images from today: the boarded-up Evers house; the concrete driveway; the vacant lot across the street; Joe's Drive-In up the way; the courtroom itself and the attendant courthouse and Jackson scenes.

—The possible camera images of time having passed: the old gray-haired blacks in the courtroom; the black deputies; the *jury*; etc.

—Perhaps consider going first and at considerable length with black-and-white, documentary-type film footage of Mississippi in 1963, Evers's murder, Beckwith and the 1964 trials: then on in color to the new investigation and trial of the 1990s.

The characters:

—Surely you have your hero in the Assistant D.A. DeLaughter.

—The D.A. Peters, a brilliant older courtroom lawyer who supported DeLaughter in his investigation in some measure because of the new black vote in his district.

—Jerry Mitchell, the local reporter who broke the stories that led to what followed.

—Myrlie Evers, the widow who was here throughout the trial, and her children—a real heroine who should share equal billing with DeLaughter.

—*Beckwith* himself! Surely an Oscar here.

—The jury, especially the old black preacher who was the fore-man and got them to pray before the final deliberation. (Morgan Freeman in a cameo role? He's a Mississippian and lives only one county away from the preacher's.)

A profoundly moving and dramatic story which I think envelopes what movie-goers like to see:

—a long quest for justice

—time passing

—a real hero and heroine

—a stunning *search*: the lost evidence, etc., the discovery of the murder weapon

—the courtroom scenes themselves

—maybe a love story? DeLaughter's wife or girlfriend who isn't sure what he's doing?

—a beauty of a film, maybe a modern-day *To Kill a Mocking-bird*

—a compelling thought: Hackman as Peters, Dafoe as De-Laughter?

All of this is amply documented. The trial transcript would be a gold mine.

P.S. I have a new fence.

We introduced Zollo to Bobby DeLaughter, had lunch at the Mayflower on West Capital, and talked about a movie. "I didn't agree right off the bat," Bobby recalled, "especially when I found out it was the same people who had done *Mississippi Burning*. I had reservations about that movie. But the more I talked with Zollo, the more convinced I became that the movie would be done correctly."

Zollo took the idea to Rob Reiner at Castle Rock. "It would've taken me years of begging to get someone else to do this movie," he said. "It took me six years to get *Quiz Show* made. Another six for *Mississippi Burning*. Castle Rock is the dream team, you know—

everybody wants to work for it. If I'd gone somewhere else, they'd have said, 'Why do we want to do this?' or 'It's a period piece.' Movie people say incredibly stupid things. But when I went to Rob and [Castle Rock president] Martin Shafer with this, Rob said, 'Let's go, let's do it.' "

——

The second movie person to arrive on the scene was almost as foreign to Mississippi as Zollo: Lewis Colick, who had been assigned to do the screenplay. He was forty-three and had grown up in a working-class Jewish household in Coney Island, Brooklyn, migrated to L.A., and took classes at the UCLA film school. He was a serious individual most of the time, small in stature, neat, excitable, with expressive eyes and a quick, sputtery laugh. He immediately encountered a unique task on the Untitled Mississippi Project, because given the complexities of the true story he must serve not only as a screenwriter, but as an investigative reporter as well. His Coney Island upbringing would serve him efficaciously in navigating the swirling Mississippi shoals.

Colick was twelve years old when Medgar Evers was assassinated, and he did not remember much of it. In L.A. he followed the accounts of the 1994 trial on television and in the newspapers. "It was very interesting, and I thought, wasn't that great, what a fine thing after thirty years to see justice done." But it never occurred to him that there was a movie in it.

Colick and Fred Zollo had the same Hollywood agent at the time, Rob Scheidlinger, and they had known each other casually in the Hollywood way, and had discussed working together someday on some enterprise or another. About six weeks after the Beckwith trial in Mississippi they met at Zollo's estate in Beverly Hills and strolled the grounds drinking iced tea while Zollo described the story in considerable detail. John Gregory Dunne describes this aspect of the screenwriting process in his book *Monster: Living Off the Big Screen*: "It was like a matter of pitch and catch. The producer pitches ideas, the writers catch them; passed balls are not allowed." The screenwriter was immediately intrigued by the power of the tale, but he had personal reservations. He had never been to the South before. "I was frightened to death of Mississippi," he recalled. "I had a two-year-old son, Jack, whom I was madly in love with, and I didn't want to go *anywhere*. But the more Fred and I talked the more I just knew I was going to have to do it. The story was too compelling. I was going to have to go to Mississippi." He came two months later.

Colick first met Bobby DeLaughter at our house in Jackson that July. "I knew I needed to establish a good relationship with this guy to be able to write the movie," he recalls. "Well, Bobby walked in, and I'll never forget it, he was wearing tight jeans with a cowboy belt and a big buckle and big cowboy boots and a white cowboy shirt that had braids all over the pockets. From the little I'd read about him, I knew he was taciturn to begin with. I had to tell his life's story, and I looked at the cowboy gear and said to myself, how is this guy going to talk to *me*? *Brooklyn*?"

They were formal at first, the Mississippian and the Brooklynite, conferring over lunches around town, but then they began meeting at night at the DeLaughter cabin in the deepest woods, where they cooked barbecue and drank beer with the family and dogs around. "I didn't even know what a bottle tree was," Colick said. "You know, the bottle tree that Peggy and Bobby had in the garden to keep the 'haints' away because Mississippi is haunted land? Bobby is a private guy, but also warm and open. So I was able to find themes of a story beyond courtrooms and civil rights cases: personal, universal, ordinary things. I had a cartoon from the *Clarion-Ledger* that shows Bobby asking the jury, 'Ladies and gentlemen, is it ever too late?' As trite as this may sound, Bobby is one of those people who when you have a conversation with him, even on the phone, you feel better about humanity."

Pretty much everything about Mississippi surprised Colick, and like many of the outlanders on the Untitled Mississippi Project he was against all expectation mysteriously drawn to it, its soil and people and spirit. "I grew very quickly to absolutely adore Mississippi and to look forward to every visit. The burden of its past is almost like the landscape, the twisted magnolias and these cypress trees that grow out of the Natchez Trace. From the Old Capitol Building and the Civil War to the Sun 'n Sands Motel in the 1960s—these buildings have borne witness to incredible events. Mississippi is still wrestling with very deep things. Something would be wrong with a writer, no matter where he comes from, who isn't utterly fascinated by the place. It goes beyond Southern hospitality. It's beguiling to be around people who've been shaped and molded and defined by where they live. Not every place in America has this. People who stay in Mississippi and have been forged by it, they're Mississippians. They're not Georgians, they're *Mississippians,* as Faulkner was, as Eudora Welty was, as Bobby DeLaughter is. And as Myrlie and Medgar Evers were. Myrlie and Medgar's passion for Mississippi was rivaled only by their *disaffection* for it." He came to discover parallels, too, between Mississippi and his native Brooklyn. "Brooklyn is probably as legendary as Mississippi," he said. "We breed crazy characters, too. I discovered something of my own childhood in Mississippi."

The Hollywood lore is abundant with tales of the contempt writers have suffered from the studios over the years. Jack Warner called them "schmucks with Underwoods" and like other studio heads of the day assigned them cubicles in small dingy buildings. John Gregory Dunne, a distinguished member of the breed, writes that since the earliest days of Hollywood screenwriters had been regarded as "an anomalous necessity" and as "chronic malcontents, overpaid and undertalented, the Hollywood version of Hessians." "Too many people have too much to say about a writer's work," Raymond Chandler once said, after having been recruited to work with Billy Wilder on *Double Indemnity* and other pictures. "It ceases to be his. And after a while he ceases to care about it." When he gave up screenwriting, Chandler observed, "I have a sense of exile from thought, a nostalgia of the quiet room and the balanced mind. I am a writer, and there comes a time when that which I write has to belong to me, has to be written alone and in silence, with no one looking over my shoulder, no one telling me a better way to write it. It doesn't have to be great writing, it doesn't even have to be terribly good. It just has to be mine."

In the modern era scripts for the blockbusters are often cranked out by what amounts to Hollywood committees. In his *Making Movies,* Sidney Lumet cites two horror stories among the many pertaining to Hollywood writers. Once Sam Spiegel had two writers working on the same picture on two different floors of the Plaza Athénée in Paris. And then there was the time Paddy Chayefsky and Herb Gardner, who rented adjacent offices at 850 Seventh Avenue in Manhattan, received identical offers on the same day for a rewrite of the same screenplay. The producers had not noticed that the scripts were sent to the same address, one to Room 625, the other to Room 627. Gardner and Chayefsky wrote identical letters of refusal.

Castle Rock, Colick noted, had a reputation for hiring good writers to write good scripts, and for backing those scripts. "That sounds like common sense," Colick said, "but unfortunately in Hollywood it's *not* common sense. In Hollywood they put things into *development*, which means they develop the script and don't make the movie. They find many, many reasons why they don't want to make the movie, very few of which have anything to do with the script and the writing. It has to do with who the audiences are, is it commercial enough, is it funny enough, is it scary enough. I could take two hours to tell you the reasons Hollywood will come up with not to make a script that could be from a literary standpoint a great script.

"Castle Rock doesn't have a lot of projects in development. They have a realistic number of staff and development projects. Another studio might have a hundred things in development. They'll say, well, let's see what happens out of this hundred. Castle Rock has maybe twenty-five or thirty things and is planning on making those twenty-five or thirty movies, with of course a margin for error."

This particular assignment was the hardest Colick had ever had. Castle Rock was waiting for his screenplay. The process took about a year. He was personally prodded by the Medgar Evers legacy, by how to be true to it. "Medgar believed in a vision of America and was willing to die for it. He paid the ultimate price for us." Colick had never dealt with authentic and tangible recent history: "Artistically I had never been under those kinds of constraints before. There were days when I felt I didn't know how to do this. I was baffled and frustrated."

As I see now in retrospect, one of the most acute problems was that there were really four different movies in this complex story: the civil rights activist Medgar, the assassination and the suffering of the family over many years, the investigation, and the courtroom drama itself. These amounted almost to centrifugal elements. Then there were the difficult considerations implicit to a true and recent set of events: too *little* dramatic liberty versus too *much* dramatic liberty. And should it be a longer film than was planned, with a wider perspective? This movie would not be a *JFK*. There would be no really cynical, irresponsible, or generic diversions in *Ghosts*. On these and other matters there would be decisions made in the best of faith that would later be used against the film, to everyone's chagrin. The problems lay in the nature of the people, the tale, and the place and how best to film responsibly and dramatically. It would not be an easy thing, making a movie like this.

There would be a number of instances of artistic license in the finished screenplay, and it was not fully recognized at the time that this was destined to cause problems with the film's reception. For instance, how could there be a direct, dramatic clash between the Beckwith character and the DeLaughter character? Rob Reiner would be as frustrated as Colick in trying to work this out. Cross-examination in the courtroom would have been the perfect opportunity, but although Beckwith had taken the stand in the first trials, he did not in the final one. "So, I had to compensate for that," Colick said. "We are talking about entertainment, *not* a documentary, but we are also talking about being faithful to the spirit of the truth. I had to contrive a way artistically, creatively, mechanically, to have Bobby go at it with Beckwith because the audience is waiting for these guys to bump heads. I remembered Bobby once told me about a very brief meeting that he had with Beckwith in the men's room of the courthouse during a recess in the trial. This is a scene I'm very proud of because although it never happened, it *could* have. The real men did have an exchange, you know, so I extrapolated and created a two-or-three-minute scene in which Beckwith asks: Bobby DeLaughter, what happened to you to make you mean-spirited enough to turn on your own kind? Why aren't you doing what the good Lord and the state of Mississippi have got a right to expect you to be doing? Bobby asks, which is what? And Beckwith says, Going after black people for killing white people rather than the other way around. This to me was the *spirit* of the truth."

The first draft of the screenplay was finished in April 1995, but it would be almost exactly one year before the shooting began, and the script would undergo, in one form or another, five major drafts, the first two by Colick, with Rob Reiner and his Castle Rock colleague Andy Scheinman adding, cutting, and revising on the last three. As producers do at this point in the process, Zollo was in effect turning the screenwriter over to the director. With each new draft the altered parts—even the most minor of changes—would be printed on colored pages inserted into the previous manuscript, the color indicating the exact date of the changes (viz: blue, 3/13/96; pink, 3/15/96; yellow, 3/20/96; purple, 4/2/96; red, 4/8/96), so that on any given day the screenplay of the Untitled Mississippi Project was nothing if not a rainbow plethora of different colors, most indecipherable to strangers like myself.

—

Next to arrive were two people constituting Wave 3, the Mississippi location manager and the L.A. production designer, who

came to the Magnolia State in early January 1996, four months before the filming was scheduled to begin. They would be joined
from time to time by a handful of various colleagues and assistants
from L.A., Tucson, New Orleans, New York, and elsewhere: an art
director, a head set decorator, an assistant location manager, assistant set dressers, set-dressing buyers, and a picture car coordinator, who would be searching for vintage vehicles, plus a few
painters and carpenters and construction men, already beginning
work on sets. These people and producer Fred Zollo would come in
and out of the state frequently in the weeks before filming, so that
Wave 3 was constantly rippling.

Location manager Charlie Harrington was thirty-nine and lived
on Cape Cod, an Irish Catholic with four children. He liked to call
himself the real point man for the project. One of the reasons he
grew to regard Ward Emling, the director of the Mississippi Film
Office, as one of the best in the country was because Emling himself had for seven years been a location manager in Hollywood.
Harrington had worked on thirty movies across the country but
none, before now, in the Deep South. He was an assistant on the
first *Die Hard* and located the prep school for *Dead Poets Society.*
He had only recently finished locations for Arthur Miller's *The Crucible,* during which he arranged the crew's takeover of Hog Island
off the Massachusetts coast and built a whole seventeenth-century
village there. Governor Weld got Harrington dozens of National
Guard soldiers to work for six months barging everything back and
forth.

Harrington loved to deal and negotiate with many types of people and prided himself on getting on the same level with everybody; he implicitly trusted humanity, sometimes perhaps a little
too much. He was a charmer, low-key yet voluble, his eyes mirth-
ful even when he was upset about things. He was often on the road
alone conferring with landowners, businesspeople, and local
politicians to line up locations for the filming, to begin on April 30.
Many of the Mississippi scenes would be, in the movie parlance,

"period scenes," going back to the early 1960s and before, and this would demand that he confer with every business establishment four blocks or more down a street being filmed; if these displayed a sign or anything else not of the period, he had to take care of it. For this and other, more distressing reasons, he considered this movie by far the most difficult he had ever worked on. Later in the process, when the top brass came in to accompany him on what were called tech scouts of projected locations, he could fly in first-class and stay at the fanciest hostelries. "But after we start shooting," he said, "I'm back with the peasants."

The ironies and surprises of Mississippi affected him. One day he went to Woodville to meet with the mayor in his office about locations; he returned two days later and drove into the service station for gasoline, and it was the mayor who pumped the gas. Later, driving on the Natchez Trace, he got out of his car to take a photograph and spotted an alligator a few feet from him in a creek. "This state is a very *wild* place, I'll tell you," he said, "very wild and rural. I never saw anything like *this* state." He would take another location job in Mississippi in a heartbeat, he said. Near the end of the shooting he would reflect that he had made more good friends in Mississippi than he had in all his time on Cape Cod. "Even the people with old-fashioned views about race who didn't think the movie was a good idea were pretty nice people, you know? Even the guy who backed out of my deal on a mansion in Natchez at the last minute didn't seem like a bad guy. I've never been in a place where I loved so many people and hated so many people."

———

Lilly Kilvert held the position of production designer, a title that originated with the wily and resourceful William Cameron Menzies on *Gone With the Wind*. The role pertains to art direction, to all the settings both interior and exterior, to the very look and visual substance of a movie. It is a consequential job, and the production designer is always recognized prominently in the front credits of a movie, while the location manager appears in the end credits. The production designer is always one of the first to begin work on a motion picture and one of the last to finish. In Hollywood Kilvert had already conferred frequently with Reiner and others on the treatment of the scenes from Colick's script, along with rough estimates of cost and space. The set-dressing and props departments were under her supervision, and she was closely connected with the construction department as well, and also with the greens foreman and his assistants, who were responsible for trees, shrubs, grass, flowers, and various other flora.

Kilvert was fortyish, a slender blonde. She had been nominated for an Oscar for *Legends of the Fall.* The most recent of her films was *The Crucible,* and before that Reiner's *The American President.* She talked about re-creating sets in L.A. for the latter movie, and about the countless hours she spent in the White House studying, sketching, and photographing everything to the minute detail; the Clintons had taken her on a tour one of her first days there.

—

JoAnne and our cats and I had recently moved into a comfortable house in North Jackson on the banks of Purple Crane Creek, which overflows in the rains. Our dwelling was built by the son of a two-time Mississippi governor who had never actually been elected; in the 1920s and 1940s, as lieutenant governor, he acceded to the post on the death of the governor, and for this he had made *Ripley's Believe It or Not.* The next street over, indeed, was called Governor's Row. Former Governor William Winter, one of the finest and most progressive Southern governors of a generation, lived directly across the creek. Former Governor Ray Mabus, later the U.S. ambassador to Saudi Arabia, lived three doors down, and elderly descendants of two other governors dwelled in the same block. A block or so in the other direction lived James Meredith, who had integrated Ole Miss in 1962.

It was a good old neighborhood and a good old house, with big fireplaces and a subtle ambiance of vanished talk, and in the parlor a Steinway baby grand on which my mother had taught piano for half a century. Here over the months the Hollywood denizens came and went, plotted the movie's details, and talked trade.

For all the savvy required to make good motion pictures, movie people can be gullible, certainly in Mississippi, and it was not infrequent that some of their number were terrified to come across rubber snakes, rats, and tarantulas on my back lawn and plastic roaches in their quiche lorraine, not to mention occasional calls to their hotel rooms from "assistant managers" questioning their credit ratings, and when the movie people defended their financial solvency, the rejoinder: "You ain't from around here, are you?"

One night later on a group that included myself, Zollo, Harrington, and the actors William H. Macy, Susanna Thompson (who was cast as Peggy DeLaughter), and Bonnie Bartlett, who was playing Bobby DeLaughter's mother, were having dinner at Crechale's out on old Highway 80 when we were joined by Charles Evers, who had been dining alone at a nearby table. We all adjourned to my house on Governor's Row. On the way I accompanied Evers back to his FM radio station, where he was bringing takeout catfish and hush puppies to a disc jockey. On the walls of the radio-station lobby were framed photographs of Charles Evers with JFK, RFK, and LBJ, and, since Evers had turned Republican, with Richard Nixon and Ronald Reagan. Charles Evers had had a checkered and flamboyant career, but at age seventy-two he was subdued and thoughtful. At our house the talk turned to Medgar, and Charles described what a good and loveable man he was. "If Beckwith had ever met my brother once," he said, "he would never have killed him."

An enormous ice storm was predicted to descend one night that January. Lilly Kilvert and Charlie Harrington were to have dinner at our house that evening and had returned hurriedly from Natchez after hearing reports of the impending catastrophe. In Mississippi people hasten to the stores and zealously stock up during the rare warnings of snow and ice, and this day was no exception. At the supermarket I was able to get the last four remaining rib-eye steaks, the thinnest, scrawniest specimens of beef ever served outside of the U.S. Army, and had to stand in line an hour to pay for them.

Cape Codder Charlie Harrington made light of the talk about the calamitous elements to come (and to tell the truth, it turned out not to be much of a storm). Then the two visitors began talking about movie projects. In candlelight, over our dubious steaks, they discussed many arcane details, logistical and otherwise, of the Untitled Mississippi Project. What town within forty miles of Jackson, they asked, could be the surrogate for Greenwood for the "Welcome Home DeLay" parade sequence after the second mistrial in '64? Yazoo City. Where was a likely site within forty miles to erect an old service station where DeLaughter, Crisco, and Bennett would stop for gas during a futile point in their investigation and from where Bobby would telephone Myrlie Evers in Oregon— a setting that would effectively capture the brooding atmosphere of the Delta? The county road from Satartia to Holly Bluff. What about a lumberyard within forty miles where Bobby, Crisco, and Bennett could confront the aging alibi witnesses of 1964? Bentonia. What about a really scary country road that Bobby, Crisco, and Bennett had to drive to their secret meeting with the Ku Kluxer? Perry Creek Road in Yazoo County.

In addition to these, Kilvert said she had to find five distinctive location scenes that would overwhelmingly establish the mood and look of the whole movie. Two John Grisham blockbusters, *A Time to Kill* and *The Chamber*, were then being filmed in the state, and she felt it important not just to search for locations not used in these films, but to find a different look and character integral to their story. She asked for one specific site that would establish the texture and feel of Mississippi early on in the movie, some place that audiences would not easily forget. The Windsor Ruins.

During one interval of several days in the nadir of the 1996 winter, since all the others had returned home for a while, Charlie Harrington was the only Untitled Mississippi Project person in the state. To me it was incredible that less than three months before the location shooting of a large-budget Rob Reiner movie involving hundreds of people and props and equipment, he was the only one in the vicinity. "I got it all to myself," he ruefully admitted. His lone vigil was not unlike what the Scarlet Pimpernel's solitary presence in revolutionary Paris must have been, and someone suggested this to the location man. "After me the deluge," he said. That was Louis XV, he was corrected, and he replied, "Well, it's the same principle anyway." So we escorted him through Yazoo County looking for locations, including the forlorn rural hamlet of Bentonia with its main street right out of a woebegone era. "Do you think we could *buy* Bentonia?" he wished to know. We even got him a date with our neighbor Eudora Welty, and at dinner Harrington sat entranced as Eudora described having written "Where Is the Voice Coming From?", her fictional re-creation of Evers's murder. She started the short story right after she read of the shooting, she said, and stayed up two straight nights writing it, and when it appeared in *The New Yorker* a couple of weeks later, she received more mail on it than she ever did on any other stories.

During this time various knowledgeable people in the state were being inundated by telephone calls and faxes from Hollywood quizzing them about interminable factual minutiae. These queries were coming from Lilly Kilvert and her assistant prop masters, from Reiner, from Zollo. Homer Best, the lawyer for the Sheriff's Department, was one of the main targets. "I was stunned," he said, "by the absolute attention to the actual physical details, which they later reproduced down to the little specks of dust. What always amazed me was this utter attention to physical details juxtaposed with the willingness to play fast with certain historical details." Concerning the Hinds County Courthouse premises alone, and not to mention all the other Mississippi locales: How many deputies were in the courtroom during the trial? How many deputies were in plain clothes in the courtroom? How many deputies in uniform in the courtroom? How many black deputies in the courtroom? How many white deputies in the courtroom? How many deputies escorted Beckwith? What was the physical setup of the security outside the courtroom? What exact sort of walk-through metal detector did you have? How long were the folding tables that made up the barrier next to the detector? What did the press passes look like exactly? What does a Hinds County sheriff badge look like exactly? What does the Hinds County sheriff uniform look like exactly? Please send photographs, badges, press passes, and the forms the press had to fill out to get the press passes. Local set dressers, such as the bartender Shoeless Jack Stevens, who had been present at Ground Zero on the movie, were scouring the state for props from the 1960s, including mannequins, girdles, candy boxes, talcum-powder boxes, soft-drink coolers, Moon Pies, bubble gum, TV's, and radios. The man in charge of period vehicles dipped in and out from L.A. His most zealous search would be for a 1962 Valiant matching Beckwith's, which seemed impossible to come by. He also needed to hire an ox.

Charlie Harrington was having his own problems. The Mississippi Department of Archives and History, an overly protective institution, was beginning to give him difficulties over historic locations considered to be under state purview, including the Evers house, the Windsor Ruins, the archives building itself where Bobby DeLaughter had gone to examine old newspapers and documents, even the courthouse. Unlike Governor Weld of Massachusetts with his unqualified support of *The Crucible,* the extreme right-wing governor of Mississippi was not volunteering to help. Worse, sometimes right up to two or three days before actual shooting people would back out on location deals after handshake agreements or even signed contracts. "This was unusual for me," Harrington said. "I make good deals with people. I'd never encountered this before. Most of this has to do with what the movie was *about.* A lot has changed in Mississippi, and a lot has stayed the same. It takes generations for attitudes like this to go away, I guess."

Location managers like Harrington frequently gravitate to

churches because they have parking lots that can accommodate the base camp for vehicles and equipment, with space enough for the extras to change into period clothes—more than two hundred extras in Woodville, Mississippi, alone had to be dressed to look like they lived in 1934. A number of white churches around the state turned Harrington down, although they never told him why. In one instance, the pastor of a white church in Bentonia enthusiastically made an arrangement after Harrington offered the usual donation to the church, then the congregation itself voted not to cooperate. Also in Bentonia, the manager of the lumberyard, where an important scene was to be filmed, shook hands on a generous rental fee, but when the owner, who lived in Memphis, discerned what the film was about, he vetoed the agreement. Harrington went next door and arranged to use land around the Blue Front Cafe, a black-owned establishment. (Ironically, Peggy DeLaughter's father had worked at that very sawmill for thirty-five years. She was shocked to learn much later that the owner had gone back on the bargain. She said she wished she had had the chance to talk with the mill people first.)

In Natchez Harrington had a handshake deal with the owner of Dunleith, an antebellum mansion, where a luncheon scene was to be shot. He and a representative of the Natchez Film Office had sat at a kitchen table in that impressive manse and enumerated for the owner their needs for that scene in the movie. They jostled with the price for a while and then got up to big money. The man wanted ten thousand dollars, which Charlie agreed to. In the days before the shooting Harrington kept telephoning the owner because he had not faxed back his contract. "He told me he was going to fax it," Charlie said, "but it never came through, and then I'd call his secretary and she'd say, 'Well we already sent it,' and then the man finally phoned and said, 'I'm really sorry I didn't call you back, but I just can't do this. I just don't feel right about y'all making a movie about the sixties in Mississippi.' " To be safe Harrington had previously made a backup arrangement with the owner of the Monmouth mansion in Natchez, who was amiable and help-ful and settled for a less outrageous price, and that was where the scene was ultimately shot.

There were difficulties with black people too. In one southern Mississippi town Harrington promised fifteen dollars an hour to policemen to help with traffic and other details, and one cop, who was black, asked that he be given the money and he would distrib-ute it to the others. Harrington caught him giving the others eight dollars an hour and keeping the seven-dollar difference.

Then there was the problem with a black Natchez alderman and his brother. The location to be re-created was the Jackson NAACP headquarters of 1963. Harrington and the alderman had a few drinks and got along well. Since the elections were in a month, the alderman invited Harrington to follow him around while he cam-paigned and introduced him to the pastors of churches and the owners of stores. Kilvert and Harrington had already selected an old gas station for a period shot; they would have to turn the entire block into 1963. The alderman said fine, and that since his brother owned the whole block there would be no difficulties. The brother signed the contract and was paid twenty-five hundred dollars for one day of shooting, an exterior scene with the property as a back-drop. (This would turn out to be one shot that took three hours of filming.) A day before the actual shooting the alderman telephoned Harrington. "You goddamned movie people," he said, "you're tak-ing advantage of my brother. He ought to get at least six or seven thousand for this."

A flustered Harrington replied that the brother had already signed the contract for a fee that was considerably higher than the standard industry rate for that kind of filming. The alderman threatened to get the Natchez sheriff to shut the whole movie down. Harrington said, "You've got to be kidding. Are you threat-ening me?"

The alderman said, "You're damned right I'm threatening you."

They arranged a meeting at the pool hall and beer joint that the alderman and his brother owned. Harrington brought along Jeff

Stott and Charles Newirth, executive producers for Castle Rock on the film. Harrington had asked them to come with him because he wanted them to see what he was experiencing on such matters in Mississippi; Stott and Newirth had never set foot in Mississippi before and were a long way from the Castle Rock Entertainment offices on North Maple Drive in Beverly Hills. The brothers were sitting at a corner table in the back of the dark, smoky pool hall. "So the three of us," Charlie remembered, "looking like pretty Hollywood guys, walk into this pool hall surrounded by black Mississippi guys and sit down and make introductions. It's highly polite at first, but the brothers have got stern faces, you know. They're really pissed off. They were asking now for seventy-five hundred dollars. 'What's going on here, Charlie?' the alderman asked. 'What the fuck's going on?' 'Okay,' I said, 'it's all in the contract. We're going to shoot for one day—tomorrow. We're not even shooting your business. We're shooting across the street from your business. We don't need to put the camera inside. We're paying you a really high price because we've been painting here and want your cooperation as agreed to. We're all set to shoot. It's all about Medgar Evers. It's about Medgar Evers's life, for Christ's sake. It's costing us big money. You can't back out the night before.' I reminded them of the signed contract for twenty-five hundred dollars, and they said that's nothing but *chump change*." The exchange continued in this temper. After half an hour or so Charles Newirth, shaking his head, got up and walked away; Jeff Stott stayed on longer, then he got up and walked out too. The brothers eventually settled on an extra two hundred dollars. "As a matter of fact, you know, I didn't say it," Charlie remembered, "but I always wanted to spread the money around more in poor neighborhoods like this one than I do in rich white neighborhoods or anywhere else I rent from. I really do. Anyway, I was exhausted."

Finally, there was the elderly black gentleman whom Harrington, affectionately almost, came to call the Eight-Thousand-Dollar Man. He lived directly across the street from the Evers house on Guynes Street in Jackson. He and others living nearby had feared back in 1963 that someone might try to kill Medgar near his house, and they had discussed what they would do if this ever happened. They had agreed that the first one of them outside would sound the alarm. On the fatal night the neighbor fired a pistol in the air and shouted, "There's a killer in the neighborhood!" It was he and another neighbor and friend of Medgar's who had put him on a mattress in the station wagon and driven him to the hospital where he died. It was they who had heard his last words: "Turn me loose." The other neighbor, whose house was next door to the Evers's, was an invalid, and the interior of his house needed to be lighted for the night scene; his wife assented, so Harrington gave her what he considered a generous fee. All along the street Harrington paid residents for moving their cars and allowing 1960s vehicles to be parked in their driveways. For the use of the Evers house a sizeable donation had been made to the foundation that was planning to make a museum of it.

Harrington needed to rent the front yard of the house across the street for camera positions during the filming of the assassination scene. They also were to put up bushes and honeysuckle in this neighbor's side lawn to simulate the spot at which Beckwith had secreted himself in his lair with the deer rifle, which in actuality had been a little farther down from the house. "I would go to his house and sit down," Harrington remembered. "His wife would make me a cup of coffee. They were wonderful people. He was kind of stone-faced." This was six or eight days before shooting, and Harrington offered him fifteen hundred dollars, which he refused, then two thousand, but Medgar's friend and neighbor kept shaking his head. He said he was thinking about ten thousand dollars. Harrington replied that they were too far apart and that he could not approve of a fee that extreme on his own. "He wouldn't return my calls, and it got down to a couple of days before the filming. I wanted to talk to some black leaders and have them call him and say, 'Please cooperate with us, we're making a movie about *Medgar*. You should be the last person causing problems.' " A prominent and respected black leader, state senator John Horhn, helped in getting Medgar's neighbor down from ten grand to eight. "Medgar's old pal was sharp as a tack," Harrington said, "and he wasn't going to budge too much. He was a very willful man." Why shouldn't anybody try to get as much out of Hollywood as they could? someone eventually suggested. "Yeah," Charlie replied, "God, I know. I'm just a locations guy. But still . . ." Yet they were all over the man's yard most of the night, and it was eventually considered money well spent.

Chapter 6

THE DIRECTOR AND HIS PLAYERS

Another wave of the Untitled Mississippi Project was led by the director himself, who made preproduction forays into the state, the first time he too had ever been to Mississippi. On his maiden trip he flew straight from a meeting at the White House to be met by Zollo. On later ones he would be joined from time to time by his wife, Michele Singer, by executive producer Jeff Stott, by Allegra Clegg, the Castle Rock production manager, and by Lilly Kilvert, the peregrinating production designer.

Much had been transpiring in Hollywood in the previous months. As soon as there was a go-ahead on the film, in the Hollywood ritual the director had begun consulting with the studio departments on Colick's screenplay, actors, sets, costumes, makeup, music, camera technique, and lighting. He would be the final arbiter in deciding the key question of how the camera itself would interpret the story and in the development of the script, which I would soon learn would be the most important consideration of all. Such technical factors were of overwhelming consequence, yet it was his task, too, to make sure that these complex mechanical aspects remained subservient to his own personal vision of the movie.

He had already put together his team. Jeff Stott and Bob Leighton, the film editor, had worked with Reiner on all his pictures. Frank Capra III, the first assistant director, had already done three movies with him; the costume designer, Gloria Gresham, had done five; the sound mixer, Bob Eber, eight; and the script supervisor, Lyn McKissick, five. John Seale, the director of photography (the title was "cinematographer" in older days) had recently filmed *The American President* for him. He had been nominated for Academy Awards for *Rain Man* and *Witness*.

A budget of forty million dollars had been set, a very big budget for a movie on civil rights. Was this a gamble? From the beginning the production manager and the assistant directors had been planning budget allowances and schedules. Technicians were breaking down the 150-page script into small cards, each representing a scene, which would be displayed in strips on a large script board, and this would accurately show how many days would be required to film the picture.

—

Rob Reiner was eighteen years old when Medgar Evers was assassinated. His father, actor-writer-director Carl Reiner, was always politically aware and supportive of the civil rights movement, and they discussed these things in the household. Both his parents were active in the anti–Vietnam War protests, and his mother, Estelle, a member of the organization Another Mother for Peace, helped design the WAR IS UNHEALTHY FOR CHILDREN AND OTHER LIVING THINGS poster so popular during that era. He was a student at Beverly Hills High School at the time of the Evers murder. "You remember where you were when you heard about JFK. It was like that for me with Medgar too. Then Fred Zollo came in and said, 'Hey, what about making a movie of this?' He had been following the trial in the media. Martin Shafer and I jumped at the chance. My God, there's an incredible backdrop. It was astonishing that someone was tried thirty years after the crime."

For many years he had wanted to do a movie about the race issue but had never felt comfortable with the idea. As a white man he did not feel he could depict what black people in America were going through. Zollo's story fascinated him. "If it's just getting a guy after thirty years, it becomes only a TV docudrama. There has to be a point of view. When Fred talked to me about Bobby DeLaughter, I said okay. It's not just the Beckwith story or the Myrlie Evers or Medgar Evers story, it's also the DeLaughter story. Here was a white person who walked into this civil rights case and had to face his own feelings of racism. I can tell this story through this guy. I can start examining my own feelings through this character."

The fateful decision to go with DeLaughter as the hero was no cynical or sardonic one at all; rather it was carefully and honorably considered by the director, who comprehended the hazards as much as anyone.

There had been one film done on Medgar Evers—a not especially satisfying 1983 ninety-minute PBS docudrama in the American Playhouse series starring Howard Rollins, Jr., as Medgar, Irene Cara as Myrlie, and Paul Winfield as a black turncoat, adapted from Myrlie's memoir, *For Us, the Living.* The film was shamelessly abundant with huge artistic liberties and fabricated details and events (much more so than the future *Ghosts*) including one scene that had Medgar brandishing a pistol at drunken whites and another in which he shows a visitor the small printing machine in his NAACP office and says it had once been used to print Confederate money! But the locations were very close to reality, and it *was* visceral, especially the scenes of Delta poverty, of Medgar's investigation of Reverend George Lee's murder in Belzoni and of Emmett Till's near Money, of the Jackson mass demonstrations, and of the murder itself, and it remained faithful to the stark fear of that time in Mississippi and Medgar's courage.

At the time *Ghosts of Mississippi* was conceived, Reiner was forty-eight years old and one of the five founding owners of Castle Rock Entertainment. He was born in the Bronx, but in 1960 his family moved to L.A., where he became a standout baseball player. He spent three years at the University of California, during which time he and his friend Richard Dreyfuss formed an improvisational company. In 1971 he joined the cast of *All in the Family* as the comical bigot Archie Bunker's son-in-law, Meathead, for which he received two Emmys. He would act in a number of films, some good, some not. When he followed his father to become a director, there were raised eyebrows, criticism, and envy in that competitive milieu. His critics would later say his oeuvre would be characterized by an uncanny perception of popular tastes; his movies had earned a great deal, and he was noted as a moneymaker. The Untitled Mississippi Project would be the tenth movie he had directed. He had emerged as one of the most admired and popular of Hollywood directors. His work included *Stand by Me, When Harry Met Sally,* and *A Few Good Men*, all of which were nominated for Oscars, and *The Princess Bride, Misery* (surely one of the scariest movies ever made, it won Kathy Bates an Oscar for her portrayal of a psychopath), *This Is Spinal Tap,* and *The American President*. He had been nominated for three Directors Guild of America awards but had yet to be nominated for an Oscar for directing. His first wife was Penny Marshall, the actress and director. He was married now to Michele Singer, who had been a well-known photographer in New York. They had two little boys; his wife and sons came to Mississippi for the filming and were sometimes at his side on the set. They were a close-knit family.

Rob had always been close to his father. He recalled the time as a child that he told his dad he wanted to change his name. Carl became upset, fearing the name Reiner was too much of a burden for a little boy growing up in Hollywood. "No, Dad," Rob told him, "I want to change my name to Carl." During his summer vacations he went every day to the set of *The Dick Van Dyke Show*, which his father wrote and directed. "I wanted to *be* my father. I loved him so much. I loved what he did, how he dealt with people, how they admired him and had such great affection for him. I watched him at work very closely when I was thirteen, fourteen years old and learned a lot from him. He went to the honest heart and truth of a scene. It was always about, what are the values? What do I want to *say* in this scene? How can it reflect real human experience? That's what I took from my father: The best stories are the stories that come out of your own experience and who you are. Those are the only stories that you can bring insight into."

In his book *Film,* novelist and critic David Thomson described Reiner the director as being "not unlike Michael 'Meathead' Stivic: decent, self-effacing, reliable, and entertaining. Crushing praise? Not in these times. . . . Reiner has that old, unbeatable sense of silly things that work. But he may be at that point where he needs to deliver something more lasting, and more rooted in life."

Shortly before the filming began in Mississippi, an intelligent young Easterner in a middle-level job in the movie expressed her concerns to me that the director, a brilliant and compassionate man who she nonetheless believed had never known struggle in his life beyond Hollywood nuances, would be incapable of directing a cast and crew to illustrate justly this incredible story of struggle: of a man murdered in his struggle to gain equality for his people, of a woman struggling to have justice served and to raise her children who had witnessed this horrible event, of a white man who struggles against intense opposition to build his case, of a state struggling against its past and still ripped apart by the issues at hand. California moviemakers knew nothing about the South anyway, she suggested. It remained to be seen.

—

I met Rob Reiner when Fred Zollo brought him to our house in Jackson to talk with Bobby DeLaughter for the first time. There is no fixed equation to such things, but in the South certain people are often referred to neither by their first nor last name alone, but by both names, especially when the first initials are alliterative. He was Rob Reiner to me, and to others as well. At Crechale's that night with Bobby and Zollo, next to the jukebox with its Patsy Cline and Willie Nelson and Elvis tunes, I told Rob Reiner I once lived for a long time in a cabin on the Bogue Chitto River working on a coming-of-age novel and watched *Stand by Me* eight nights in a row on the VCR. "Yeah," he said, "I guess that's still my favorite." He was inquisitive about everything pertaining to Mississippi: history, habitudes, politics, landscapes, weather, sports, food.

In L.A. he had been talking frequently on the telephone with Myrlie Evers, he said, about things that had happened around the time of the assassination. She had recently told him that she had the stigma of only being identified as Medgar's widow. He replied, "Well, I have the stigma of only being identified as Meathead." He cried during one conversation, he said, when Myrlie told him she had been digging around in some of Medgar's old effects and found the wallet he had on him when he was killed. Both the wallet and the money inside it were still caked with blood. Later, when he went to the murder house in Jackson, he stood in the driveway and wept again. "I experienced what Bobby tells me *he* experienced there—the thought that goes through your head of being taken from your family, having some coward shoot you in front of your family and take you away from your children."

From the start, he would frequently confess, he was obsessed with historical accuracy and the constraints it placed on a dramatic plot, just as Lewis Colick had been inhibited in writing the script. "Normally I'm just creating dreams and stories and fantasies, and even if they reflect reality, they're not real people. I've never shot a movie about real people and real situations before. It's going to be difficult. I'm taking this responsibility very seriously. Most people get their history through movies, you know. When people talk about Medgar Evers, I want them to know this is what actually happened. This is not some ancient history where you can take licenses and nobody is going to question you. The people are still alive, and you have a responsibility to tell their story. I've got an audience of one. I've got Myrlie Evers. If she likes this movie, I'm happy."

The later criticism that Reiner had involved himself in "a white man's" motion picture about the race issue—that its focus was on white people in what was a black struggle for justice—would desperately haunt him and the film itself, perhaps inevitably, as it

turned out. All this was well in the future, but even in the forma-
tive stages he was sensitive to this view and defended what he was
doing.

The subject of *Mississippi Burning* would keep coming up. "The
difference here," he would argue, "is that this story is true. I understand that people might review the film that isn't there instead
of the one that is, because it's so rare that this subject gets a
chance to be opened up in a mainstream Hollywood movie. The
powers that be in this town are not so thrilled about making movies
about serious subjects like this for commercial consumption.* It's
not easy to do, so you try to find ways you can get into this arena.
We're not making up that Bobby DeLaughter was the guy who
spearheaded this four-and-a-half-year reinvestigation and reprosecution. He believed justice was color-blind, and he was seeking to
have a wrong righted. And in a way, I felt that because he was white
it was my way into the subject. I think every black person in this
country, on the surface of things, might have misgivings about a
white person portraying some aspect of their reality. But if you realize Bobby's motives come from a very good, decent, compassionate place, then those misgivings melt away. And in the case of
Myrlie, that's exactly what happened in her relationship with
Bobby. I didn't feel qualified to do the Medgar Evers story or the
Martin Luther King story. My hope is that audiences will identify
with Bobby DeLaughter and his journey. I was raised by parents
who were big supporters of civil rights, and yet, no matter what I
do, no matter how sympathetic I am, and how much money I give,
I'm white, and I'll never be black. There's nothing I could do that
would enable me to say, 'I know exactly how this feels.' The criticism of my being a white person making a movie that has civil
rights as a backdrop is very unfortunate to me because we're living
in a time where everybody is so divisive." (Months later, with the

* One of the most unusual stories I ever heard in this regard was of the Hollywood producer who wanted to film Richard Wright's 1940 novel *Native Son* with
an all-white cast—including the actor playing the protagonist, Bigger Thomas.

release of the movie, one reviewer would call it "Rob Reiner's biggest mistake" and praise him for his courage in doing "such an obvious non–box office film.")

Getting financing from studios had never been an easy thing for black directors. An exception was my fellow Southerner Spike Lee, whose *Malcolm X,* based on the Malcolm X–Alex Haley book, I considered a searingly honest and powerful film. I recently viewed Lee's *Malcolm X* again and, in the absolute height of modern American ironies, had the spooky comprehension that Lee's film was attacked in the established national media for markedly similar reasons that the singularly different *Ghosts of Mississippi* was. Both motion pictures emanated from similarly tragic, intrinsic American wellsprings, miles and regions and interminable heartbeats apart, yet at their core were the big, complex racial aspects of the nation, and each was fated to be ensnared in separate crossfires of a turbulent America. Lee was still trying unsuccessfully to raise money for a major film about Jackie Robinson. He claimed no white studios, Hollywood being a staunchly white town, would allow him this.

Initially Myrlie herself had had "legitimate misgivings," Reiner said, and she would remain passionate in her hope that someday someone would do a film centering on Medgar, herself, and her children. But there were delicate negotiations, and she would cooperate fully in the film, at least to a point. Reiner consulted frequently with her, sending her every draft of the script, and she gave him notes and ideas, which he tried to incorporate as much as he could. Early on, he said, Castle Rock agreed to pull the plug on the project completely if at any time Myrlie felt the story was not being told accurately. (In May of 1996, only days after the cast and crew left Mississippi for the three months' filming in L.A., I introduced Myrlie to a large biracial audience at the Natchez Literary Festival. In her speech she praised Castle Rock and Bobby DeLaughter but expressed her concerns that the movie would not adequately capture the suffering she and her family had endured since the assassination. These remarks were not quoted in the national press.)

Recognizing early on the potential for an uneasy reaction toward the movie among black Americans, Castle Rock officially retained Myrlie as a consultant. They cast the three Evers children in the film as well as their friend Yolanda King, daughter of Martin Luther King, Jr. Their L.A. premiere would be planned as a benefit for the NAACP. They contributed to the future Medgar Evers Museum in Jackson. And they were producing for school use a CD-ROM on Medgar and the history of the civil rights movement. Their dedication to this movie, $40 million plus whatever else it took to eventually get it out there, was to a film that in all likelihood would not make any money. There was no way to question their faith.

Now, in early 1996, the director and his associates were committed to moving forward, and this became widely known in the state. The first printed attack came from an ultra-rightist Mississippi journal, which called Reiner the ranking leader of "the Medgar Evers cult."

———

In time Rob Reiner would be impressed by elements of Mississippi. "I'm amazed by how beautiful it is. I had some notion of it as hot and flat and dry and dusty, but it's very green and verdant, and every road you take, it's gorgeous. It's got a mythic quality to it— the Spanish moss and the kudzu, those vines that grow. And then the people. Being a Northerner, a liberal, you expect a strain of racism that's worse than anyplace else in the country or in the world. What you find out isn't that there's not any racism here, but it's very different from what you think. The vast majority, I found out, are good, decent people whose minds are in the right place, which is why I still don't understand how Kirk Fordice got elected governor."

He wanted to see the Delta, where a number of important scenes would be shot, and especially Greenwood, Byron De La Beckwith's hometown, and Money, the little town near which Emmett Till had been murdered in 1956.

Strangers are intrigued by the Delta, as indeed they should be. Bobby and Peggy DeLaughter and I had previously taken Zollo and Colick on a tour of the region. "I'd never seen a landscape like the Delta," Colick recalled. "When you see the little churches and juke joints and shotgun shacks and the Parchman prison, you realize— *blues.* The blues sprang out of the place, and the blues still haunt it. Yeah, the blues hang in the air like the humidity." The Hollywood fellows, Zollo and Colick, had wished to see Belzoni, hometown of the famous movie producers Larry and Chuck Gordon. Colick asked us to stop so he could take a photograph of a large road sign that said: BELZONI: CATFISH CAPITAL OF THE WORLD to give the Gordon brothers, and when he walked along the edges of the cotton field to get his camera angle, he asked, "Am I okay in here?"

"Just watch out for the rattlesnakes," someone said, and the screenwriter took his photograph fast.

When we drove past the dusty village of Little Yazoo, the Yankee visitors were advised this was the hometown of Leonard Bernstein; farther up the way the hamlet of Midnight had produced Helen Hayes, and Silver City was the birthplace of Bela Lugosi; it took them an honest time to realize we were putting them on. Behind the wheel of his car Bobby told stories about his most unusual court cases, bank robberies, rapes, murders, embezzlements. Our trip culminated at Doe's Eat Place in a decrepit wood-frame house in the black section of the Mississippi River town of Greenville, which had produced the writers William Alexander Percy, Shelby Foote, David Cohn, Walker Percy, Ellen Douglas, Charles Bell, and Beverly Lowry. We dined on the tamales, one-and-a-half-pound T-bones, and marinated french fries in the kitchen itself, and as the City of Angels intruders discussed the Untitled Mississippi Project they also engaged in badinage with the farmer patrons, country waitresses, and cooks about catfish farms, soybeans, rice irrigation, local black running backs going on to the Ole Miss Rebels, the Great Flood of '27, and Delta murders, especially the first white society woman from down the way ever sent to the

Parchman Penal Farm—for murdering her consort with garden shears in the 1950s; she was once temporarily released to attend her daughter's debutante party, and later permanently set free out of Delta gallantry to host her weekly bridge games. It was a long remove from Spago on Sunset Boulevard or the Palm Restaurant on Santa Monica, not to mention the Polo Lounge of the Beverly Hills Hotel. Assistant D.A. DeLaughter also soon had the fender of his car dented in a motel parking lot in Indianola, got a ticket from a state trooper for having an expired inspection sticker, and ran out of gas on the way back to Jackson and had to walk several miles in the 100-degree heat to the nearest service station. The Delta does that to all of us.

To me the Delta is the Old Testament in its ageless rhythms and despairs—in the violence of its extremes, the excesses of its elements, the tension of its memory. The few who own this richest land in the world are among the wealthiest people in America, and the black laborers among the poorest. Once this land, in the words of one nineteenth-century traveler, was "a jungle equal to any in Africa," a dark impenetrable forest of towering trees and thick undergrowth, and panthers, bears, alligators, giant mosquitoes and spiders and blue-backed scorpions, rattlesnakes and cottonmouths, and swarms of gnats that would follow men around to crazy distraction. Historian James C. Cobb calls it "the most Southern place on earth." Novelist Richard Ford calls it "the South's South." Faulkner's Ike McCaslin described it as a place "where white men rent farms and live like niggers, and niggers crop a share and live like animals, where cotton is planted and grows man-tall in the very cracks of the sidewalks, and usury and mortgage and bankruptcy and measureless wealth, Chinese and African and Aryan and Jew, all breed and spawn together until no man has time to say which one is which and no one cares."

Not long before I had had a conversation with an acquaintance of mine, a native of the Midwest who ran the Atlanta bureau of one of the country's largest newspapers. He had been doing a story out here in the Delta, and he had been touched by the patina of this older, inward Dixie. "In all the South it's the other extreme from Atlanta," he said. "Southerners hate to be strangers to each other. That's why Atlanta is so traumatic for Southerners to visit. Southerners like to see you and say, 'Hi, how are you?' and the Yankees in Atlanta just don't respond to that. As for the native Atlantans, there's a city they remember that no longer really exists. But the Delta! It's still here. I've never seen a place where people talk so much to each other, and not just whites and whites, blacks and blacks. Damned if the whites and blacks don't carry on a conversation together all day long."

Now, on this latest trip with Rob Reiner, Zollo, Bobby, and his teenaged son Burt, I recalled the countless visitors I had taken through the Delta over the years: peregrinating Northern scholars, writers, journalists, and civil rights workers, though never moviemakers. Their reaction had always been a singular amalgam of bafflement, titillation, anger, and, not the least of it, *fear,* yet to the person they were struck by its brooding sadness, its physical power. Reiner was no exception. He was curious about all of it. "What the hell is *that?*" he asked on the drive from Bentonia to Yazoo City, and solicited a treatise on the history of the kudzu vine. He wanted details on how the paths of Medgar Evers as an insurance salesman and later NAACP activist and Byron De La Beckwith as a fertilizer salesman must have crossed here in the Delta in the 1950s and early 1960s, in back-road towns like Itta Bena and Egypt and Hushpuckena. On these Delta roads after his investigation into the Emmett Till and other murders and his voter-registration work Medgar would almost never stay overnight but drive back at full speed toward Jackson, often trailed by cars. It was this very highway, U.S. 49, Reiner was told, on which Beckwith had driven from Greenwood to Jackson and back on that June night in 1963. "Opening scenes, maybe?" he said. In the car later he turned to Bobby and asked him if D.A. Peters would be upset if the fiery cross-examination of the alibi witness were given to the DeLaughter character. "I don't think he'd like it very much," Bobby replied. This prompted the director to speak openly, as he often would, of the problems he faced of being faithful to the essential truth of the story while at the same time giving it a necessary dramatic edge.

The two men perused my hometown of Yazoo City for possible locations. Medgar had visited Yazoo City often; in 1956 he had helped organize the school-integration petition here, to be followed by the campaign of intimidation from the White Citizens Council, the organization meeting of which I had attended that long-ago evening. The council had so frightened the Yazoo NAACP president that he was no longer able to hold meetings. "One thing, the people are afraid," Medgar said then of my town. "I would say it is worse than being behind the Iron Curtain." He wrote to the NAACP president in New York: "Honestly, Mr. Wilkins, for Yazoo City there doesn't seem to be much hope."

In his book *Rising Tide,* John M. Barry reported how Ho Chi Minh, then a French journalist, collected clippings from Southern and Mississippi newspapers about the viciousness of the countless Delta lynchings years ago, including an article in the *Vicksburg Evening Post* about the murder, in the early 1900s in a county not many miles west from where we were driving on this day, of a black husband and wife accused of killing a white man. Barry quoted the article:

> "The blacks were forced to hold out their hands while one finger at a time was chopped off. The fingers were distributed as souvenirs. The ears of the murders [sic] were cut off. Holbert was beaten severely, his skull was fractured, and one of his eyes, knocked with a stick, hung by a shred from the socket. . . . [A] large corkscrew . . . was bored into the man and woman . . . and then pulled out, the spirals tearing out big pieces of raw, quivering flesh." [Barry continued,] Then the crowd burned them at the stake, after partially filling their mouths and nostrils with mud to prevent a fast death from smoke inhalation.

In a similar town across the way, another mob, Barry reported, "had bound a black man's hands and legs and placed him inside the body of a dead cow with only his head sticking out, so he would die slowly while insects and birds were attracted to the moisture of his eyes, mouth, and nostrils, and crawled in his ears." On the river levees of the Delta at the turn of the century, he wrote, "mules were worth more than blacks. Black levee workers recited a saying, 'Kill a mule, buy another. Kill a nigger, hire another.' "

We drove past the big houses and the derelict shacks, the endless fields, the catfish ponds, and the dismal, half-empty little hamlets where black men, women, and children sat on the stoops of forlorn dwellings "as if an ancient civilization had died out," Easterner Peter Applebome wrote, "leaving behind only a desultory colony of black survivors and ramshackle houses and ghost towns baking under the Mississippi sun." Then directly through Tchula, the kind of Delta town where Martin Luther King, Jr., had wept in 1966 over its terrible, wrenching poverty. And then on to Money, the minuscule settlement on the banks of the Tallahatchie near which the black youth Till, from Chicago visiting his relatives, was beaten, mutilated, shot, and dumped in the river with a cotton-gin fan tied to him for allegedly having whistled at a white woman in a grocery store—and the two white men after being acquitted of the murder sold their story of how they killed him to *Look* magazine. Faulkner wrote a letter to the Memphis *Commercial Appeal*: "Any society that condones the killing of little children does not deserve to survive, and probably won't."

It was getting on toward dusk as the five of us lingered in front of the very grocery store, collapsing and boarded up now. The director was curious to know about the circumstances of the Till murder, also about Beckwith's grandfather Yerger, who once owned ten thousand acres of cotton land around here when the family was prosperous. He then asked young Burt DeLaughter what it was like growing up in Mississippi these days, and what kinds of responses had he gotten five years ago among kids his age to his father's reopening the Evers murder case. He said he had encountered hostile reactions.

In Greenwood Bobby took us to the convenience store where in 1991 he had secretly arranged to meet one of Beckwith's alibi witnesses behind a garbage bin to ascertain whether he still stood by his 1964 testimony. We dutifully inspected the contours of the garbage bin, touching it gingerly, as if it were a movie prop. Then we walked about the lawn of the courthouse where the local citizens had given a welcome-home party for Beckwith in 1964. Reiner and Zollo wanted to take photographs of the Confederate monument that Beckwith's grandmother had helped finance, she herself having been the model for one of the stone figures: a woman nursing a wounded soldier. Curiously, several white teenaged Greenwood girls were here taking pictures of this too.

I had momentarily lost my bearings, and I rolled down the window of the car to ask an old black woman the way to Lusco's, which, like Doe's Eat Place in Greenville, is one of the distinctive restaurants of the Deep South with all the appurtenances of a joint, on a murky, ramshackle Greenwood thoroughfare. She gave me elaborate directions.

"I didn't understand a single word she said," Rob Reiner declared as we drove away. In a private banquette in Lusco's, as the five of us dined on gumbo, pompano, and fried chicken, patrons came in and out to get Meathead's autograph. On the long drive home he asked if the Civil War was fought over slavery, inquired about the history of the Jews in Mississippi and why precisely Beckwith was not convicted in the two 1964 trials. He wanted to understand the people, the circumstances, the mood, what Mississippi thought then, what the young people were like then.

—

The fifth and final wave of the Untitled Mississippi Project would arrive a little later on, in April of 1996, and this would comprise the entire undertaking—the hundreds of cast and crew.

In the lead roles Reiner had cast Alec Baldwin as Bobby DeLaughter, Whoopi Goldberg as Myrlie Evers, and James Woods as Byron De La Beckwith. Tom Cruise was his first choice as DeLaughter, but Cruise was about to film another movie, *Jerry Maguire.* "I think Alec is an incredibly powerful actor," Reiner said.

"I wanted someone who has the strength of character to be at the center of this—from his edgy film noir roles to the role of being a warm and loveable human being whom everyone can identify with. If this movie's a success, he'll be seen in a new light." Reiner had talked with Cicely Tyson, Oprah Winfrey, and Alfre Woodard about the Myrlie Evers role before deciding on Whoopi Goldberg. She felt the pressure of carrying the mantle of Myrlie Evers but actively sought the part, as did James Woods his.

Other principal members of the cast were William H. Macy, fresh from the lead male part in *Fargo* (for which he would be nominated for an Oscar), as Charlie Crisco; Craig T. Nelson of the television show *Coach* as District Attorney Ed Peters; Susanna Thompson as Peggy DeLaughter; Bill Smitrovich and Michael O'Keefe as Beckwith's defense lawyers Jim Kitchens and Merrida Coxwell; Diane Ladd as DeLaughter's ex–mother-in-law; Virginia Madsen as Dixie DeLaughter; Jerry Levine as Jerry Mitchell; Wayne Rogers as Morris Dees; Brock Peters as Walter Williams, Myrlie Evers's second husband; and Bill Cobbs as Charles Evers.

Among the unique choices would be the casting of the adult Darrell Evers, Medgar's eldest son, to play himself; of Medgar's younger son, Van, to play himself; and of his daughter, Reena, to play a member of the jury. The role of the adult Reena would be played by Yolanda King. There were indigenous touches. Both William H. Macy and Diane Ladd had Mississippi backgrounds. Benny Bennett, Bobby's other investigator, would play himself. Finn Carter, an actress living in L.A. who had grown up in Mississippi as the daughter of the writer Hodding Carter III and granddaughter of the crusading journalist and editor Hodding Carter, Jr., would play Assistant D.A. Cynthia Speetjens.

James Woods had heard of the Beckwith role at a party in Hollywood. Woods had a long history of playing hateful villainous roles, including a moocher pimp, a brutal gang boss, a double-crossing hit man, a drug-addicted investment broker, and a sleazy political operator. He had gotten a copy of the screenplay, then studied the assassin's speech and mannerisms on videotapes and constructed the character from the outside in. "The challenge of this guy!" Woods said later. "Call it crazy, the stuff he does, the sniffing, all of those strange gestures. I just couldn't resist it. Part of the challenge for me is playing someone who is as far from my personal values as you can be, and that's Byron De La Beckwith. I loathe his values, I loathe his racism, I loathe his hatred, I loathe his bigotry, I loathe everything about him, and that provides a degree of difficulty for me as an actor. And as an actor, I want to do a four-and-a-half-twist double gainer off the high board." He came to Reiner and Zollo to audition for another part but told them he really wanted to play Beckwith. "Jimmy, I'm concerned about your age," Reiner said. Woods was forty-eight but would have to portray a seventy-three-year-old in many critical scenes.

"I can make you believe it," Woods replied. "Let me show you." He began reading.

"I was blown away," Reiner recalled.

"Before our eyes he became Beckwith," Zollo said.

Since Whoopi Goldberg was to play Myrlie Evers both in her thirties and in her sixties, she had to get to know her. They would meet in person and talk on the phone on the West Coast throughout the period before filming. "Myrlie and I are from two separate eras. Her cadence and her manner are so vastly different from mine. I had to get into her from the sixties forward to an adult. I was a kid in the sixties. Playing a real character as opposed to a fictional one carries with it a responsibility." To her, Myrlie was a powerful presence from the moment she entered a room, not unlike Coretta Scott King and Shirley Chisholm, she said. "She loved her husband with every fiber of her being and is able to pass the idea that justice is real to Bobby DeLaughter. When Myrlie talks to me about Bobby in real life, she glows." Myrlie told her that after the assassination she was tempted to hate every white person she saw. Over the years she had heard from various lawyers, "Yeah, sure, we'll reopen the case." Bobby DeLaughter was as rooted in the South as the others, Whoopi said, so Myrlie originally had little faith in him. In the script, every time Bobby calls Myrlie, she says, "Uh-huh, thank you for your call, Mr. DeLaughter."

William H. Macy had gotten the role of Charlie Crisco through the usual Hollywood channels. His agent sent him the script, and he was moved by it. Macy's mother had been raised in Pascagoula, Mississippi, and he spent a lot of time there when he was growing up. "Being a transplanted Southerner," he said, "I liked the script so much because it's about the South that I know in my heart. It's about the South that has a conscience as deep as can be, and about a people who are righting a wrong that they know must be righted at great personal costs. I loved the script because it wasn't just a bunch of Northerners coming down to teach Southerners how to be good guys." *Fargo* had recently been released and was causing a national stir with rave reviews and word-of-mouth praise. "Rob Reiner's one of those great directors who doesn't drive actors nuts with auditions," Macy said. "He gave me the part on the spot."

How Macy had gotten the role in *Fargo* as the car salesman who plotted to have his wife kidnapped for ransom and ultimately ended up being responsible for, by my tally, eight gruesome homicides, is in itself a story. He went in to Joel and Ethan Coen and auditioned for a bit role. The Coen brothers liked what they saw and asked if he wanted to audition for the lead. "I said to myself, oh, *brothers*, do I ever? I went out in the hall and worked on it for about twenty minutes and came back in. They said, 'That's real good. Do you want to work on it some more and come back in and read again?' So I took the script home and called up every actor I knew and made them come over and read the scenes with me." He worked on it all night and went back the next day. "They said, 'That's really good. Okay. Thanks a lot.' Then I found out they had gone to New York for more auditions. So I flew to New York. I walked into their office and said, if you don't give me this role, I'm going to shoot your dog. *Fargo*'s a killer script and they're great filmmakers, the Coen brothers."

Macy would not consciously "study" the real Crisco because when he arrived in Mississippi for the filming Charlie was in the hospital with a recurrence of his acid stomach. Macy tackled the role much as screenwriter Lewis Colick had months before. "The way I got to know Charlie was through his legend, which is very large in Mississippi. So I'd talk to Bobby and the folks around there about Charlie, and they told me tales. This gave me freedom to go anywhere with the role I wanted because his legend was that he was whoever was needed at any given time. That was his personality. He's an excellent cop, they say. I would try to capture that."

—

On his second preproduction excursion to Mississippi, this time with his wife, Michele, Reiner wanted to meet Bobby's other police investigator, Benny Bennett. We met in our house and began talking with Bennett about the new job he had taken shortly after the 1994 trial with the criminal-intelligence division of the State Gaming Commission. He was just then investigating organized criminals coming into the state's new gambling casinos with devices to cheat the slot machines. "They call it a monkey's paw, or a kick stand," he told us. "It's really a light device they can slip up inside the payout shoots of a slot machine. When certain slots pay out, the coins drop down and break a beam of light. When they punch the button the device floods the interior of the machine with light and defeats the counting device, so the machine keeps dropping out coins because it doesn't know it's broken a beam. It was an international ring, and we followed them to Mississippi from Missouri and got 'em—made a lot of arrests."

"Was it the same gang?" the director wanted to know.

"It all goes back to the same person, yes sir, Mr. Reiner." Then he talked about "the adrenaline rush" all good cops get on such undertakings.

Reiner asked him about various facets of the Beckwith search. In his low, deep drawl Bennett described a number of these, including the secret rendezvous with Delmar Dennis, and then the time he saw on Bobby DeLaughter's desk at the courthouse the dusty photograph of his father, a detective, at the murder scene in 1963.

"Have you ever done any acting?" Reiner asked.

"No sir, I never have."

"Would you like to try out for this role of yourself?"

"Yes sir, I sure would."

The next morning Benny read several scenes from the script. "Would you like to have the job?" Reiner asked.

"Yes sir, I would." That meant he would have to come out to L.A. for a long time. "That's just fine," Benny said. "I've never once been to L.A. I'll have to work it out about getting off from the slot machines."

Minutes after this transaction, he telephoned our house. "I got the role. Right now I'm goin' out to tell my little daughters their daddy's a Hollywood actor!"

———

The first read-through of the screenplay by the principal cast took place in the Culver City studios in Los Angeles in April 1995, in a back-lot soundstage converted into a rehearsal hall. Susanna Thompson, who would play Peggy DeLaughter, would remember how impressed she was by Reiner's introductory remarks that this would be the most important movie he would ever do and that it would be important to America. He warned his players and crew members that there would be unnerving racial epithets throughout the film against blacks and Jews, mainly in the words of the Beckwith character, but that these were necessary to the true story. "There were a lot of black people both in the cast and crew," Reiner said later, "and I told them that we were going to hear these words over and over and that that was what this movie was all about, exposing this kind of racism and coming to grips with it." He asked for comments. "Okay, Jew boy!" James Woods replied in his Beckwith voice. Emotions ran high during the reading of the script. With all three of the Evers children there that day, Reiner's voice cracked and he could not finish reading his stage descriptions of the murder.

Alec Baldwin came to Mississippi in early April of 1996, three weeks in advance of the filming, to get to know Bobby DeLaughter. Baldwin was thirty-eight years old and had grown up in Massapequa, Long Island. One of the reasons he was pleased to get the DeLaughter role, he said, was his admiration for Medgar Evers and the chance to make a movie that would make Medgar be remembered. Another was the influence his father, who was also named Alec Baldwin, had had on him when he was growing up. "When I was a kid, he was very involved in liberal causes. He was active in civic affairs, and in Little League and Boy Scouts. He had grown up in the Fort Green neighborhood of Brooklyn, a rough section. He didn't have a racist bone in his body." For twenty-seven years the elder Baldwin taught American history, government, and economics at Massapequa High. When his son was ten years old, the elder Baldwin took him into New York to Bobby Kennedy's funeral at St. Patrick's Cathedral.

"When I was a kid, if I wanted to communicate with my father, I had to meet him on his own ground. So I'd come home from school every day, and he'd be reading *The New York Times* and then we'd watch the Vietnam War on TV. If I wanted a meaningful relationship with my dad other than just small talk, I had to learn what Dien Bien Phu was, and the DMZ." Once the two of them were watching a violent civil rights demonstration on television. His father said, "If you were black and lived in this country, how would *you* feel about things?"

"I'd be with them," the younger Baldwin said.

"That's it. That's all you need to understand," his father replied.

"You never heard him say a disparaging word racially against any people, and that rubbed off on me forever. And then an opportunity to play a role like this in a movie comes along. I think Dad will like my role as Bobby DeLaughter." Alec and his father had remained close. After the final shooting of the movie, many weeks hence, he would miss the wrap party in L.A. to return to Massapequa for the dedication of a new school auditorium named in honor of his father.

Only a few days before he came down from L.A. to Mississippi, Baldwin had been acquitted in a widely publicized lawsuit in which a tabloid paparazzo who was taking pictures of his wife, actress Kim Basinger, and their infant daughter as they arrived home from the hospital accused him of having broken his camera, and then of assaulting him. Now Baldwin was traveling incognito through Mississippi absorbing its atmosphere and places. This was his first trip to the state. "I'm married to a Southern girl from Athens, Georgia, and I really grew to like Mississippi," he said.

But he encountered notable exceptions. He walked into a jewelry store in Natchez where two middle-aged women were behind the counter. One of them recognized him. "She knows who I am, but I'm not getting that warm feeling that usually accompanies that recognition. I'm familiar with this, but hers was kind of on the cusp, you know? She's looking at me and she starts to get this little odd, twisted grin. I know exactly what's going on. So I stick my hand out like I'm the mayor of the city and say, 'Hi, I'm Alec Baldwin.' She says, 'I know who you are, Mr. Baldwin.' I say, 'We're down here visiting your town for a while because we're going to be shooting a movie in three weeks.' And she goes, 'Um hum, ah hah, um hum, what movie are y'all doing? Y'all aren't working on that . . .' and I could see her look at her friend because she knew she was full of shit, she was playing with me. 'You're not working on that Grisham film, *A Time to Kill,* are you?' and I say, 'No, as a matter of fact I'm not, I'm working on another movie.' 'What movie is that?' And I say, 'We're doing the Medgar Evers murder trial.' She says, 'Hooo-weee! You never gonna keep 'em down now! Hooo-weee, you never gonna keep 'em down now! All you New Yorkers coming down here telling people we're mean to our black folks, let me tell you something, we are *not* mean to our black folks down here. We give them everything, and they don't appreciate a damned thing we've done. Well, you should see the way some of these bluegums around here act.' I'd never heard that phrase before, *bluegums*. I'm doing my political backpedaling, you know. I say, 'Well, I'm from New York and we've got our share of racism there too, but the good news here is that you convicted Beckwith. We're talking about the state of Mississippi. We're going to make you look real good, because in the end you did the right thing.' "

Baldwin had never played a real person before. "When you first meet Bob, he's a very serious, sober guy. I was expecting this liberal soldier of fortune, more flamboyant and self-promoting. But he simply believed all he had to do was the right thing and everything else would take care of itself. One of the first things Rob said to me was that he thought I had to lock into Bob quickly." Baldwin, Bobby, Peggy, Reiner, and Zollo were driving one night to a spare-rib place called Doc Harry's out in Madison County. "Perhaps I was a little drunk with the importance of what we were doing," Baldwin said, "but I looked at Bob and told him he may not have gotten everything he wanted as the result of what he did on this case, but when this movie was over he would. 'It's going to change your life. We're going to make you a part of the American culture.' " Baldwin began hanging around with Bobby in his office meeting his colleagues and talking about the Beckwith case and going with him into the courtroom on motion hearings and guilty pleas.

Baldwin wanted to see the murder site. Late one afternoon he, Bobby, Charlie Crisco, and a couple of others piled into Baldwin's chauffeur-driven Town Car and drove out to the Evers house. Baldwin was talking at length on his cellular telephone. When they arrived the others got out of the car while Baldwin continued to talk on the phone. The car was parked at the exact place in the driveway where Medgar had been shot. Two little black kids, a boy and a girl about eight or nine years old, were walking in the direction of the house; they were the only people around. As Baldwin was getting out of the car the little girl put a hand on her mouth, pointed at him with the other, and yelled, "Is it *you*? Is it *you*? You're the Shadow, ain't you?"

"Yeah, sweetie, I sure am," Baldwin said.

She started stomping her feet and dancing in circles on the lawn, then shouted to the little boy who was with her, "I just met the Shadow!" and the boy began dancing around too. The girl said, "I know who you really are, you're Alec Baldwin, and I've seen all your movies." She reeled off about a dozen, beginning with *The Shadow.*

Baldwin asked the kids what they had in their hands. They said they were selling raffle tickets for their school. He reached into his pocket and withdrew a stack of twenty-dollar bills. "Will that cover it?"

The girl's eyes grew wide. "Sir?"

"I want to buy all your raffle tickets." And to the boy, "Yours too." They handed him the tickets. The girl gave him a pen to write his name on all the tickets. "No," Baldwin said, "You put *your* names on every one of them. I hope *you* win the prize." It was at this point that Bobby decided he was being played by a pretty nice guy. The kids left the boarded-up assassination house with the money and the raffle tickets as they blew kisses and shouted, "Bye-bye, Shadow!"

—

What was in hand now was a big-budget project on a true story set in turbulent racial times; a talented, high-profile director; a screenplay by a solid Hollywood professional; a cast from top to bottom that would have been the envy of any studio (with past Oscar nominees in even some of the smaller roles); and a personnel that had worked closely together on good movies in the past. On the eve of the shooting there was every reason to be sanguine.

On the surface, at least, matters were relatively calm, but underneath there was an eddying undercurrent of potential problems—these implicit in the nature and dimension of the true story itself. Reiner and Zollo had privately worked hard to eliminate, or at least reduce, these existing tensions with reason, diplomacy, meetings, give-and-take. Most seemed to have disappeared by the commencement of the filming, but they were probably destined to flare up sooner or later in the public eye. This, I perceive now with the acute wisdom of hindsight, was more or less unavoidable. There were a number of specific and likely volatile facets.

• The Mississippi people versus the national media, *Mississippi Burning,* and Zollo. Since many were horrified by the image of the state in *Mississippi Burning,* the most persistent question Mississippians were asking about *Ghosts* was: "Is it going to make us look bad all over again?" This applied to nonracists who did not want old problems aired to the world, as well as to racists who did not think Beckwith should have been retried at all.

• Many American blacks and white liberals versus the precedent of *Mississippi Burning* for, in their view, having glorified white FBI men and made blacks too passive and subservient.

• District Attorney Ed Peters and his office versus Bobby De-Laughter and Castle Rock. This contretemps was a smoldering one and had to do with interoffice jealousies, misunderstandings, and strict historical accuracy. Copies of the script were making the rounds. There had already been a particularly agitated confrontation in the D.A.'s office with Reiner, Zollo, Peters, and some of his staff during which Bobby was also present. Bobby had told the director that some of the people in his office were displeased with the way they were being portrayed, and Reiner had offered to meet with them to answer questions. It turned into a shouting match. Members of the staff angrily complained about one scene that suggested political motives for the 1994 trial. A major aspect was whether Peters had done anything for political reasons during the Beckwith investigation, as part of the script implied. Black leaders in Jackson had charged that the D.A.'s office had covered up certain things, including the discovery of the murder weapon. The script indicated that Peters had pandered to the black community, to which he strenuously objected, and that he had asked Pat Bennett, a very able black prosecutor in the D.A.'s office, to either replace or join Bobby for political motives. Peters argued that he had only wanted Bennett to help Bobby because other cases had slid. In the meeting Bennett said she was asked to come on not because she was black but because she was a good lawyer, and that she had decided not to do so on her own. Another contentious point was that the crucial cross-examination of the alibi witness was being given in the movie to Bobby rather than Peters. The meeting with Peters and the others was not pretty. Reiner told the district attorney the film would never work unless Bobby and Myrlie's eyes met after the devastating cross-examination of the alibi witness—"the enlightened Southern boy and the grieving widow," Peters would later scoff. When Reiner arrived on the film set the next morning, he threw a temper tantrum while describing the session. He turned to Zollo: "What was that last night, Fred? I don't like it, Fred." Pacing furiously, he said the paranoia he had encountered in Mississippi reminded him of the paranoia he had seen in Marine Corps officers when he was shooting *A Few Good Men*. "I've never seen him go off like this," a young assistant whispered. "That meeting must not have been too well planned."

• Bobby DeLaughter versus Castle Rock. This mostly regarded the factual accuracy of the script. Bobby was concerned that his parents were portrayed as racists, and also that his ex–mother-in-law was depicted as hostile to him when he came to her house looking for the murder weapon when, in fact, he said she was cooperative; also, that he did not barge in during her bridge party. He voiced such reservations. At times Bobby was emotionally confused about the movie; after all, he and his family would be living in Jackson long after the Hollywood people left. He was helpful and cooperative as a consultant, but he is a modest man and was concerned that he was pictured as too much the hero. He had a warm regard for his boss, D.A. Peters, and worried that Peters's role in the investigation was being minimized. He was concerned, as well, about the animosity toward the film among others in the D.A.'s office. With Bobby and the film, it would come down to who he was as a person, and he is a complicated one. He was having a hard time with these matters, but as yet had said nothing publicly. To some it seemed the movie was putting more pressure on him than the investigation and retrial ever did.

• Myrlie Evers versus Castle Rock. From the start, Myrlie wanted this to be Medgar's story, or her and her family's story, or both. Reiner and Zollo were straightforward with her from the beginning about the fact that the plot would focus primarily on the investigation and trial but would have opening flashbacks. Myrlie, like Bobby, is a proud, complex person whose feelings about *Ghosts* would vacillate throughout.

• Lewis Colick versus Castle Rock. The screenwriter was privately expressing displeasure over changes from the second draft of his screenplay in the third, fourth, and fifth drafts.

• Some state officials versus Hollywood/Castle Rock. "This is a film about a verdict," the highly capable director of the state film office straightforwardly told the home people. "If you have a problem with that verdict, then you're going to have a problem with this film." This was the third movie with racial and legal themes set and filmed in the state that year. On *Ghosts* Governor Kirk Fordice was distant.

• Tensions about the murder and the case itself as they would be dealt with in the movie. This touched upon Myrlie's feelings about the Mississippi that murdered her husband and the present complexities of white-black relationships. This also pertained to the conservative white Mississippi view of Bobby and the Beckwith conviction. More specifically, this likewise involved Jerry Mitchell, the reporter who broke the jury-tampering story in 1989, who thought Bobby's role in the screenplay and movie shortchanged his own in the real investigation. Mitchell emphatically saw himself, Myrlie, and Bobby as a triumvirate that together got the case reopened.

All of this was the froth on a cauldron, and Mississippi to the marrow.

Chapter 7

HOLLYWOOD COMES TO YAZOO

Having grown up in a small, isolated Deep Southern town in the pretelevision age (and the Hollywood heyday), I never grew inured to movies. The main reason for this, I believe, was memory itself: the remembrance of being a lonely little boy in the darkened air-cooled movie theater of home on a hot summer's afternoon and seeing on the screen before me the magic images of those people from the exotic, faraway world, especially New York City and Los Angeles—how they smiled and talked and danced and kissed and sipped their drinks, the things they said and did, the clothes they wore, how they hailed taxicabs, the way the men always ordered for the beautiful women in the fancy restaurants, how long it took to dial a call on a New York telephone (our own telephone central being oral and in the three digits). Our imaginations were aroused by these fantasy characters and places, as we tried to figure out some of the unexperienced mysteries of things through them, I guess—and then, when it was over, being suddenly back again on the broiling little Main Street of summer's reality.

The Dixie Theater! It was a tall, gaunt, rectangular edifice at the corner of Main Street and Broadway in Yazoo City, with gritty concrete floors and the wafting smell of salted popcorn and faintly acrid butter, and a high, dark balcony where the Negroes sat (white people called the balcony "the buzzards' roost"), having their own entrance to it off to the side. The Dixie was the repository of my questing dreams. I can remember simple specific gestures on its magnetic screen—a move of the head, for example, or a wisp of conversation—to this day more real and enduring to me than the real words and gestures of the real movie people I later met and knew in New York and Los Angeles.

I was eleven years old when I saw my first in-the-flesh movie star. I opened the door to the tiny lobby at the Dixie, and who should be sitting there next to the popcorn machine signing autographs but the cowboy actor Lash La Rue! I stood staring at him. He noticed me. "What's the *matter,* kid?" he asked. "Ain't I real?" As an added dividend, a year or so later Don "Red" Barry, another cowboy actor, came to the Dixie, followed by other Western luminaries such as Sunset Carson and Al "Fuzzy" St. John.

When I was in junior high school Hollywood sponsored an ambitious public-relations campaign by dispatching movie stars, three or four in a group, to small towns across the country: "Main Street Meets Hollywood," I think it was called. The Yazoo Chamber of Commerce erected a platform in front of the Dixie Theater in the middle of Main Street only a stone's throw from where the Untitled Mississippi Project would someday film a raucous and colorful scene. The high school band was there to play Sousa marches. A good part of the town turned out. Ushered to the platform to vigorous applause, the three lustrous visitors sat down in easy chairs provided for the occasion. One of them was the actor David Brian, another the starlet Adele Mara (*The Sands of Iwo Jima*)! Her young, shining beauty, her bright blond hair lightly tossed and glowing in the sunshine, her perfect gleaming teeth seemed to exhilarate the very air of Main Street on that faraway day, and I even admired her fingernails. I cannot recall the third celebrity, but I do remember gazing at the sparkling Adele Mara for a very long time—did she have any idea how I was looking at her?—and I wondered to myself whether I would ever know a girl like that; later I wrote to Republic Pictures and got a poster of her, which hung by my bedside for years. Finally, when the band finished playing for these stars, the mayor, who was also one of the town's barbers, took to the microphone and said, "It's a real honor to welcome these three characters."

One of the prides of my existence as a junior in high school was to have my photograph taken, also in the lobby of the Dixie, with Huntz Hall, movie sidekick to Leo Gorcey in the East Side Kids, also variously known as the Dead End Kids and the Bowery Boys, this photograph having been arranged to celebrate my recent election as the high school's "wittiest boy," while Mr. Hall was in town on a publicity tour. I still have that photograph, and there I am in the 1952 Yazoo High yearbook with Huntz Hall, I in a yellow plaid shirt laughing self-consciously, while the celebrity visitor, wide-eyed and with an exaggerated smirk, is pointing his finger to his temple as if it were a pistol. Moments later I was interviewing Huntz Hall for our school paper, the *Flashlight*. He was not especially laughable now and, in fact, seemed rather bored. I asked him if they had lines for their movies that had to be memorized. "Christ, kid, whatcha think we do," the comic said, "make it up as we go?"

—

It is a necessity of modern moviemaking that two weeks or so before shooting is to begin, the location manager takes the director, producers, and key technicians on tech scouts to locations that have either already been selected or are being considered for scenes. The Untitled Mississippi Project group traveled in two fifteen-seat vans and included Charlie Harrington, Reiner, Zollo, executive producers Newirth and Stott, production manager Allegra Clegg, first assistant director Frank Capra III, director of

photography John Seale, production designer Lilly Kilvert, key grip
Robin Knight, and gaffer Mo Flam. They rode around to every lo-
cation in the script and discussed how to shoot the scene. In Yazoo
County itself they had visited Bentonia, Satartia, and Yazoo City.

The main street of Yazoo City had been chosen as the surrogate
for Greenwood, Beckwith's hometown, where after his second
hung jury in 1964, the citizens had erected a WELCOME HOME
sign for him, given him a reception in the county courthouse, and
presented him with a check for his legal expenses. Yazoo City was
only forty miles from Jackson, where the numerous cast and crew
were quartered, but Greenwood was ninety-six miles away, and
contracts required that all these many people be paid from the
hour they left their hotels to the hour they were dropped off afterward: hence Yazoo City rather than Greenwood. Harrington and
Ward Emling had a meeting with Mayor Hugh McGraw and seven
or eight civic leaders and warned them what the movie and this
particular scene were about. Since this would be a period scene,
Harrington had to negotiate twenty-eight contracts with owners of
the different storefronts along Main Street. The mayor and citizens of Yazoo City, he said, were the nicest and most unhesitatingly
supportive of any town in the state.

———

In an early morning's sunlight I drove down the precipitous Yazoo
City hill called Broadway, the flatland Delta looming before me
like an ocean, which indeed it once had been. At the corner of
Main Street was the site of the noble Dixie Theater, now a depart-
ment store. I could still ascertain the familiar contours of the COL-
ORED ONLY entrance, long since cemented over.

The street transformed by Hollywood into the way it was more
than thirty years ago played ruses on my emotions. A few yards
south of the filming were the remnants of another movie house
where my mother and grandmother had given me, age eight, a
quarter to see *Gone With the Wind* for the first time. One block be-

yond that was the precise spot where a policeman had shot a black man, then stood over him with his pistol and refused to allow anyone to help while he bled to death. Down the street had been the radio station where I was a disc jockey as a teenager: "This is WAZF, twelve-thirty on your dial, in downtown Yazoo City, Mississippi, with studios high atop the Taylor-Roberts Feed and Seed Store." We drove our girlfriends up and down this street on Saturday nights before the late picture shows. Here in 1950 we had our *own* parade, on the day our baseball team won the state championship; we sat in the back of pickup trucks with our girlfriends and dogs and basked in the invigorating applause.

Today there was a large WELCOME HOME DELAY banner across this street so familiar to my heart, dozens of vintage cars, and hundreds of extras. The extras, many of them carrying miniature Rebel flags, were emerging from a warehouse down the way that served much as a human-being assembly line, each of them having dutifully filed one-by-one through Wardrobe, Makeup, and Hairdressing. These extras had been recruited by announcements a couple of weeks before in the *Yazoo Herald* and other local outlets giving the place and time for them to congregate. They were told to bring recent snapshots of themselves. Here they had filled out forms, which categorized them by gender, race, and age, and they were eventually selected by the extras casting director. The turnout at the National Guard Armory in Yazoo City had by all accounts been torrential. "I've been in this business of extras a long time," an assistant extras director said. "I've never seen so many people who wanted to be in a movie so much as they did in Yazoo City, Mississippi. They were passionate about it, to say the least. Everybody in this town wants to go to Hollywood."

In this warehouse a carnival atmosphere prevailed. The extras were eating breakfast while they waited to file into the dressing area for costume. Then they moved in a line through the doorway to the barbers' chairs. Men were getting their hair shaved a little and slicked back. Women were having curlers put in. Then they moved to the makeup tables, above which were taped photographs of women from 1964 magazines. At another table the women's rollers were removed and hair spray liberally applied after extravagant teasing and styling. For some reason all this reminded me of the first version of the movie *Invasion of the Body Snatchers*. When they finally emerged from this elaborate and systematic transformation, the extras seemed beside themselves, squealing with laughter at each other. "I wouldn't have known *you!*" one young woman said to another. "Well, I wouldn't have known *you* neither."

Even with the passing of the years, I recognized a number of the older extras. Many of the men wore close-fitting, short-hemmed pants with short-sleeve, button-down polyester shirts, white socks, and loafers. Others, representing country people, wore overalls. There was hair grease on the teenaged boys. The women had on cigarette pants, Keds, print dresses that fell well below the knees, eyeglasses with rhinestones around the rims, with scarves tossed over their bouffant hairdos. Every building, every store on Main Street, was on a map on my consciousness. The Black and White Store window displayed men's and women's clothing of that era. The windows of the appliance store were filled with period TV's and radios. Another set of windows displayed a mannequin dressed in the high fashion of 1964—a woman's suit with matching hat, gloves, and shoes. Yet another re-created a 1960s ladies' boutique with mint-condition hats and purses. Every price tag was authentic 1960s. In another window Shoeless Jack Stevens was putting a girdle on a mannequin.

Frankie Capra, the assistant director, bellowed through his bullhorn to herd the extras onto the sidewalks. A man began driving a red 1963 Chevrolet convertible up and down the street for camera angles; James Woods's stand-in was in the back. At this moment Rob Reiner arrived on this strenuous set. He sat in his chair and scrutinized the scene through his monitors. Pleased with the angle, he ordered the driver to repeat his movements. The director and his assistants counted the seconds the drive would take and plotted the exact moment the reporter in the crowd would come running to the car and ask DeLay a question.

Suddenly a jaunty figure in a shiny blue cotton suit with a red tie, red socks, and white belt, shirt, and shoes strutted onto the set. It was James Woods. He was chewing on a cigar as he approached Reiner; throwing his arms upward, he struck a pose as if to say: "Good? What do you think?" Everyone, extras and onlookers, cheered and applauded. I stood behind Reiner's monitors as he oversaw the first of countless takes from various angles of Woods perched in the back of the convertible smoking the cigar and haughtily gesticulating to the adoring throngs. For what would eventually be little more than thirty seconds on the finished film, this work took all morning and much of the afternoon.

Friends from my distant past gathered round and we talked about vanished times and those we had known who were long or recently dead, while Reiner and Woods dipped into the crowds and shook hands and signed autographs. An extra picked up one of Woods's cigar butts off the street as a souvenir. Fred Zollo said he wanted me to meet someone. He led me down the sidewalk and introduced me to the former Klansman and FBI informer Delmar Dennis, who wore a 1950s-style fedora and did indeed resemble the actor who had played him at the Windsor Ruins, though frailer and considerably more worn. He had come all the way from his home in Tennessee to watch this Yazoo shooting. His wife and two daughters stood next to him in 1960s garb; they had been hired as extras. "I knew Beckwith back then, you know," Delmar Dennis said. "That actor looks a lot like ol' *DeLay*." Then we shook hands and I departed—just another Untitled Mississippi Project circumstance. Three weeks later I opened the newspaper to find that he had died suddenly of a heart attack.

—

The Yazoo County village of Bentonia is a sleepy settlement of 390 souls, about half of them white and half black, with the Illinois

Central railroad tracks paralleling the main street near a depot that had closed down years before. The Big Black River down the road was infamous in the folk tradition among local black people for having been the site of a horrible mass lynching in the 1870s, the circumstances of which had been hushed and strange and mordant when I myself first heard of them as a boy. Bentonia was known for the black blues singers who had lived there over the years, including Jack Owens, the oldest performing Mississippi Delta blues man and last link to the blues' golden age, who at ninety-one performed for Yankee and Mississippi visitors on the porch of his little shack with his dogs all around and drank straight gin chased by Nehi strawberry and still carried a .22 pistol in his boot. He occasionally could be heard here at a juke joint called the Blue Front Cafe. The Blue Front and the big lumberyard next to it would figure in the Bentonia filming the day after the Yazoo City parade sequence. This was the lumberyard whose owner at the last minute had reneged on the location agreement with Charlie Harrington because of the subject matter of the movie. Harrington hastily made an arrangement with the three black brothers who owned the Blue Front, since their property was adjacent to the lumberyard, with the tall stacks of lumber that Reiner wanted in the background of the scene. For a half day's rental the brothers got four thousand dollars.

Surely never in its history had Bentonia known such commotion. The forlorn dirt strip across from the feed-and-seed store on this early morning was a maze of the usual identical industrial-size trucks with their logos of an Atlanta rental company, trailers, big rigs, and cars. The black Lincolns parked next to one of the luxury trailers signified the presence of Alec Baldwin and James Woods on this day's shooting. The first scenes on the Blue Front property would be re-creations of the separate meetings DeLaughter, Crisco, and Bennett had had in Greenwood in 1990 with the two former cops who had been alibi witnesses for Beckwith at both 1964 trials and still stuck to their story. (In actuality it was just Bobby and Crisco, and they spoke with only one cop. The other would not talk to them.)

Hundreds of people scurried to and fro. On the porch of the Blue Front, a small shotgun building, three black men were drinking beer and observing the activity; they seemed in a highly amiable mood, smiling and laughing, which was understandable when I learned they were the siblings who owned the property. Under a structure that had nothing but support poles and a roof Reiner and his assistants were discussing the angle of the first shot. All around them was much debate about the decoration of this set. The lumberyard owner's decision had caused messy logistical problems.

The confusion about the shots with the stacked lumber in the background was such that the shooting moved to a house up the road for another scene while the problems with the original one were solved by the technicians. Everyone got in vans and departed in a grumbling mood. The new scene would re-create a verbatim interview Beckwith had had in 1993 with a reporter for a Jackson television station at Beckwith's house in Signal Mountain, Tennessee. The house for the filming was on the crest of a small hill a few hundred yards from the main street with a broad front porch displaying a large Confederate flag. On the edge of the lawn was a tent for the director and the monitors. On the porch the cameramen were getting ready. Townspeople were watching from their cars, from across the road, and from the lawn next door, some of them relaxing on blankets and quilts. A man standing nearby was holding a tall glass filled with ice and what appeared to be straight bourbon whiskey and happily talking with the local spectators; he was the owner of the house, and when someone commented that he had reason to celebrate since he was most probably being paid very well, he tilted his glass to that.

Suddenly James Woods's makeup artist emerged from the front door of the house. The town of Bentonia would likely never again see the likes of her, certainly not in daylight. She was a petite woman with long hair dyed the color of a ripe plum. Her arms were covered from wrist to forearm with silver bangle bracelets. Her neck, too, dangled with trinket jewelry. She made a jingling sound as she came out the door of the house, followed by a few other workers. She gave Rob Reiner a thumbs-up signal. Reiner then bellowed to assistant director Capra, "Frankie, can we do this?"

Capra, wearing a baseball cap turned in reverse, shorts, and a Hawaiian shirt, shouted through his megaphone: "Quiet, please! We need total silence. Lock it up!" A Bentonia dog began to bark in the distance. All the crew strained to see if they could spot this intruder. "Get that damned dog out of here!" someone shouted. Capra withdrew his walkie-talkie and ordered someone to run the dog away.

Shooting began as the front screen door of the house opened and James Woods abruptly appeared as the seventy-three-year-old Beckwith, thirty years older than the man he had played in Yazoo City the day before. He had been in makeup for three and a half hours, and his resemblance to the authentic Beckwith was chilling, right down to the liver spots on his head. He waved his hand and tugged at his trousers as he walked down the steps. With each break between takes the plum-haired makeup artist, carrying a large black bag of supplies, powdered his nose and dabbed the sweat off his face while someone else held an umbrella over him to protect his makeup from the blazing Yazoo County sun. Soon the Video Village with its monitors and personnel moved to the side lawn to shoot the verbatim footage of the 1993 interview, with TV reporter Ed Bryson playing himself. The angle would be over the reporter's shoulder looking up at Beckwith's angry face. From the screenplay:

UNTITLED MISSISSIPPI PROJECT

As THELMA BECKWITH *moves out of frame*, BECKWITH *straightens his tie and clears his throat.*

BRYSON (*offscreen*)
Tell me, Mr. Beckwith, do you think it's a crime for a white man to kill a black man?

It's obvious that BECKWITH *is enjoying the attention and the opportunity to tell the world the way things are.*

BECKWITH

God put the white man here to rule over all the dusky races. It says so in the Bible.

BRYSON (*offscreen*)

Did you kill Medgar Evers?

BECKWITH

I did not kill him.
(*laughs*)
But he sure is dead. I didn't shed a tear.
(*laughs again*)
And he ain't coming back.

BRYSON (*offscreen*)

I'm just wondering what happens if you're indicted again, Mr. Beckwith.

BECKWITH

I'm gonna tend to my business like I always have. I'm gonna look out for my God, my family and the whole State of Christ's church.

Now that don't encompass anybody but white Christians. All these other races, colors and creeds, they're anti-Christ. Many of 'em believe in human sacrifices and voodoo. And the Jews are what God made 'em. Children of the devil. And anybody who says Jesus was a Jew is a damned fool, and they're gonna suffer in hell.

BRYSON (*offscreen*)

Mr. Beckwith, according to your way of thinking, how can justice be done in the Medgar Evers murder case?

BECKWITH

First they gotta find out who killed the nigger.

BRYSON (*offscreen*)

Then what?

BECKWITH *smiles the mocking smile of a man who has gotten away with murder.*

BECKWITH

Well, just do whatever the law says that you can do *if* you're big enough to do it.

Woods had Beckwith down so realistically that there were only about three or four takes of this scene—the fewest I ever saw in this movie. Weeks later, this scene was the teaser trailer that would be shown in advance of the December release date in theaters all over the country; in several of these movie houses, members of the audiences stood up and shouted at the screen, and in one of them a man threw a box of popcorn.

After they finished filming the scene, Woods came over to the director under the tent and asked to see the shot. Reiner ordered a replay on his larger monitor. There was absolute silence among the people under the tent. The scene had cast a haunted mood over the whole set. I had grown up with this diabolic hatred, and the remembrance of it evoked by these images flickering in front of us overwhelmed me now. "This is creepy stuff, Jimmy," Reiner said. James Woods turned away from the monitor and whispered, "Ooh! I scare myself."

—

There was the day they built an old run-down service station and grocery just off a gravel road in the Delta out from the Yazoo River town of Satartia, where Ulysses S. Grant had gotten hopelessly drunk in 1863 and on returning to his lines around Vicksburg got on his horse and proceeded to run over his own men. The set dressers were creating a dirt driveway in front of their half-completed service station, and it was so hot that day the dirt was like cement. Others were carrying worn Orange Crush and Coca-Cola coolers, old clocks and gas pumps, a pay telephone, a DELTA 76 sign, and various minutiae. Although this scene would be set in the 1990s, the props were of the earlier time, appropriate to an establishment that would have been unchanged for years, as are many things in Mississippi. The paraphernalia for the gas station had been shipped in from ten or twelve states through movie catalogue orders. I had gone with Shoeless Jack Stevens and the other set dressers as they did business with an old fisherman and trapper who lived in a house trailer on cluttered premises a quarter of a mile from the set, a macho fellow with slicked-back hair, tattoos, mustache, gold-framed glasses, somebody Stanley Kowalski might have played cards with on poker night. He hand-wrestled big catfish in the Yazoo River and boiled his own chitterlings. For the upcoming set they rented some things from him: sixteen old tires, old outboard and inboard motors, yard junk.

Under a gray sky against the copious Delta horizon the rich, flat land with its faint touch of early cotton stretched as far as the eye could see; there were glimpses here and there of the muddy and meandering Yazoo—Indian for "River of Death." This was spectral ground, and well known to me. Only a few miles northwest of this spot, where the Yazoo and Sunflower rivers ran their course from the upper Delta and came closely together, are the remnants of a highly advanced Indian settlement occupied continuously from at least 700 B.C. to A.D. 1600. There are many Indian mounds, including a huge central one, a forested promontory rising out of the flat cotton fields, where on stormy winter nights locals claim to hear ghostly shouts and wails. Twenty-five or so miles southwest of this location, in the last remnant of the old primordial Delta forests, was the setting of the fictional deer camp of William Faulkner's "Delta Autumn," one of the finest stories in the language.

In the distance a local black man driving a tractor through the fields was rehearsing his movements. "How much was a gallon of gas down here in 1991?" someone shouted. "Anybody know?" He was carrying a big sign that would display the cost per gallon.

"I'll call the Highway Department," another replied, and withdrew a cellular telephone.

In the hardworking Hollywood terminology the set dressers were calling this the "Gas and God" set because the contrived service station was directly across the road from a real church, a small wood-frame structure belonging to a black congregation. To the side of the church was a cemetery full of homemade tombstones. An official military stone bore the inscription of a black soldier who had fought in France in World War I. This set was a clash of universes, very American in its unfolding. Several elderly black people, gray-haired men and women, sat in straight-backed chairs on the porch of the church and on the steps leading to it, wordlessly gazing out at what was transpiring before their eyes: a Hollywood apparition springing full-born from the Lord's alluvial earth.

A black man in his seventies sat next to me on the steps. This was his church, he said. It was more than one hundred years old. He asked me to explain what was going on across the road. I tried. He talked to me about the countryside. "This is my land," he said. "I don't own it, but it's *my* land." He and his wife had raised thirteen children on this land. Twelve of them were still alive. They lived in Chicago and Detroit and came home to Mississippi once a year. He had forty grandchildren, also quite a few great-grandchildren, but he was not sure of the exact number. He paused. "Medgar Evers, you say? A movie?"

On the grassy lawn Hollywood people were sitting on tall canvas chairs, all of them speaking into cellular telephones. On a blanket a young white woman was having a picnic with her three children. I suspected she was the daughter-in-law of the cotton planter who owned these many acres. Soon, before the actual shooting began, men drove in from the sprawling base camp down the main county highway with trays and containers of that morning's snacks; today's specialties would include cappuccino, possibly the first and last time cappuccino would ever be served in the cotton fields abutting Satartia, Mississippi.

When Reiner and the actors arrived at the completed set, they did take after take, over the course of hours. It was a brief scene involving Bobby DeLaughter, Crisco, and Benny during a futile juncture in their search, and in the finished film the scene would last less than a minute:

EXT. GAS STATION OFF THE HIGHWAY—DAY
BOBBY's *Blazer pulls into a gas station and up to a pump.*

BOBBY (*voice-over*)
I was hoping I'd have some good news for her today.

BENNY (*voice-over*)
Who's that?

BOBBY (*voice-over*)
Mrs. Evers. I call her every Friday and tell her how the case is progressing.

CRISCO
Bobby, I got a flash. This case *ain't* progressin'.

BOBBY, CRISCO, *and* BENNY *get out to stretch and gas up.*

BOBBY
I think about her keeping this thing alive all this time. Imagine a woman loving a man so much.

CRISCO
Hell, I can't even get a woman to love me while I'm still alive. You know what I did after my last divorce? I

took up golf. Man needs a hobby to occupy his mind. Otherwise you wind up doing crazy things like drinking too much or chasing twenty-six-year-old murder cases across the Mississippi Delta.

Chapter 8

ON THE SET

The inherent personal stresses that had spilled out here and there had disappeared and would be in remission for a good while. The cast and crew seemed to be enjoying what they were doing and gratified by the story they were telling. Many of them remarked on the camaraderie on the set. Castle Rock, nothing if not efficient, was beginning to plan its impressive publicity campaign of teaser trailers for movie houses and national television channels well in advance of the scheduled December release, including the arresting Beckwith/Woods TV interview. The Jackson media was friendly and enthusiastic. Rick Bragg, a new star in the *New York Times* diadem who had just won a Pulitzer for his stories, came to Jackson from Atlanta to research a substantial piece on the making of the movie, which would be a major spread on the front page of a Sunday Arts and Entertainment section early in the summer. Everything was going well. Perhaps *too* well?

———

"If one goes to the root of the matter," screenwriter and playwright Sidney Howard once declared, "motion pictures are neither written nor acted, but made." In one of Rob Reiner's many colorful asides, this one during a break in filming in front of the Hinds County Courthouse one afternoon, he surveyed the animated tableau before him and recalled a recent conversation he had had about moviemaking with director and producer Andy Scheinman. "We agreed on this phenomenon. You start with a script, which is basically anywhere from one hundred to one hundred fifty pages long, and it's about the size of an eight-by-ten. It's this little thing that weighs maybe a pound. From that comes an explosion of production. There are schedules and deals and plane reservations and rehearsals and equipment and crew members and lighting packages and teamsters and hundreds of people. Hundreds and hundreds of people working over a period of three months of pre-production and three of production and three to five of postproduction. All of that energy, and you wind up with these two cans of film about the same size as the script and then a videocassette even *smaller* than the script. It's what's in those two little cans of film that matters."

Everything on the set became so familiar and contained that away from those Mississippi and later California sets I would experience bizarre recognitions not dissimilar to the ones on my first arrival in New York City years ago, where I would mistake strangers for real people I had once known in Yazoo City as a boy. All they had to do was bear some vague resemblance to someone who had once had meaning for me. This, too, became my own peculiar and haphazard off-the-set eyesight. When we were in L.A., for instance, the young man smoking a cigarette at Sunset and Doheny was Frankie Capra. Why was Whoopi Goldberg walking a Dalmatian in broad daylight on La Cienega? The fellow sipping a smoothie in front of Jerry's Famous Deli in Westwood was Todd Murata, the second assistant director. And wasn't that Bobby Joe Garren, the greens foreman, waiting for the light at Yucca and Las Palmas?

The set was not only a communal phenomenon but also an acutely hierarchical one. Everyone had a function, and the chain of command, even given the banter and boisterousness of frivolous moments, began at the top with the director, producers, and stars, moving on down through the entire assemblage to the most obscure grips and gaffers. The Hollywood phraseology could not be more specific: "Above the line" meant "talent"—directors, producers, actors, screenwriters; "Below the line" meant the technicians. This hierarchy was more tangible than any I had ever observed, even in Washington, D.C., a caste town if ever there was one, and it dutifully extended even to the specific dimensions of the private trailers always parked near the shooting area: forty feet in length, or thirty, or twenty, two-room or one-room, the director and stars with the larger and best-appointed down to the actors of lesser stature with the more diminutive ones. A few dine privately in these air-conditioned trailers with kitchenette and bathroom and bedroom and television, while the members of the crew are outside, under a tent, serving themselves buffet. And everyone is eating well.

—

The logistics of filming a big movie are in themselves staggering, and the daily canon is the call sheet, which the production office distributes to everyone in midafternoon for the next day's shooting. These sheets specify the address of the location with precise directions on how to get there, the weather forecast including sunrise and sunset, the time of the crew call and shooting call, and the numbered day of shooting out of the total projected days. Each scene is briefly described with the number of the scene from the scheduling board based on the numbers from the final script. There are numbers representing the actors working on that day, then their names below numbered consecutively, the characters they are playing, the time they are to be picked up, the time for makeup, and the on-set time. Below all this, under "Atmosphere and Stand-Ins," is a list of the extras, and under "Special Instructions" the camera and wardrobe requirements, special equipment, special effects, vehicles, set dressing, greens, and props. There is also a page count for each set. Shooting scripts are distilled into eighths of pages, and one set might be four eighths or two eighths or five eighths. A director tries to shoot between two to three pages each day. The reverse side of the daily call sheet contains an elaborate maze of technicians' names and titles with their call times, times for breakfast, crew lunch and extras' lunch, transportation, equipment trucks, drivers, and the address of the nearest hospital. My God, was that modest little memo I wrote after the broken-fence night Shoeless Jack Stevens called Ground Zero responsible for all *this*? It made me feel both godlike and scared witless. What if it didn't *work*?

Moviemaking requires a bewildering galaxy of vehicles alone. Movie trucks are easy to spot because they display the logos of the firms that rent equipment. One typical day's filming in the L.A. area required five fifteen-passenger vans to transport the crew and extras from the checkpoint to the set, one fuel truck, two stake beds, one camera truck, one production truck, one grip truck, one prop truck, one wardrobe truck, one water truck, one five-ton set-dressing truck, three two-room cast trailers, one electric truck, one generator truck, one craft-service trailer, one makeup and hair trailer, one schoolroom trailer, one bus, and one honeywagon, a euphemism for the portable toilets. The wardrobe truck, for instance, was an eighteen-wheeler with a steel stairway leading up to a glassed-in back area. This rig was air-conditioned, had hardwood floors, and was filled with a great volume of vintage and contemporary clothing in excellent condition, each article tagged by size.

—

On the set everyone and everything are at the service of the camera. "If my movie has two stars in it," Sidney Lumet once said, "I always know it really has three. The third star is the camera." The lighting of a set is often lengthy and complicated, which explains the legendary delays. If the angle of the camera has to be changed more than fifteen degrees, the whole setup has to be relit. During the later filming in Hollywood, in the Culver City Studios courtroom with its removable or "wild" walls, the various camera angles on Wall A or Wall C would consume many hours. Night filming is especially trying, with even more prolonged waiting. A camera holds a thousand feet of film and has to be reloaded every eleven minutes, and this means further delays.

Australian John Seale is regarded as one of the best directors of photography in the trade. As early as 1981 he was the camera operator on the Australian classic *Gallipoli.* He is the only DP whom Reiner has worked with more than once, their previous film having been *The American President,* since DP's usually make two or three pictures a year and it is difficult to synchronize with their schedules. "I would do every picture with John Seale," Reiner said. "His movies look terrific; he works very fast. He has no ego problems, and he's got a great sense of humor. He's everything you could possibly want." It is he who is in charge of filming the actual scenes. He almost never touches the camera but centers his attention on the setups on a focusing screen. He leaves the technicalities of camera movement to the main cameraman and a crew of three or four assistants. He and his crew are skilled artisans in the complex aspects of lens, stop, light, and filter, all of which remained a continuing enigma to me.

—

The systematic organization necessary to get significant images on several miles of celluloid is vast. The perpetual waiting around on the set, the moods, the anxieties, the personalities, the ennui, the flippant and cynical Hollywood humor and extravagant one-liners provide their own histrionics. "Once a movie starts shooting," John Gregory Dunne has written, "it resembles a freight train without brakes; it gathers speed and goes, and it is best to keep out of the way. . . . Tension is the given of a movie, and it has less to do with ego than with the intensity of short-term relationships, a lifetime lived in a seventy-day shoot."

There are lengthy intervals of immense noise and frantic movement, suddenly followed by moments of great stillness and silence:

"the purring generators, the whirring cameras, the whispering technicians," as Truman Capote once described a little of it, "dancing in and out among thick cords of electric cable." Sometimes in late afternoon of a long working day, assistant directors and technicians who have been up since 5:00 or 6:00 A.M. can be seen catnapping in chairs, on lawns, against walls. Yet in the midst of all this, carefully plotted work is going on. After the seeming anarchy and confusion of the first shooting I saw at Windsor Ruins, long days on many locations became a lesson in order and correlation. I grew to know what Orson Welles meant when he said making a movie is like owning the biggest electric train set in the world.

It is a clamorous calling, the constant shouting: "Clear the eyelines!" "Video Village coming through!" "Watch your feet!" "Holding traffic!" "Lockup!" "Can we have an apple box?" "First team!" "How much time are we talking about?" "Print!" Director Sidney Lumet knows something of this: "In the studio, as you're shooting on a set, they're building another. A door opens and you hear that ear-splitting screech of the buzz saws in the carpentry shops; hammers going constantly; the thuds of sandbags being dropped; the hum of conversation among the extras; the squeak of nails being pulled; the shouts of electricians as they focus their lamps." And the incessant movement, even on the smallest set: the camera operator rehearsing with the dolly grip, the heightening and lowering of the camera, the positioning of the dolly, the lowering of the boom, the birdlike descent of the makeup artists during lulls, the actors strutting about rehearsing their lines, the director and his cinematographer pacing the room, the carpenters nailing some object or another in place. Since much of the day is consumed waiting about for the scenes—the setups—to be readied, the rush and hurry between takes has to do with time and costs. The filming of fifteen or twenty setups a day is considered prolific.

—

Hollywood stars are sanctified, the screenwriter Robert Towne observes, with having "features that are ruthlessly efficient," so much so that their very faces and physiques send out considerable information before any lines of dialogue were spoken at all. This was true of Baldwin and Goldberg, and especially so, in this film, of James Woods because of the circumstances. Around the set one of the most mesmerizing of all sights would continue to be him made up as the seventy-three-year-old Beckwith. Pieces of preformed latex and gelatin were glued to his face and then colored in. "It was like maple syrup poured on you at five in the morning," he said. It was so much like real skin, he said, it changed temperature when he walked into a cool room. "Do you know what it's like having something glued to your eyelid?" A rubber cap was applied over his hair, and old-age freckles were dotted on by brush. "Cataracts" were also added, and hair and ears and teeth. They had to color the teeth and use makeup at the gumline. Everything was rubber except his nose, eyeballs, and eyelids. Even his lips were under a latex sealer. He likened this state to being in the air force, a Top Gun pilot. "They give you the training and give you all this equipment, and then you go out and fly."

A gregarious presence, Woods relished strolling up to people he knew with his Beckwith swagger as they failed to recognize him. Even his own driver didn't know him. "Dammit!" he shouted. "It's me, Jimmy!" In the infernal summer Mississippi sun his skin could not "breathe," and his perspiration had nowhere to go. He drank electrolyte liquids all day long and almost fainted twice. A crew member was assigned to hold an umbrella over him between takes so he would not melt. To look at himself aged by twenty-five years or so was painful, he confessed. His girlfriend would comment on how depressed he looked when he came home from work, and he was so down that they broke up for a while.

Whoopi Goldberg usually spent no more time on the set than was necessary. She stayed in her trailer, in front of which she had staked several plastic pink flamingos, until the last minute. Each day's call sheet listed her by her real name, Caryn Johnson. Sometimes her mother was with her on the set. Whoopi was singularly consistent with her own iconography, acutely intelligent, funny, and candid. Between takes she was totally out of her Myrlie Evers character—back to the voraciously foul-mouthed Whoopi: fuck this, fuck that. She was a product of the Coney Island projects, and one day on the set she sadly remarked about the divide that had developed between her childhood chums and herself when she became a star, and how much this inevitable chasm worried her, as if nothing could be done about it. She sometimes talked about her granddaughter and said she wanted to do movies the little girl could watch, and how difficult it was for her to find them. If people with racist feelings see this movie, she said one day, perhaps they'll be able to take a step here, a step there. "But it's important that we get to the kids. If we can get to the kids, then we have a real shot." On a side trip from Jackson one off day she took Darrell Evers for some gambling at one of the riverboat casinos in Vicksburg.

In Walker Percy's novel *The Moviegoer,* the protagonist, Binx Bolling, sights William Holden strolling through the French Quarter in New Orleans on a torpid afternoon. "Holden has turned down Toulouse shedding light as he goes. An aura of heightened reality moves with him and all who fall within it. Now everyone is aware of him. He creates a regular eddy among the tourists and barkeeps and B-girls who come running to the doors of the joints." As the male star, Alec Baldwin cast something of this spirit.

I first met him at the Windsor Ruins shooting, where he was reclining on the hood of his Lincoln Town Car during a break smoking a cigar and bantering with a few young crew members. At a gathering at our house one evening, locals kept asking him how his Southern accent was coming. "I'm considering playing Bobby this way," he said, and proceeded to put on the thickest, most rural Mississippi accent imaginable, straight from the deepest boondocks. "No," he quickly said, "I'm not doing it that way." Even on the set he was persistently approached for autographs by the extras and civilian onlookers, and he seemed to try to treat such things with a certain egalitarian élan. During mealtime recesses he often spurned his private trailer and dined under the base-camp tent with bit players and crew, who even in their tough nomadic professionalism conducted themselves with a certain deference. At other times he could be seen playing around with the child actors or tossing footballs with the grips and gaffers. He was an intelligent, articulate young man who within this odd, rigorous systematic order wanted to be a good guy, and he was. But during the extensive filming of the Untitled Mississippi Project I perceived in him a concern about his reputation as a serious Hollywood actor after a recent succession of undemanding parts. He took the Bobby DeLaughter role earnestly and worked hard on it, as if he judged it a turning point in his career. "Bad guys are kind of easy to play," Gregory Peck once said. "The real trick is to make the virtuous character interesting."

—

For many years, about the only film-crew positions available to women were as script girls and in the editing office. The crew on the Untitled Mississippi Project was still preponderantly male, just as the executive offices in most Hollywood studios were still sometimes called "the boys' club," although there were more women and blacks on this film than was the Hollywood norm. Shooting a movie is a strenuous and often dirty job, and since this was a spring and summer schedule, rarely did you see the crew in anything other than very casual shorts, T-shirts, and tank tops. In contrast, on the more open sets, the gawkers absorbing the spectacle, usually women hoping for a glimpse of a star, were dressed in party finery and cosmetically resplendent, especially on the Mississippi locations.

The crew roster of a Hollywood movie is broken down into arcane categories and nomenclatures that illustrate its highly specialized calculus. Under "Makeup and Hair" on this film, for example, were the following positions: key makeup, special f/x makeup (James Woods's), makeup, Mr. Baldwin's makeup, Ms. Goldberg's makeup, key hair, and hair. Under "Grips": key grip, best boy grip, dolly grip, three grips, rigging key grip, rigging best boy grip, and five rigging grips. Under "Electric": gaffer, best boy electric, four electricians, two rigging gaffers, rigging best boy, and three rigging electricians. Under "Camera": director of photography, camera operator, first assistant camera, first assistant "B" camera, second assistant camera, loader, and four members of the camera helicopter unit. Under Assistant Directors: first assistant director, second assistant director, and second second assistant director. The organizational table of contents of the crew list enumerated thirty-four such categories, and these did not include the director, producers, coproducers, and executive producers, or the cast of 110 people with speaking lines. There was one medic, one masseuse.

A set also includes the production assistants, known as P.A.'s, who are the hardworking gofers, usually college film students or relatives of the movie's executives; and carpenters ("carps"); set dressers; and stand-ins, called the second team, on whom all the lighting is prepared before the actors, the "first team," are summoned. For lighting purposes the stand-ins must wear the same color clothes as the actors will in the forthcoming scene. They do not necessarily have to look like the stars. Alec Baldwin's stand-in was a young man from New Orleans who owned a bric-a-brac shop in the French Quarter. Whoopi Goldberg's was a young college graduate whose ambition was to write novels and whose favorite writer was Mississippi's Ellen Gilchrist. These stand-ins had worked with Alec and Whoopi on many films.

Indeed, many of the people had worked together before in locales all over the United States and the world. On this movie, the director was noted for running a relaxed and amiable set, thus the familylike mood. Here are a few of the people one got to know:

Frank Capra III, grandson of *the* Frank Capra and son of the director-producer Frank Capra, Jr., was the assistant director and coproducer. He and the second assistant directors, George Bamber and Todd Murata, were almost constantly on the move except during actual filming. In large scenes involving many extras, Capra sometimes used an old-style megaphone to direct them. He was all business—always working, rarely acknowledging or speaking to others on the set unless giving directions. People called him Frankie, and if asked when he wasn't working, he was not averse to talking about his grandfather. Does anyone know, for instance, that *It's a Wonderful Life* caused practically no stir when it first came out and was a box-office flop?

In actual filming, after the long preparations that preceded it, the center of all activity was the camera operator, Scott Sakamoto. His job was a complicated one: to turn the wheels that point the camera to the contours and movements of a scene. His motions often appeared chaotic but had been assiduously planned and rehearsed. Often there were six, eight, or ten movements of the camera in a shot, each having been numbered with chalk on the floor beforehand. Changes in the height of the camera had to be delineated and the actors' positions plotted with tape, called marks, with different colors of tape representing each actor. In the actual shooting Sakamoto had to work in intimate unison with four other men: the focus puller in charge of keeping focus between the camera lens and the actors, a grip handling an opaque board that reduced light, another grip on the tongue upon which the camera was raised and lowered, and yet another maneuvering the crane, or dolly, which also has several alternating positions. The proper movements of these men in these moments of shooting often resembled a miniature rugby scrum to me. I never fully comprehended what was transpiring, and if my description taken from my hastily scribbled notes and conversations misses by a little, I at least tried.

There was Lyn McKissick, the script supervisor, who was always at the director's side behind the monitors taking detailed notes involving timing, use of props, and camera angles. When they filmed over Alec Baldwin's shoulder earlier, she might tell Reiner, he picked up his pencil in the middle of his lines. Now he is doing it at the *end*. This would be confusing to the movie viewer.

There were two other Baldwins, neither related to the actor but both hired at his behest as part of his contract because they had worked together before. Still photographer Sidney Baldwin, a black man with a graying beard and small braids of hair, was as perpetually on the move as the assistant directors. With several cameras draped around his neck and a small mountain of film in his satchel, he was responsible for the hundreds of photographs to be used in publicity, magazines, and theater lobbies and for still shots of sets in Mississippi so that when the crew returned to L.A. the production departments could re-create them on the soundstages for close-ups. Dialect coach Brooks Baldwin of New Orleans and New York instructed the actors on the Southern accent before each take, their heads juxtaposed and bent low as they went over the lines word-by-word. It was Brooks Baldwin who once observed that he had carefully studied both Medgar and Myrlie Evers's accents and found they were more mainstream American than most Mississippi *white* accents, which signified to him that they had wished to communicate to a broad national audience and constituency.

There was the welfare worker, also called the studio teacher, a middle-aged woman named Marge Schlaifer. She was in charge of teaching the six children in the cast their prepared curricula from their schools and for making sure they ate on time and did not work beyond the industry regulations. While on location in Jackson she also took them on sight-seeing tours with a teamster driver and visited the Old Capitol, the planetarium, and the museums. The most notable child ever in her charge had been the actress Jodie Foster. She had been doing this for many years and had some stories to tell.

There was Bostic Beard, a young black man who was Rob Reiner's assistant, a graduate student in film at Columbia whose master's thesis would be a finished screenplay. He had discussed that craft with Lewis Colick and likened a movie script to an item of "architecture." There was teamster Olivia Conklin, one of twenty or so drivers attached to the project. When the cast and crew left Mississippi for the filming in California, she drove the director's thirty-foot, three-room-and-bath trailer the seventeen hundred miles from Jackson to L.A. In Mississippi there was the director's personal bodyguard, a fellow with a shaved head from L.A. named Dick who might have passed for a crew technician. He sat close to the director behind the monitor, and I was not sure who he was until the afternoon during a break when I took Rob Reiner on a tour of the Hall of Governors in the state capitol and he trailed right along behind us. A pouch attached to his belt might have passed for an electrician's tool kit.

There was Carl Fullerton, Alec Baldwin's makeup man, his makeup box with Kleenex, combs, brushes, and powders always at hand, whom I first spotted in the woods of the Windsor Ruins sitting on a small folding stool reading the latest *New Yorker,* a double issue on African-Americans, opened to a portrait of Myrlie Evers. Each movie was different, he said. On *Philadelphia* he was responsible for several people, but on this one only for Baldwin, which was in the latter's contract, so he always brought along something to read.

There was Steve Mann, the picture car coordinator, third in the transportation command behind the transportation coordinator and the transportation captain. Mann's job was to find old vehicles. On the set one day he talked at length about his calling. Many people make a living, he said, out of renting old cars to the movies. When he went on location he first started calling the antique car clubs. One phone call usually led to other people, and this became like the branches of a tree. He had problems in Mississippi. Most of the people he contacted who could afford to fix up old cars and keep them as a hobby did not like the theme of the movie and refused to rent. "Eventually the dollar bill overrode some people's political objections," he mused.

He had trouble finding a 1962 Valiant, the model Beckwith had owned—"one of the ugliest cars ever made," he judged. The Mississippi tax personnel ran computer records on all the old cars he needed. There were six computer "hits" for '62 Valiants in the state. He wrote letters and made phone calls, but none of the owners cooperated. The state police helped him search. The entire state, it seemed to him, knew he was looking for a '62 Valiant. He eventually found one only a few blocks from his own house in Santa Clarita, California, and shortly after that he found a backup in San Bernardino. He had both Valiants shipped to Mississippi. A little later Mann got a tip from a Beckwith relative in Beckwith's hometown of Greenwood, Mississippi, that another relative owned Beckwith's *real* Valiant. But by that time they already had the two they needed, and the relative likely would not have let him use it anyway, although you never can tell about Delta people.

His other most demanding responsibilities were to find matches for Medgar Evers's 1962 Oldsmobile and Myrlie's 1957 Chevrolet 210 station wagon. He was talking with a man in Florida about microwave antennas on news vehicles who told him that someone in Pennsylvania owned a '62 Olds of that model. The person in Pennsylvania told him he had just sold the car to someone in Vermont. The Vermonter faxed Steve Mann a photograph, and he bought the Olds over the telephone, then flew a man to Vermont to load it onto a car trailer and bring it to Mississippi. A match for Myrlie's '57 Chevy wagon was difficult to locate because it had to be a four-door, which was not a major collector's item. He eventually found one lying in a vacant field out by Clinton, Mississippi, but it was in bad disrepair. Then someone phoned out of the blue to report that he had that very model in the backyard of his house, which happened to be only six blocks from the Evers murder site. Mann went there, only to discover that weeds were growing up through the Chevy. He hauled it out to a paint-and-upholstery shop, and they repaired it for the movie.

Going beyond the call of duty, Mann had to find an ox for a scene set in 1934 in Woodville, Mississippi. He tracked down a man in Brandon named John Wayne Blow, a veritable Dr. Dolittle who owned all kinds of animals. Mann took a picture of Blow's ox, whose name was Tex. Just before they were ready to shoot, the production designer, Lilly Kilvert, said they needed a smaller ox. John Wayne Blow had a long-haired Highlander ox named Scotty, who looked like something out of *Star Wars*. Scotty fit the requirements and was paid four hundred dollars a day. In a stretch of the imagination, someone suggested to Mann, oxen might be considered vehicles, and then reminded him of Norma Desmond, the aging silent-screen crone played by Gloria Swanson in Billy Wilder's *Sunset Boulevard*. She had gotten a phone message from Cecil B. De Mille and descended on the Paramount lot thinking the director wanted to discuss an impossible screenplay she had written, only to find that what he really wanted was to rent her vintage Isotta-Fraschini touring car with its leopard-skin upholstery.

—

During the waiting around between setups, the talk was about politics and baseball, Hollywood murders, suicides, and scandals, restaurants in Jackson and L.A., Mississippi mores and Southern California mores, and movies, movies, movies. One conversation in particular concerned a neurotic movie actor whose mother had subjected him to a painful "stretching machine" when he was a teenager because she thought he was too short. And whenever something out-of-hand occurred on the set, you could usually count on someone to shout, "Well, this is Hollywood!"

There was constant talk of a title. The Untitled Mississippi Project had lingered. Perhaps *that* should be the permanent title? Shoeless Jack Stevens liked *Justice Delayed*. What about *Delayed Justice*? *The Last Mile*? ("This ain't a death-row film," someone said.) *Justice Postponed*? *Search for Justice*? *Mississippi Yearning*? *Mississippi Turning*? *Mississippi Churning*?

On the very first day's filming, which had taken place in Woodville, sixty miles south of the Windsor Ruins, there was an unusual occurrence. Woodville was used to represent the town of Decatur, where in 1934 the ten-year-old Medgar Evers and his twelve-year-old brother, Charles, sat off by themselves on the lawn of the courthouse as a large crowd of whites had gathered to hear Senator Theodore G. Bilbo, the most virulent racist ever to sit in the U.S. Senate, deliver a white-supremacy speech. The re-creation of the event involved some two hundred extras, period vehicles, and horse-drawn wagons. "Educating the Negro or even associating with the Negro in any way whatsoever," the actor playing Bilbo harangued, "is a dangerous enterprise, ladies and gentlemen, make no mistake about it." And as happened in real life in Decatur in 1934, he noticed the two kids: "If we fail to hold high the wall of separation between the races, we will live to see the day when those two little nigger boys right there will be asking for everything that is ours by right." After the final take of this scene, one of the extras came up to the actor, J. T. Walsh, shook his hand, congratulated him on the speech, and asked if he would consider running for office soon.

During the filming at Windsor Ruins, I talked with a black man, a bit player, who was modeling the hat he would wear in the next day's shooting, a brief scene in which he approaches the character playing Medgar Evers and tells him of his excitement over having been allowed to try on the hat by a white retailer, Evers replying that this would be no victory until he could wear his hat into the voting booth. The actor began to recall his youth in Columbus, Mississippi, when even buying a Coca-Cola was a predicament for him. His presence in the store was not especially welcome. To get the drink he had to ask for a "Mr. Coca-Cola, please," then show his money. He was expected to put the money on the counter and not in the merchant's hand. The owner would then get the Coke out of the icebox, while all around the black kid were white children younger than he who were allowed to get Cokes for themselves and without having to show their money.

In the dining tent one later evening, in California, I got involved in a lengthy conversation with two young black Pasadena policemen who were part of security. They had been watching some of the filming and were curious to know everything there was to know about Medgar Evers, Myrlie Evers, Bobby DeLaughter, and Byron De La Beckwith. What was the significance of the scene being shot in the house down the way? The discovery of the gun, they were told. Did DeLaughter really find the gun in his ex–father-in-law's den? Surely that was made up? Where was Beckwith now? Why wasn't he in the state prison?

Killing time:

One afternoon, during a half-hour break in the Jackson City Hall, where a room was being used as the grand jury chamber in the Beckwith indictment, Rob Reiner walked across the hall to look at a tall stepladder, which the art department had been using. Zollo and several others joined him there. "Look at these instructions they put on ladders these days," the director said. It was not unlike the old *60 Minutes* show that reported that for every type of injury caused by a ladder a label had to be put on *all* ladders. There were three or four dozen metal labels on the City Hall ladder. A small crowd now gathered around it. People put on their glasses to read the labels required by the Federal Occupational Health and Safety Administration (OSHA). All was solemn as the producer of the Untitled Mississippi Project slowly read the instructions out loud, attracting more hushed onlookers from outside. His recitation took at least ten minutes. Here is a sampling of the many instructions:

• Do not use ladders if you tire easily or are subject to fainting spells or using medicine or alcohol or are physically handicapped.

• Face ladder when climbing up or down; keep body centered between side rails.

• Maintain a firm grip; use both hands when climbing.

• Never climb ladder from the side unless ladder is secured against side-wise motion.

• Never climb ladder with your back to it.

• Do not overreach; move ladder when needed.

• Do not walk or "jog" ladder when standing on it.

• When you get to top of ladder, avoid falling off.

• Under no circumstances allow ladder to fall on your head. . . .

On the set one day Diane Ladd, the actress from Meridian, Mississippi, who had been nominated for three Oscars and was playing the widow of Judge Russel Moore, said that to discourage some of her many conservative Mississippi relatives from coming to watch she told them the movie was being filmed much farther north in Greenville rather than in Jackson. Michael O'Keefe, twice nominated for an Oscar, and Bill Smitrovich, who were portraying Beckwith's court-appointed lawyers, Merrida Coxwell and Jim Kitchens, reported during a break at the courthouse that they had visited with the men they were playing, who told them their business had suffered after the trial. We surreptitiously watched one day as Homer Best, attorney for the Hinds County Sheriff's Department, stood alone under the shade of a tree across the greensward and ponderously rehearsed his one line as a TV reporter: "Will you testify in your own behalf as you did in the first two trials?" He wanted to substitute "like" for "as," this being more Southern, so he was practicing it both ways. Someone later assured him he was certain to be nominated for Best Supporting Actor.

Loitering along with everyone else, the greens foreman, Bobby Joe Garren, explained that far from having had a background in horticulture he had never worked a day in his life until he was in an L.A. bar telling someone he was looking for odd tasks and the man told him some movie people were looking for a person to work with plants. He told a tale of the first scene of the movie in Woodville. They directed him to go to the water tower and cut down three trees. He got there to find three of the most beautiful crepe myrtles he had ever seen. He went back into town and asked, am I really supposed to cut those crepe myrtles? And they said, absolutely, the mayor says it's okay to cut them. He returned to the water tower and was admiring the trees again when an elderly lady drove by in her car, rolled the window down, and asked if he was going to cut down those trees. He said, well I'm supposed to, ma'am, but I'm trying to figure out a way to save them. She said, my husband was the mayor for thirty years and he donated these trees to the town. She came by and looked at them every day. He went back and told his bosses the only thing this lady's got to live for is those crepe myrtle trees. So they hired a company from Louisiana at eight hundred dollars a day to dig up the crepe myrtles and replant them in front of the Presbyterian church, which needed some trees. On the national-cemetery set in L.A. Bobby Joe reported he had just been back in Woodville the previous week replanting the crepe myrtle trees in front of the water tower. The present mayor is the nephew of the old lady and her husband, the former mayor. He went to the greens foreman and said, "I sure do thank you for that. She never would've forgiven me."

Jamie Gordon, who grew up in Boston and was the assistant to Charles Newirth, discussed one afternoon how much she disappointed her Eastern friends who envied her glamorous Hollywood life. "If only they knew," she said, and explained to them "the endless waiting, the wheels spinning, the hours, the very hard work." She displeased them even further by describing the lengthy preparations that went into the illusions and effects. I was reminded of one of the experts' comments: that he always smiled at the cliché that film is truth twenty-four times a second, because film is a *lie* twenty-four times a second—"events prearranged, predigested, rehearsed, meticulously thought out, and eventually photographed. It's the *appearance* of truth twenty-four times a second because it's all organized." In Gene Kelly's famous *Singing in the Rain* sequence, he said, even the *puddles* were organized.

——

If the camera is everything, the director's monitor is its agent. And the director himself is at the epicenter. The job is physically demanding, with killing hours, and does not end with the day's filming; there are the dailies to be viewed after that. With the exception of his petulance on the set the day after the stormy meeting in the D.A.'s office, Reiner moved from one task to another with facility and cheer. Over an hour and fifteen minutes on one particular afternoon, for instance, he did the following: When several onlookers approached him for his autograph, he gave it, chatting with them about the weather and the Mississippi landscape. Two middle-aged men passing by on the sidewalk shouted at him, "How ya doin', Meathead?" "It's amazing," he said, "because

I look so different now. I'm an old man—gray beard, bald head. My kids can't even recognize me. I guess I could win the Nobel Prize and the headline would be MEATHEAD WINS NOBEL." Then he withdrew his cellular telephone and called his young sons: "How are my little buddies doing? I sure love you."

After this he rose from his canvas chair and had a long conversation in undertones with John Seale, the director of photography, about the setup then being prepared, then returned to confer with his script coordinator, who was taking notes. He turned to Zollo. "Those helicopter shots in the Delta in the dailies yesterday. They were magical and special. That's what making movies is all about." The still photographer came up and asked him to pose with a couple of the bit players who had requested a picture. That done, he surveyed the scene being arranged and shouted directions to Capra. "How much time, Frankie?" he asked.

"Ten minutes for lighting," Capra said.

Just then a man came under the tent and presented Reiner with a sack of homegrown Mississippi vegetables. "That's sweet of you," Reiner said. As the donor departed, he said, "That fellow said, 'I like what *y'all* are doing.' I thought you couldn't use *y'all* in the singular." Someone advised him the man was using it to include not only him but everyone in the crew. "Well, it sounded like he was referring just to me." An assistant reported that reservations had been made for the whole cast and crew at the Jackson Generals' game the following Sunday. "Good! I'll buy all the tickets, but they'll have to pay for their own hot dogs and beer."

The scene was now ready. The shot would gravitate around James Woods. "And . . . Action!" The first two or three takes went awry. In exasperation, Reiner slapped a towel against the monitor, then went out and talked to the actors and assistant directors before returning to the monitor. After the next take, Woods asked, "Am I on camera?"

Reiner laughed. "You know every second when the camera's on you!" Often it takes several hours to light a setup. Sometimes the director would get it on Take 4 or 5, requiring no more than fifteen or so minutes; sometimes it required thirty takes and more. This one took eight. "Cut!" Then, "Okay with you?" he asked the camera operator. "Print!" And to the actors, softly: "That was absolutely great."

The next scene included dozens of extras, and one by one they came filing onto the set, eliciting from the director this not-atypical disquisition as he gestured toward the swirl of humanity: "Look at this. No two people look alike. This feeling goes through me all the time I'm in crowds. God or whomever you want to credit finds a way to make each of these people look different—they're all individual snowflakes. What's interesting to me is that what's processed through their mind is also different. The idea, you know, of a true Christian ethic, of loving thy neighbor and doing unto others and those things we hold very dear, and treating your fellowman with a certain amount of decency and respect, is so far afield in another person that has two eyes and two ears and a nose and a mouth and legs and arms just like us, and he's thinking, 'I've got to eradicate that guy. I've got to kill that person over there.' It's funny to me that you've got something that seems so obvious and so universal and that we should all be embracing, that there are not just one or two or a handful but millions of people around the world that have these weird, distorted views of what's right and ethical and godlike and religious and all of those things. Anyway, that's just always interesting to me."

—

Reiner's family, Michele, five-year-old Jake, and two-year-old Nick, were sometimes on the set. One day the boys brought him some peacock feathers from their visit to a farm. A scene in front of the Mayflower Cafe in Jackson was being filmed. The boys sat on his lap as he coached Craig T. Nelson on his lines. He told Alec Baldwin his last take "had a good feel, a good flow to it," then he kissed Jake on the cheek. "This is only Nick's second film," he said. "But Jake's a veteran. He was with us for *A Few Good Men, North, The American President*. This is his fourth film." Michele commented on that day's set that she was not accustomed to all the kindness and hospitality shown to her in Mississippi. People would not let her pay for boat rides and other such things. "I grew up in New York and have spent twelve years in Los Angeles. I *expect* people to be mean." I invited them to an organized nocturnal tour of the cemetery in Yazoo City the next evening. They arrived there at twilight with a driver, a nanny, and a bodyguard. (I never saw the family with personal bodyguards in Los Angeles, although there was always security personnel on the sets.) A local woman came up and asked if the nanny, who bore little physical resemblance, was Penny Marshall, the director's ex-wife. The Reiner boys, L.A. kids, had never been to a cemetery. "What's this?" Jake asked me, pointing toward the ground.

"What's what?"

"This round thing."

"That's a grave."

"What's a grave?" I was at a loss as to how to begin.

On the sets there were many sessions in the director's trailer: powder-puff blue carpet, cream-colored sofa, matching blue valances above miniblinded windows, microwave, refrigerator. The dining area as well as the bedroom were higher by a few stairs than the main room. The television was always on CNN for the political news. Reiner sometimes wrestled on the carpet with his sons. Among the guests in Mississippi were Ray Mabus, the former state governor, who had just returned from his tenure as U.S. ambassador to Saudi Arabia, and his wife, Julie. Mabus observed that the Arabian royalty would make pleasure excursions into the desert in caravans of trailers like this one, except that their trailers were bigger.

Always time to kill. Baseball was a common theme. The director was invited to throw out the first ball at a game of the Jackson Generals, a Class AA Houston Astros club, but he asked to be allowed to take a swing at the first pitch instead. He hit it to the warning track in deep left field some 330 feet from home plate. He was pleased with this accomplishment and brought it up at every opportunity. During one day's break he confidentially took me aside and said he wanted to talk about something. I feared some earnest problem with the movie. "I'm worried Jake doesn't like baseball," he said. "I've taken him to a couple of Dodgers games. He doesn't seem to love it the way I did when my father took me to Yankee games." In his trailer and on the set baseball-trivia questions abounded. What two brothers together have hit the most career home runs? What fourteen players have won the baseball Triple Crown? Who was the second black major-leaguer, after Jackie Robinson? Name the two players who won the Triple Crown *twice*. Who was the last pitcher to win thirty games? Who was the one before that? Another of his trivia exercises involved the movies themselves, in which he would solicit five or six people to participate. They called this the Movie Game. One person would name a movie, the next would have to name the director or an actor in that movie, the third another movie the director had directed or the actor had played in, and so on, incessantly—arduous fare for the film outlander. A player dropped out after five failures, with Reiner and Zollo invariably the finalists.

Throughout the Mississippi filming the director persisted in trying to get me into one scene or another and I persistently declined. "This is your opportunity," he declared one day in the state supreme court chamber. The scene to be shot would duplicate the announcement, after the court's deliberations over the Sixth Amendment provisions of "speedy trial," of the judgment allowing the state to reprosecute Beckwith after thirty years. No sooner had I relented than a crew member escorted me outside to the wardrobe truck for a sports coat, dress shirt, and tie. Back on the set, since I would play a reporter, someone handed me a spiral-bound notebook and a ballpoint pen. Makeup and Hair descended on me like sparrows. I was directed to a seat among a throng of spectators and reporters. We waited a long time for the final lighting, and for the camera positions and focus marks. At the last minute Frankie Capra ordered me to move to another seat three chairs over. "Rob really wants you in this scene," he said. I thanked him. I had always wanted to be directed by a Capra.

During a recess at the fake gas station in the Delta out from Satartia, Benny Bennett, the Mississippi cop playing himself, described to Zollo and Bill Macy a trying moment he had had in Jackson the night before. He and his young daughters were in his apartment eating pizza when he remembered he had left his camera in his GMC truck. "You know, I don't go anywhere without a gun. Never. I don't go outside my apartment without a gun. I was rushing downstairs in a hurry. No shoes, no shirt, no gun, and I'm pretty tenderfooted. I almost ran into these three guys running across the parking lot. I knew they didn't belong there. So I hollered at 'em, 'Hey, what are y'all doin'?' Every one of 'em had a hubcap under their arms and a screwdriver. Two of 'em started cuttin' through the barbed-wire fence, the other was lookin' over his left shoulder at me. I was goin' toward him and can see him reachin' toward his waistband. He sweeps out a six-inch barrel revolver and wheels around on me. I went, 'No gun, no gun at all.' He says, 'Back off!' Well, I wasn't going to turn my back on him. I figured he was too far away from me to rush him, so I just took a few steps backwards and he went through the hole. When he did I ran upstairs and got my gun and went back down still barefooted, and I thought I could see 'em cuttin' across the apartments way off. I called the police. I never saw them again. But I got to thinkin', you know, it might've been a good thing because he was young and I really didn't want to kill anybody over a hubcap. He was a teenager. If I had had a gun, then I would've gone for it and I would've either killed him, maybe, or he might've killed me, and that really would've ruined my whole weekend."

——

Hollywood people are eating all the time, and eating abundantly well. In addition to the ritualized meal recesses, which usually lasted an hour or more, during actual shooting and the shorter breaks the available beverages included freshly squeezed fruit juices, coffee, cappuccino, various kinds of herbal tea, milk, soft drinks, and the ever-popular Evian bottled natural spring water from France. On a given day the snacks might be chicken eggrolls, meat and vegetarian pizza, egg salad, banana bread, Danish, salmon, sliced watermelons and honeydews, baby carrots on ice, granola bars, bagels with lox or butter, cheese-filled jalapeños, guacamole, coffee cake, cream cheese, barbecued spareribs, barbecued shrimp, tuna melts, pastrami melts, hamburgers, cheeseburgers, cappuccino popsicles, muffins, and cereals. Sometimes there were juicers with which you could squeeze your own orange juice.

The principal meals were served out of an elaborate kitchen truck from For Star Caterers, reputed to be the best in L.A. For the Mississippi location filming this truck had been driven all the way from California—a clean, classy, elongated vehicle with a marquee attached to the side displaying the daily menus in neon. Among the many otherworldly facets of moviemaking was its odd designations of "breakfast" for the first meal served and "lunch" for the second, no matter the time. If a day's shooting had lasted very late and the next call was for 5:00 or 6:00 P.M. the next day, people would exchange good mornings the next evening and then settle in for "breakfast." The next break for dining on such an evening would be 11:00 P.M. or midnight, and this would be called "lunch." There was never "dinner."

This would be the breakfast setting on the last night's shooting in Pasadena: The base camp had been established in a pleasant, shady side lawn of a ranch-style private dwelling only a short walk from that night's set. The marquee of the kitchen truck offered scrambled eggs, breakfast club sandwiches (turkey, bacon, egg, cheese), hot and cold sandwiches, and breakfast burritos. On a large barbecue grill nearby, turkey, beef, vegetarian burgers, and turkey and beef hot dogs were being prepared. The red-and-white commissary tent was filled with chairs and long tables covered with checkered tablecloths. A huge buffet counter was laden with items of all descriptions. The most amazing thing to me was that these fantastic spreads all came from one trailer.

In the Culver City Studios in L.A., the commissary was a spacious reconverted soundstage down the "main street" from the kitchen truck, the director's and stars' trailers, and the other working soundstages where the courtroom drama was being shot. My notes scribbled on the call sheet for Day 32 of 61 days records the cornucopia of lunch items. There were three choices for the main course: stuffed Tri-Trip with sun-dried tomatoes and spinach, roasted chicken breast with wild mushrooms, and fresh local sea bass with julienne vegetables. The extensive buffet in the commissary included sautéed green beans, baked potatoes with an assortment of toppings, vegetarian minestrone, artichoke strudel, fresh artichokes, Thai cucumber and shrimp, pastry shells with fresh strawberries, brownies, fresh sliced peaches, chocolate cake, ice cream, and baked pear dumplings.

For 11:00 P.M. "lunch" on Day 61 of 61 days, only a couple of hours before the last scenes were to be shot, these Hollywood caterers followed their final-day tradition and served four-pound lobster and sirloin steak. The mood was celebrative yet wistful. One of the gaffers at our table consumed, at last count, three lobsters.

—

Here are a few random generalizations concerning Hollywood people themselves. For the most part life on this set was pleasant, gratifying, and generous of spirit, and an interesting diversion from one's own life's work. There was nothing wrong with learning about another cosmos. And it *is* a cosmos.

• Most Hollywood people are afraid when they leave Hollywood.

• The top male directors and producers have beautiful wives.

• The top directors and producers are usually between forty-five minutes and two hours late for social engagements.

• The top directors and producers are rich.

• They call movies with special effects for killing and mutilating many people "whammies."

• With staggering exceptions, they do not drink much liquor.

• They drink a great deal of bottled water.

• They hug each other a lot.

• They never write letters, even when you write them. They are talkers, not writers. In that regard, I sometimes suspected that, with all their visual wizardry, most of them had what amounted to dyslexia pertaining to the written word. When they need you, they get you on what I call their "celluloid" phones. When they don't, they don't.

• Malcolm White, a Jackson entrepreneur involved in several recent movies in Mississippi, wrote these observations on a napkin in his restaurant, Hal & Mal's, about working with them on planning an event: "They have a whole bunch of people making arrangements, changing their minds. You never see or deal with the person in charge. All these others work on the head person's behalf. But you know the name of that person like you know your own child's. Finally at whatever event you've been involved in the head person greets you with a big smile and open arms like your best friend. Then they're gone and you never hear from them again."

• Hollywood people work very hard when they work. Celluloid telephones are rampant and ubiquitous among them and are in use at all times. The Industry would collapse overnight without them. One can spot Hollywood people talking into their celluloids while standing in shrubs when privacy is called for, or perched in the branches of trees, or on real lawns or the contrived appurtenances of soundstages, or while leaving the honeywagons. Even the child actors use them. During one recess in filming, on a lawn in Pasadena, I sighted eight or ten executives seated in a casual semicircle on their high black canvas chairs. Every one of them was talking into a celluloid telephone. I had the oddest divination that they were all talking to each other.

Chapter 9

APPARITIONS IN SUNLIGHT
AND DARKNESS

The promoters in buoyant solicitude chose to present Jackson, Mississippi, during the waning years of the century as the Bold New City. I prefer to call it the Old Bold, for my clandestine aspect of it, in truth, exists in another time, when it was nothing if not a somnolent state-capital town, drowsy in those wartime summers, and indwellingly rooted. Although I was brought up in Yazoo City, I was born in Jackson, and I spent every summer of my childhood here with my grandparents and eccentric great-aunts. A barefoot boy in a sailor's cap could venture about the Old Bold then and absorb the familiar prattle of the ladies in their iced-tea rituals from the decaying verandas shrouded in the crepe myrtle, for this was his inheritance. Everything—people, places—seemed of a piece, palpable and connected.

When the Untitled Mississippi Project people descended on Jackson, they would find a different place, considerably brisker and more up-to-date, of course. By the late 1950s and 1960s much of the public élan of the city was shaped by entrenched entrepreneurial Babbitts who lacked the vision, as noted by Ole Miss historian

James Silver in his *Mississippi: The Closed Society,* to contemplate "the inevitable social and political changes bound to accompany economic progress." So many of the serene and stately old domiciles on North State Street and elsewhere were torn down for parking lots, apartment complexes, motels, and smart insurance and mercantile establishments, a destruction in not unequal measure to the pyrotechnic Sherman's eight decades before. Capitol Street, the main thoroughfare, became an amalgam of the older high-rises, crumbling storefronts, immense parking garages, and the brutal aspect of overshadowing modern structures that could pass for Cleveland, Ohio. Across from the magnificent governor's mansion, the second-oldest executive mansion in the country next to the White House ("built for giants," one local cynic pronounced in 1994, "inhabited now by pygmies"), the Lamar Life Building remained, the town's first skyscraper, a white-marble Gothic of fine proportion, ten stories high with the clock towers on top. Eudora Welty's father had it built in 1925, and I remembered the wonderful gargoyles around the main entrance, in the form of alligators, so appropriate for Mississippi, which not long ago were sandblasted away by renovators. The first blocks of Farish Street, once the vivacious and flavorful main thoroughfare for blacks, is now dotted with boarded-up storefronts. Farther north is the lengthy row of shotgun houses from that time, remarkably unchanged. A white boy in the 1940s could stroll the neighborhood free and unchallenged, assimilating the high-pitched laughter and the doleful music: the life of the street at once alien to him and familiar as his own heartbeat.

As in many other American places, much of the town of my childhood is lost forever—the majority of its edifices and landmarks and green country spaces, so much so that when I wander now in my voyeur's paranoic heart, I suspect someone has been preceding me with a giant eraser. As elsewhere there are drugs and crime in plentitude—92 homicides out of a city of 196,637 in 1995 alone—and flights to suburbias sprung full-born in the affluent white vicinities of Madison County, giving the city a majority black population of 52 percent in 1996. Guns were readily available in pawn shops, of course, and at Jackson's notorious "gun shows." Someone observed that it was much easier to get a gun than a driver's license in Mississippi. One of the most depressing facts was that many children were being killed in this mad and gratuitous butchery. As in many other cities, usually the local TV evening news shows feature one account after another of murder and mayhem, more often than not black upon black, causing the viewer to wonder: Is anyone in town still alive and unscathed?

The rich white precincts of Belhaven and North Jackson frequently experienced waves of fear when solitary young black men demented on crack cocaine drifted in to commit theft and even murder, sometimes in broad daylight. In recent months five people I personally knew were victims: a federal judge and his wife held at gunpoint for their jewelry; my dentist robbed of his cash and wristwatch and shot in the hand as he left his office; a woman who organized the book signings at Lemuria Bookstore abducted as she was opening the store and threatened with death—she jumped from the moving car, shattering her ankle; the director of the state public-radio station robbed of his money and locked in the trunk of his car and driven around for hours before the thief finally let him go. One white man in Belhaven claimed to carry a .38 while he mowed his lawn. The black neighborhoods were known by all to be populated by countless young males crazed on coke and armed with blades and pieces, usually murdering one another. There seemed no solution to this at all. What would Medgar make of such things?

Yet beneath the transient exteriors of the contemporary town lie the elusive yet immutable reminders, the lingering landmarks, and a number of these would be locales in the Untitled Mississippi Project.

———

Truman Capote once wrote an essay on the movie made of his *In Cold Blood*, some scenes of which he watched being filmed and which were eerily faithful to actual individuals, events, and places. He called the essay "Ghosts in Sunlight": "It was like swimming into a familiar sea only to be surprised by a muscular wave of sinister height . . . not, unfortunately, the victim of a bad dream, or of 'just a movie,' but of reality." I had already experienced a little of that at Windsor Ruins, Yazoo City, and Bentonia, and some of the Jackson scenes would be even more oracular.

There was extensive shooting, both exteriors and interiors, at the Hinds County Courthouse, the white-granite 1930s Art Deco structure where all three trials had taken place. Scenes would move back and forth within that thirty-year hiatus, causing the observer to ponder whether he himself were ensnared in a warp of time. At one point during a break in one day's filming the real newspaper reporter Jerry Mitchell was talking with Jerry Levine, the actor who was playing him. Real and ersatz deputies with guns mingled everywhere. Sheriff Malcolm McMillin conversed with the actor playing Sheriff McMillin. Bobby DeLaughter's teenaged son, Burt, had a job in "crowd control" and, since he had outgrown himself, was being played by an actor. A couple of women from Arkansas were visiting the set during a break in one of these crowded scenes outside the courthouse. They approached Orley Hood of the Jackson paper, who was writing in a notebook, and asked if he was a movie actor.

"No, ma'am," Hood said. "I'm a newspaper writer."

"You're playing a newspaper writer in the movie?"

"No, ma'am. I'm playing myself right here today."

"You look familiar."

"Honest, I'm just a real person."

One day they were shooting a scene in which Woods as the seventy-three-year-old Beckwith emerged from the courthouse during the 1994 trial surrounded by a swarm of reporters. There was a collective gasp from the local onlookers, many of whom at one time or another had seen the real Beckwith. Just as I had been at the earlier filming in Bentonia, they were visibly stunned by the stark resemblances, by the identical loud voice and haughty mannerisms. He proceeded down the sidewalk with the actress playing his wife, who likewise looked like the true-life Thelma, as the reporters followed them. One asked him what his feelings were about being on trial for the third time. "I feel like an Indian let loose in a brewery," he declared. Another wanted to know if the pin on the lapel of his coat was a Confederate flag. "Son, if you don't recognize the Confederate flag, you're doomed to go to hell in Africa." Gregory Peck once observed that "when the cameras are on you, you become a little intense and crazy. You want to do everything." This had to have been intensified with Woods, because he was *playing* a crazy.

Only fifty yards or so from this feverish activity was the real Beckwith, alone in his ten-by-ten-foot cell, where he considers himself a political prisoner, spending his time writing racist literature, the postage and handling paid by the state of Mississippi. At that very moment he could have been standing on a chair looking out his window at the Hollywood commotion. A little earlier, during a jail "scout," Rob Reiner had seen him asleep in his cell strewn with racist pamphlets. "It's just as well he was sleeping," Reiner said, "because I don't know if I could've talked to him." James Woods said, "I had no desire to meet the guy. Let him sit there and stew and be ignored." (Because of the jail's strict policy, none of the movie people would have been allowed contact with him anyway.)

Later that day, during a break in the scenes inside the courthouse, Whoopi Goldberg commented to the crew that if you kill a man, you shouldn't be able to have your postage paid for. As she spoke, Woods in his Beckwith makeup strolled toward her, took her hand, and waltzed her down the corridor. "I swear," he said in his swaggering Beckwith drawl, "if I'd met a woman like this in my prime, I'd of changed my views on segregation." Observing this vignette, Rick Bragg of the *Times* wrote, "How surreal can Hollywood be?"

That night a colossal simulated storm descended on the courthouse, with shrieking wind, torrential rains, crashing thunder and

lightning, just as it had in 1994 after the jury withdrew to deliberate for the evening, trapping me and the others in the courtroom
and corridors for a long time. Frankie Capra was shouting, "Close
your eyes! Lightning coming!" as the man-made flashes illuminated as if by the devil's own fire the wood-carved eagles on the
courtroom ceiling and the frieze panels in the hallway depicting
head-scratching slaves pushing cotton toward a steamboat and
Civil War soldiers of Mississippi. It was so faithful to the actual
storm on the actual day that I and the others who had been there
that earlier night felt its spooky sorcery.

After this man-made tempest, the crew was preparing a set for
the following day in the lobby of the courthouse. The scene would
re-create the handcuffed Beckwith's being brought in after his arrest in 1963. To the side of the lobby is a large semicircular reception desk dominated by an enormous glass top. Old courthouse
denizens told Reiner that on this spot in 1963 there had been a
concession stand. The reception desk was a permanent fixture that
could not be removed because it weighed a ton and was securely
fastened to the floor, so Reiner told the set dressers they had to
turn the desk into a 1963 concession stand, that they had come all
the way to Mississippi to shoot on location and had to get everything right. They had twelve hours to do this. Shoeless Jack
Stevens and Andrea Fenton, the set-dressing buyer, set to work.

Stevens had always been an enthusiastic collector of arcane period items, traveling the back roads of Mississippi to old stores,
warehouses, attics, and junkyards in search of them. "It was a
scramble," he passionately confessed, "and that's the nature of the
business. This was like the amusement ride at the fair. You're going
to hit a bump. Think of what a concession stand was like there
then. Think of what I've got at home. Think of what we can go buy
now. You keep your warm-up jacket on when you're in this line of
work because they're gonna send you out, especially *these* people.
We were up to the task, by God." Old magazines from June 1963—
Life, Saturday Evening Post, Look, Time, Newsweek—were flown in

from L.A. Shoeless Jack brought from his house a ROSS BARNETT FOR GOVERNOR and other political posters. He also had an old revolving rack with postcards of Jackson of the era, an old cash register, a penny gumball machine, and one of those big glass containers for Planter's Peanuts. "Potato-chip sacks. They can't be foil. It's all going to foil. Go to Tom's Vending. Jujyfruits, Beech-nut Chewing Tobacco, Moon Pies." Another set piece, prepared earlier, would be a stack of specially printed Jackson *Clarion-Ledgers* of June 23, 1963, with the lead headline: FBI NABS GREENWOOD MAN IN EVERS MURDER. Beckwith's two-column photograph had been replaced by a photograph of James Woods; in every other respect the front page was like the original. In the film-ing of the scene, when the deputies brought James Woods in, he was downright chipper as admirers fawned over him. He noticed his photograph on the *Clarion-Ledger* at the concession stand, picked one up with a handcuffed hand, and gingerly said, "Nice likeness," holding up the paper for the extras playing the reporters to see. Someone later gave me a copy of that newspaper as a keep-sake. Among some of the other front-page headlines were: RACIAL AGITATORS CONTINUE TO FOMENT TROUBLE IN U.S.; STATE BAR VIGOROUSLY RAPS CIVIL RIGHTS PROGRAM; and NEW CONCES-SIONS MADE TO NEGROES.

What would prove to be the most troublesome scene in the en-tire Untitled Mississippi Project was Myrlie Evers's appearance after the 1994 verdict. After the real trial this had been hastily arranged in a small unused courtroom and proved to be a highly emotional moment, but the staged version took place on the front steps of the courthouse before a large crowd of reporters, deputies, and onlookers, nearly three hundred extras in all. With Whoopi Goldberg on the steps were her movie offspring Darrell and Reena; Alec Baldwin and Susanna Thompson and the child actors; Craig T. Nelson as Ed Peters; and Jerry Levine in the audience as Jerry Mitchell. Everyone was shaking hands and embracing, and then Whoopi Goldberg went behind the microphone to give a much

longer version of Myrlie Evers's real speech, ending with the words
"I've gone the last mile of the way, and"—raising her head upward
and clenching her fists, tears streaming down her cheeks—"all I
want to say is . . . yeah, Medgar. Yeah!" This was projected as the
next-to-the-last scene in the movie, and it was not working; it
seemed to lack emotional resonance. Reiner ended up doing numerous takes on this scaldingly hot day. This was not the first time
I was struck by the sheer *patience* required of movie people in delivering the same lengthy lines over and over again, twenty or thirty
times or more, without saying to hell with it and going on home to
Beverly Hills. From such moments I saw what exhausting work
good movie acting had to be, out at the edge and direly repetitive.
"I think they get bored with it," screenwriter William Goldman
once commented. "It will get them a table at Spago. But it's hard
to be a movie star."

The director was displeased with this scene, and so was Goldberg. She later maintained that she had to do this scene before she
filmed the murder and funeral ones and failed on that day to have
the warmth and feeling demanded of her. As a consequence, and
for technical and organizational reasons, her speech would be shot
over and over again in a Culver City soundstage in front of a
replica of the Hinds County Courthouse.

———

The thoroughfare was called Delta Drive in 1963. It is now
Medgar Evers Boulevard, and two miles or so from the site of this
night's shooting is the Medgar Evers Public Library, with a statue
of him on the lawn. This is a nearly 100 percent black neighborhood, and one of the most crime-ridden in the entire city. As with
the old Delta Drive, the present Evers Boulevard is also Highway
49, which comes down on a straight north-south radial through
the Delta from Greenwood to Yazoo City to Jackson.

The scene tonight would be Number 9 in the finished movie, the
re-creation of Joe's Drive-In, a hamburger and beer establishment

with gas pumps and a garish neon sign, only two hundred feet west of the Evers house. It was to this site that the assassin drove his muddy white Valiant on that night and parked it in the parking lot. The carhop named Barbara Holder saw the long whiplike antenna on the Valiant and remarked to friends, "It looks like a police car." She was twenty-two years old when she testified at the 1964 trials, fifty-two at the conclusive one.

As with the gas station set that had been built in the Delta outside Satartia, Hollywood had constructed a 1960s drive-in on a vacant lot not far from the original Joe's. These were exterior scenes entirely, but in the gas station there were windows and a door where you could see inside, and Shoeless Jack Stevens and the others had stocked this interior with their period pieces, including a hardware-store revolving key rack that had been flown in from L.A. While they were working, a man pulled in. "What do you mean, you're not a gas station?" he said. "Where am I supposed to go with this tire?" An aged black woman hobbled in on a cane to buy a hamburger and something cold to drink, and all Shoeless Jack could give her was water. Much the same had happened a few days before in Yazoo City, when Shoeless Jack and the others had fabricated a circa-1964 bridal shop on Main Street, and a woman came in to have a dress altered and declared the town had always needed a bridal shop.

Jackson's stifling springtime heat wave, hot even by Mississippi measure, was just beginning; there was a festive county-fair atmosphere around the set. Hundreds of black people of all ages stood across Evers Boulevard, some of them drinking from cans of beer, and they were in a celebrative mood, drawn from the whole vicinity to the luminous Hollywood simulation. Joe's Drive-In was indeed right from my own youth, and the pretty carhops with wavy hairdos, one of them played on this night by the real Peggy De-Laughter, and the food trays on the cars, and the youngsters sitting at the wooden tables drinking beer and smoking cigarettes reminded me of long-ago Saturday nights in Yazoo. The song from a rock-and-roll station on car radios, to be dubbed in later, would be the Four Seasons' "Sherry." The scene called for twenty-five 1950s and 1960s cars, and the cameras began to catch this cavalcade as it proceeded up and down the main drag.

When the black spectators caught sight of James Woods walking from his trailer down the way toward the set, they began to cheer and applaud enthusiastically, and Woods caught the mood and amiably waved back at them. He came to the director's tent. "Jimmy," Fred Zollo said to Woods, "why don't you cross the street and introduce yourself to them? 'Hi, I'm Byron De La Beckwith.' "

The drive-in scenes were shot over and over, including the final ones in which Woods, his Valiant parked in a darkened corner of the lot, opened the trunk and withdrew the Enfield 30.06 deer rifle, an exact replica of the real murder weapon. For days after the filming, and long after the cast and crew had left Mississippi en masse for L.A., Joe's Drive-In remained there. Cruising past it one afternoon, I saw only a security guard eating a hamburger on one of the tables outside. But it was gradually stripped of its appurtenances and soon vanished from the face of the earth.

—

One of the most affecting moments was the filming of the assassination itself, another painful duplication of reality. Only two American movies in history, I had been told, had ever been filmed at the actual house where a murder had occurred: *Death of a Centerfold: The Dorothy Stratton Story* and *In Cold Blood*.

When the Hollywood people arrived at the abandoned house, the windows were boarded up, the paint was peeling from its sides, and the lawn was nothing but dirt and weeds, with scraggly growth everywhere. During the initial filming the house was kept in this condition, since an earlier scene had Alec Baldwin as DeLaughter visiting the home with an aged homicide cop from 1963, and then another scene capturing a moment before the 1994 trial when Bobby, doubtful over his investigation and fearing its effect on his family, drove to the spot at night and relived the murder in his mind's eye. After these scenes were shot, the carpenters, painters, landscapers, and decorators restored the house and grounds to their 1963 condition, planted grass and flowers, and got permission to transplant a towering live oak tree in the front yard, which had been planted by Myrlie and Medgar and was small at the time of the murder, to an open area down the way that would someday be the parking lot and visitors' center for the Medgar Evers House Museum when it opened to the public. Since there was no equipment in Mississippi for transplanting such a mature tree, a Louisiana firm was brought in to do the job at a cost of thirty thousand dollars.

The day before the filming, the head set decorator, Karen O'Hara, took visitors around the inside of the house. Brief scenes would be re-created here of Myrlie and her three children watching JFK's civil rights address on television, and their rushing frantically through the rooms to the driveway when Medgar was shot. In the kitchen was a vintage 1960s aqua refrigerator and stove just like Myrlie and Medgar's. The refrigerator was dented in the exact spot where the .30-caliber bullet that had pierced Medgar's body, shattered a front window, and gone through a wall into the kitchen had ricocheted off the refrigerator before settling on a cabinet next to a watermelon. The living room and bedrooms had been furnished with pine and early American pieces. In the bedroom near the TV was a framed wedding photograph of Whoopi Goldberg and Jim Pickens, the actor playing Medgar, and other photographs of Whoopi, Pickens, and the movie children. The prop people had a fitted sheet on the single bed mattress on which the neighbors would put Medgar to drive him to the hospital. Someone asked the set decorator whether fitted sheets indeed existed in 1963. Yes, they did, she said—they had checked this out in the Sears, Roebuck catalogue of that year.

They filmed on two nights, the last of the Mississippi schedule before returning to Los Angeles. It was oppressively hot, just as it had been on the real night, with a cloying, humid heat that sharpened the palpable tension on the set. Along the main road that led to the security point and the Evers's street many black men, women, and children stood silently watching. The street is now

Margaret Walker Alexander Drive, named after the noted writer who lives a few houses down, but it was Guynes Street in 1963, situated in the first middle-class black subdivision in Jackson, a neighborhood of small, neat, ranch-style homes. Earlier that afternoon, in a day scene to come later in the movie, they had filmed Goldberg as Myrlie Evers as she tried to wash away her husband's dried blood from the driveway.

Because the area was so confined and security so tight, this was a crowded set. Black families from the adjoining houses stood watching on their front lawns, beyond range of the cameras. These spectators, unlike those at Joe's Drive-In the night before, were hushed and respectful, the atmosphere almost funereal. A number of older people among them had been here on the night of the murder. Along with the friend and neighbor across the street who had put Medgar on the mattress and driven him to the hospital, the other man who helped him still lived in the neighborhood. Power lines ran along these lawns to huge trucks in the distance. Whispering artisans deftly stepped over these thick coils of wire on their mysterious appointments. Across the street at an angle from the Evers house a small growth area with honeysuckle vines had been created; this simulated the spot where Beckwith had crouched with the deer rifle. All along the street were 1950s and 1960s vehicles.

When filming began, Jim Pickens as Medgar drove toward the house in a '62 Oldsmobile. This was filmed time and again. Reiner directed the actor in rehearsals: to park the car in the driveway, to get out of the car and walk toward the house, to fall at a certain angle. A package of fake blood, consisting of chocolate syrup and glycerine, was hidden under his shirt, and when Pickens pulled a cord in front of him the blood would explode. Every time the special-effects man attached the package of blood under the shirt, he shouted to the director: "He's live." A blank shot was sounded, and the blood suddenly appeared all over his back. Many new shirts were used on these two nights, and many packets of blood. The scene would eventually be run in the movie in slow motion.

In the dwelling directly across the street, behind the lights and cameras, the woman who owned the house came out to watch. With her was her little boy, no older than five. Someone in the crew brought him a Coca-Cola. From behind the director's monitor, Reiner's wife, Michele, noticed the child and his mother. She asked Charles Newirth, the executive producer, to inquire of the mother if she shouldn't take her son away since the scene was so bloody and traumatic. Newirth asked the woman, but she said it was fine. After one of the early takes and the firing of the blank bullet, the mother said to the boy, "Did you hear it? That sounded like Eddie's gun, didn't it?" The child nodded in assent.

I noticed Charles Evers, who was standing in the shadows as if he wished to be invisible. Reiner greeted him and warned him that there would be take after take of the murder; was he sure he wanted to watch? "No, no," he replied. "I'll be all right." The director remembered Charles's presence was like "a moth to flame," as if he had a deep interior need to be there, as if he were saying good-bye to his brother again. Jim Pickens looked like Medgar, Charles said—same height, same build. Before one of the countless takes, he watched as Reiner, because of lighting problems, stopped the action just before the gunshot—as if stopping the murder itself. What if it were that easy? This gave me the same strange feeling I have every time I watch the old film clips of President Kennedy's caravan turning left toward Dealey Plaza: "Please, God, don't let it happen this time." At one point, I walked over to the staged woods, the shrubs and honeysuckle of Beckwith's lair. From the driveway of the house I heard Whoopi Goldberg's screams, and the screams of the children. When what was supposed to be Medgar's body was being lifted into a station wagon, the older Evers neighbors were out in the street saying, "They wrapped him in a blanket—*then* they put him on a mattress."

Lewis Colick flew in from Los Angeles the first night of the murder scene and drove straight from the airport to the Evers house. "It was absolutely eerie," he said. "The last time I'd seen the house was a year ago, on the anniversary of the shooting. I stood in the driveway and looked at this decrepit, boarded-up shack. Was this what had become of Medgar's dream? And here was the house now restored to what it was, the cars in the driveway, Myrlie's and Medgar's. Reality was being created, not an illusion. It was incredibly powerful and gratifying. I want to tell you, what I experienced that night of the filming didn't have anything to do with moviemaking anymore. But by the same token it had *everything* to do with moviemaking."

Chapter 10

TINSELTOWN AND
THE CULVER CITY STUDIOS

The Culver City Studios had once been Selznick International Pictures. David O. Selznick had married Louis B. Mayer's daughter in 1930, and around town it was observed, "The son-in-law also rises." Here Selznick had shot many movies including, of course, *Gone With the Wind*. In the back lot he had filmed the movie's first shot: Using the discarded *King Kong* sets, he had burned down Atlanta. Outside Soundstage 11 he had filmed the opening of the Twelve Oaks barbecue scene, the day Rhett, Ashley, and Scarlett learned the war had started. It became a place of apparitions for me: of Vivien Leigh and Clark Gable, Leslie Howard and Hattie McDaniel, Fredric March and Joan Fontaine, not to mention Gary Cooper, Lawrence Olivier, Janet Gaynor, and Lassie. Selznick himself felt something about ghosts, and the apocalyptic town. In a lugubrious mood one dawn on its deserted streets he told Ben Hecht, "Hollywood's like Egypt. Full of crumbled pyramids. It'll never come back. It'll just keep on crumbling until finally the wind blows the last studio prop across the sands."

Selznick's offices were to the side of the famous main building, an imitation of Mount Vernon, which was always shown at the beginning of his movies. The corridor outside his office, where he plotted *Gone With the Wind* and dispatched his thousands of memos, is lined with photographs from that film as well as *Rebecca*, the first *A Star Is Born*, *The Garden of Allah*, *Intermezzo*, and *The Prisoner of Zenda*. In one of the nearby bungalows, now production offices, the elder Joseph Kennedy during his motion-picture days had had his trysts with Gloria Swanson, and here he had fired Erich von Stroheim for directing an actor to dribble tobacco juice on her in a movie scene. Cecil B. De Mille had also made movies here when the lot was Fox-Pathé Studios, as had Howard Hughes years before he let his hair and fingernails grow long. The pioneer visionary filmmaker Thomas Ince had built these studios in 1918. He met his death under enigmatic circumstances in 1924 aboard William Randolph Hearst's yacht sailing off the coast of Southern California. Rumors about what happened linger to this day, the most persistent having it that Hearst had caught Marion Davies kissing Charlie Chaplin and fired a pistol, killing poor Ince by mistake. A different rumor is that Hearst suspected Ince of an affair with Marion. Whatever, Ince's ghost is frequently seen walking through walls on the old back-lot soundstages wearing a bowler hat. The street leading to those stages is named for Ince.

Now these haunted premises had been transformed into Jackson, Mississippi. In various soundstages had been created in nearly precise facsimile the courtroom of the Hinds County Courthouse with the Jackson skyline seen out the windows, the spacious corridors, the D.A.'s offices with their web of hallways and cubicles replete with authentic documents and memos on the desks and bulletin boards, even the exterior of the courthouse steps and main entrance. This was altogether unsettling. I felt I had come seventeen hundred miles only to arrive home again.

The Culver City Studios were like a walled, self-contained town with a small mountain in the background, the same mountain that the innovative production designer William Cameron Menzies had had to obliterate through trick photography when they were filming *Gone With the Wind*. A little main street ran all the way through it, bordered by a mailroom, an electrical shop, a masseuse's office, a production department, a general store, a TV and sound department, a grip office, props, carpentry, set construction, and commissary. Slightly to the side was a small village of neat bungalows, tiny plazas and sidewalks and cul-de-sacs adorned with shrubs and flowers. The back portion of the lot was dominated by the huge, hangarlike soundstages numbered 1 through 15, and not far from these the snack trucks, the caterers' trailer, and the trailers of the stars. When I developed an infected toe, I went to the medical dispensary next to the production office, and the medic fixed me up. When I came down with a cold—from the smog, the natives advised me—I adjourned to a trailer that stocked vitamins, laxatives, Preparation H, eyedrops, jock-itch and athlete's foot ointment, and eight kinds of cold pills.

The director took us on a tour of the premises. We explored the cavernous soundstages with their musty resonance of vanished voices. You could close your eyes and hear Cecil B. De Mille. *"Lights . . . Camera . . . Action!"* On which of these stages did Jane Russell reveal her cleavage in *The Outlaw*? On which did Scarlett try to seduce Ashley to go with her to Mexico? Which comprised the great medieval hall of Manderley? In the main building up the way we dipped into Selznick's old office, then Joseph Kennedy's across the corridor. On the front greensward we ran into Mel Brooks, a jaunty figure in his seventies and one-time comedy partner of Carl Reiner. He had an office in a newer structure next door. "I'm over there writing," he said, "and they have all these TV writers there and they're all eleven years old. They say, 'Mr. Brooks, can I go out in the hall and have a glass of water?' " He pointed to Rob Reiner. "I knew this guy when he was four years old. His dad and I did improvised comedy acts after dinner. The kid sat right there on the floor looking up at us with a totally serious expression. He wasn't even laughing at us."

"Oh," Reiner said, "but I was laughing on the inside."

—

The home base of the Mississippi contingent in L.A. was a small, endearing family-style apartment hotel situated in a quiet middle-class residential neighborhood halfway between the jostle of Sunset and Santa Monica in West Hollywood. We were only a couple of blocks from the House of Blues Cafe, a converted cotton gin that had been shipped all the way from Clarksdale in the Mississippi Delta. Peggy and Bobby DeLaughter were here, and the homicide cops Benny Bennett, who was playing himself on the set every day, and Charlie Crisco, who had come out to sample the ambiance. Someone observed of Bobby and the others that they were about as Hollywood as, well, Mississippi. The young boy actor Lucas Black of Danville, Alabama, who was playing Burt DeLaughter (and would soon become a star in the movie *Sling Blade*), was staying in our hotel with his parents. Someone ran into him in the hotel's laundry room. "Will you miss Hollywood?" he was asked. "No, sir," he replied. "I just want to go home and do some fishin' and be alone by myself. Hollywood ain't Alabama."

From our rental Honda on long, aimless excursions we took in the eclectic panoply of the city. This was Joan Didion's town, or one of them, and her words were burned in me. At first the visitor's eyes burn also, and it does not take long to learn why: We grew to discern different kinds of smog—shimmering smog, lackadaisical smog, cumbersome smog, wispy smog that comes in on little cat feet—the price to be paid in the swathing unabashed eternal sunshine for being twelve degrees or so cooler on average than the deep imperishable summer of home. And everywhere the exotic miscellany of trees, shrubs, and flowers that bedeck the whole rambling town fixed against its mighty backdrop of dark blue, snowcapped mountains, sloping down into the foothills like a surf, encompassing its final flatness: the pale yellow avocado, the oranges and lemons with their slick white blossoms, the palm, eucalyptus, and red-berried pepper trees, the oriental wisteria and roses and bougainvillea and birds of paradise and violet-blossomed jacarandas set against the brick and stucco and asphalt and tile— and even a plethora of neatly trimmed versions of my state's own *Magnolia grandiflora*.

Avoiding the freeways, the Dixie visitors found the town more comfortable to negotiate than one might think. The major boulevards took us where we wanted to go. La Cienega, which led you from West Hollywood out to the Culver City Studios, was my favorite, with body-sculpting gyms and restaurants with names like the Stinking Rose. We drove among the mansions of Bel Air and Brentwood and down the little unprepossessing streets among the valleys and canyons and gorges: the humid film-noir streets of *Double Indemnity* with row after row of "those Spanish stucco houses everybody was nuts about ten or fifteen years ago," as Fred MacMurray described the dwelling of his homicidal sorceress Barbara Stanwyck.

A placard on the back of a car on San Vicente declared UN- KNOWN ACTOR SEEKS BIG BREAK and provided the man's name and telephone number. At Selma and Wilcox, a young woman waiting at a traffic light wore a T-shirt that said JESUS: PROTECT ME FROM YOUR FOLLOWERS. Substantial billboards on the principal thoroughfares proclaimed straightforwardly in reference to O. J. Simpson, GUILTY! or NOT GUILTY! Why, in Culver City, was there one large sign after another, for several miles toward Venice Beach, advertising *dentists'* offices? And does anyone know there is a memorial to the Confederacy in the Hollywood Memorial Cemetery? And that Truman Capote's crypt is only ten yards from Marilyn Monroe's in the Westwood Cemetery? In the mixed black, Asian, and Latino neighborhood that was once proclaimed America's "New Ellis Island," the burnt-out places stood as reminders of the upheavals after the Rodney King case of 1992. As we drove in Zollo's car one morning along the Pasadena Freeway to a filming location in the little town of Sierra Madre the temperature gradually climbed from 84 degrees to 96. Another day, tooling down the same reckless freeway in a production assistant's convertible, sipping a strawberry-banana smoothie and dodging around equally breakneck vehicles to the beat of ear-splitting rock on the stereo, I felt a little like an Angelino, except for being pretty much scared to death the whole journey.

We were having lunch one day on the patio outside the Polo Lounge of the Beverly Hills Hotel, that magnet to the affluence and hedonism of the wealthiest zip code in our land, with its unstinted gardens and well-appointed bungalows where Gable and Lombard and Chaplin and the reclusive Howard Hughes had dwelled long ago, and the famous swimming pool where people were always paging themselves on the telephones. Dining at a nearby table was a coterie of native souls who in their laid-back sartorial polish and garrulous badinage could have passed as Tinseltown stereotypes; I was certain the names Coppola and Scorsese and Nichols came up at least twice. One of the men wore Gucci shoes without socks and a light cashmere pullover draped casually about his shoulders. His manner, idiom, and attire breathtakingly resembled the actor John Marley's in *The Godfather,* in which he played the craven director who refused to give Johnny Fontaine the movie role he wanted until Marlon Brando had the director's Arabian stallion's head chopped off and put in his bed while he was sound asleep.

Across the way was another absorbing sight: two dozen or so elegant and handsome young women in their early twenties engaged in a bridal shower. Bottles of Moët & Chandon were placed here and there in tall silver ice buckets. They nibbled serenely on herbs, salads, fruits, and little plates of caviar. Their exquisite raiments and perfect physiques, their rich and unblemished epiderma, their light and sophisticated banter, their gay young laughter and good-hearted applause when the bride-to-be gingerly opened her multifarious gifts from the shops on Rodeo Drive and admired them one by one with a relishing attention at once supple and bemused— these were a mesmerizing frieze for the outlanders. Surely these merry young women would never grow old and die, would they? JoAnne and I found ourselves comparing this *tableau vivant* before

196 | *The Ghosts of Medgar Evers*

us with a bridal shower in the Mississippi Delta, a planter's daughter perhaps, and her Chi Omega sorority sisters from Ole Miss, who would have been equally merry and beautiful and elegantly attired, but there would have been more noise, and more embracings, and something brawnier than the bubbly, and the gifts would have been not from Rodeo Drive but from the shops in Memphis.

After this lunch we drove up into the hills beyond the hotel, along manicured, gently curving lanes called Coldwater Canyon Drive and Loma Vista Drive that extend like fluttery cats' whiskers into cool canyons and steeply undulating foothills lined with the motion-picture people's luminous estates, some of which one L.A. writer called "high-tech igloos," their sunken gardens, terraced lawns, onyx patios, tennis courts, and swimming pools mostly obscured by great crests of hedges and walls. The only traffic on these verdant thoroughfares this afternoon were BMW's, Mercedeses, Lincolns, and Rolls-Royces, but when an unprepossessing station wagon unexpectedly happened by, one was tempted to shout at the top of his lungs: "Get that Chevrolet off this road!" Suddenly, at the dead end of Crescent Drive, I caught sight of an impossible coincidence from my imaginings on the hotel patio, and I recognized it immediately: Set elaborately behind wrought-iron fences and a giant contoured greensward was the very estate itself in *The Godfather* where the poor horse had lost its head. At the apex of the next highest hill, we turned to look down on the evanescent city laid out before us, grand and elusive in its gleam of smog, a lavish phantom it seemed, an oasis encampment in the vast and peremptory desert beyond.

———

There may be no two more disparate places in America than Hollywood and Mississippi, which exist so distantly in the Great Republic as to be nearly untranslatable to each other: the unmitigatingly tragic, memory-obsessed Mississippi earth on the one hand, the fashionable boulevards of popular tinsel dreamland on the other.

Yet there had always been a Mississippi connection in Hollywood, which had intrigued me, primarily in its embodiment in the unique and unlikely duo of William Faulkner and Elvis Presley, each of whom spent considerable time in the motion-picture calling. The state had produced a roster of playwrights, actors, actresses, and producers who dwelled out here: Tennessee Williams, Beth Henley, James Earl Jones, Morgan Freeman, Diane Ladd, Mary Ann Mobley, Ray Walston, Oprah Winfrey, Larry and Charles Gordon, Dana Andrews, and Stella Stevens. The latter was a couple of years younger than I. Her real name was Bootsie Eggleston, and I remember her less for her roles as Daisy Mae in the *Li'l Abner* movies and others than for her climbing trees and building castles in sandboxes with me before her family moved away from Yazoo to Memphis. As for Dana Andrews, he was the son of a Baptist preacher from Collins, Mississippi, and at the height of his stardom in the late 1940s the publicist for Fox dispatched a telegram to the mayor of Collins suggesting that the town officially change its name to Andrews in honor of its native son. The mayor wired back: "We will not change our name to Andrews. Have Andrews change his to Collins."

Faulkner was chronically broke and in debt in the 1930s and 1940s, his books total financial failures, and he was forced to spend months at a time writing scripts in Hollywood, often miserably homesick. The money was really not as good as he claimed it was, but unlike Scott Fitzgerald in the same period, who had pretensions of elevating movies to an art medium, money was all Faulkner ever came out here for. He sometimes slept during story conferences. Once during an interview for a job on a script, he asked Irving Thalberg if he was the man who did the Mickey Mouse cartoons. He drank more heavily than ever, even by his own admission, and became the model for the drunken screenwriter in the Coen brothers' movie *Barton Fink*. "I've got the world's greatest writer working for me for peanuts," Jack Warner, known as the most pernicious of the Warner brothers, boasted. There was more money in Hollywood, Faulkner said, than in all of Mississippi. "One day a leaf falls in a canyon out here," he said, "and they call it winter."

Faulkner wrote scripts for bad movies and for good ones. One of the dregs was an improbable epic called *Land of the Pharaohs* requiring ten thousand extras playing slaves building the pyramids and being entombed alive for their malfeasances. Faulkner complained that neither the director, Howard Hawks, nor he knew how pharaohs talked, so he modeled them after Confederate generals. His closest Hollywood relationship was with Hawks, who some thought kept Faulkner on the payroll just for his company. But Faulkner did two screenplays for Hawks that became superb movies, vital to this day: Raymond Chandler's *The Big Sleep* and Ernest Hemingway's *To Have and Have Not*. And it was his friend Hawks who provided the most memorable, and accurate, story about the Mississippian in Hollywood:

> Faulkner and I were going hunting down in Imperial Valley after doves, and Clark Gable called up and said, "What are you doing?" I said, "We're going hunting. I'm going hunting with a fella named Bill Faulkner." And he said, "Can I go?" I said, "Yeah, if you can get over here in half an hour." So he came charging over, and we got in the station wagon. We had a couple of drinks on the way down. We started talking, and I don't know what, the conversation got into literature and Gable said, "Who do you think are the good writers, Mr. Faulkner?" Faulkner says, "Thomas Mann, Willa Cather, John Dos Passos, Ernest Hemingway, and myself." And Gable looked kinda funny and said, "Do you write, Mr. Faulkner?" Faulkner says, "Yes, what do you do, Mr. Gable?"

He continued to write his own work while in Hollywood. In my own Hollywood peregrinations, ancillary to the Untitled Mississippi Project, I had visions of him in the solitary nocturnal walks he took around Beverly Hills and downtown L.A. He bravely wrote *Absalom, Absalom!* here, pecking away with two fingers on a small typewriter in a house on Sweetzer Street, one of four small "alpine" châteaus a block away from Sunset Towers. "It's a tortured story," he told a friend from Mississippi, "and a torture to write it."

Elvis's spirit likewise stalked me here. We were almost exactly the same age and from small Mississippi towns, but I never once met him. He was a movie usher as a boy, "studied" Brando and James Dean, saw *Rebel Without a Cause* countless times and memorized Dean's lines, and always *wanted* Hollywood, which was a very long way from the tiny shack where he grew up across the tracks. Back home his mother worried incessantly about him in Hollywood, fearing he might be corrupted. He made thirty-four movies in all, most of them downhill from his early movie days. "He made more films than Eleanor Powell," one critic noted. Michael Curtiz, who had directed *Casablanca*, feared that Elvis would be pompous and difficult but found him "a lovely boy" with the potential to become "a great actor." Elvis fell in love with Judy Tyler, a beautiful young actress who played opposite him, but she died in one of those freakish Hollywood car wrecks. This killed something in Elvis. With intelligent scripts and coaching, could he have fulfilled the Hollywood promise? "He was just a piece of clay in the hands of the bigshots," his old Memphis girlfriend lamented. Another Hollywood casualty, one wondered? Yet Mississippi loved him and was proud of him and, in the same way I'd pictured Mr. Bill Faulkner's long walks when he was struggling with *Absalom, Absalom!,* I conjured the Tupelo boy in his pink Cadillac convertible tooling down Sunset or Santa Monica in the expansive nighttimes, practicing his next day's lines, I will bet, as he went.

—

It would prove refreshing to observe L.A. through the eyes of the Mississippi visitors, especially Crisco and Benny.

Crisco had arrived to view the filming and ended up spending much time with Bill Macy, who was playing him onscreen. Crisco was not the least homesick, he said, and kept putting off going back to Jackson. JoAnne and I were having dinner with the De-Laughters on the patio of an Italian restaurant on the Sunset Strip when a car pulled up parallel to the curb and Crisco stuck his head out the window and shouted, "Y'all aren't from around *here,* are you?" It was Crisco cruising the Strip, just the way we used to do on Grand Avenue in Yazoo City. As he got out to greet us, there was an unidentified commotion from somewhere across the Strip. "What was *that*?" he exclaimed, and whirled around in that direction and extended his hand as if instinctively going for a .38.

Rob Reiner said it was rewarding to have Benny Bennett on the Hollywood sets because he helped make the others act "real." Everyone was nice to him in L.A., Benny said. Macy helped him hit his marks (indicating where he should position himself) before the cameras, which Benny knew nothing about, and both Alec Baldwin and Macy said they would help him get a Hollywood agent. The teamster driver in charge of getting Benny to the various appointments back in March did not have the slightest notion who he was, especially when he complained, "I just feel lost without my gun." A few days before that, during a break in an interior scene set around a desk in the fabricated D.A.'s office, he had been asked what kind of weapon he particularly liked, and he told them he preferred a Glock 9-millimeter because he was able to come back with a double tap to the head a lot quicker. Alec Baldwin jokingly asked him where he went wrong in his youth to be double-tapping someone to the head.

There were differences between Mississippi humor and Hollywood humor, Benny had discerned. For instance, rather than using the phrase "when the shit hits the fan," the Hollywooders say, "when the feces hits the oscillating rotor." There were other instances. "We're around dead people a lot," Benny went on, "and the scum of the earth, I guess you would say. We can make jokes about murders and stuff, which is our way of staying sane. Black humor is what we have. Well, a friend from Mississippi came out the other day to watch me in the film. During the week he coaches and is very well respected in the school system. On the weekends he dresses up like a biker. He rented a motorcycle while he was out here. Well, we're on the set. He's wearing a bandanna and a leather vest." On the Culver City set Baldwin was talking about his incident with the paparazzo and said he was concerned that although he had beaten the assault charges, the man was now suing him for a million dollars. "My friend looked at him and said, 'We'll get rid of him for half of that.' Alec didn't say anything, he just looked at us. I think for a few seconds he thought we were serious."

Benny's mother back home wanted to know all about Hollywood, so he had already taken about ten rolls of film. "She wanted to know about the actors, how they treated me. I just told her how they filmed things, and how accurate the sets were." During his Hollywood stay he had wanted to visit the Spahn Ranch, where the Manson family once lived, having group sex and smoking a lot of pot, but found out it had been bulldozed and some kind of subdivision was going up on the spot. One night he had a ride-around with some hospitable L.A. cops in the neighborhood called South Central, a ten-square-mile area that sees more murders each year than does all of Jackson, Mississippi. He also had been hanging out with a motorcycle club at Barney's Beanery on Sunset with its 226 brands of beer, including Rattlesnake, erroneously attributed to Mississippi. "Pretty good people, they're working-class. Of course out here you've got multimillionaires ridin' Harleys." The only unpleasant incident he had experienced was on Venice Beach, where a black fellow who had noticed his T-shirt that said HARLEY-DAVIDSON OF JACKSON, MISSISSIPPI bumped into him. "Excuse me," Benny said. Then the man ran his shoulder into him. "When he bumped me that second time, I just grabbed him, jerked him, and shook him real good, up and down good, and then he went right on off." In restaurants in L.A. as well as in Mississippi, Benny never liked to eat with his back to the door; he called this "the cop instinct," although he felt more comfortable out here than back home because people didn't know him here: no released scoundrels, for instance, whom he had once helped send to jail. In his line of work, he said, he had always been paranoid when it came to watching his back and surveying the surroundings.

In Malibu one Saturday night, Rob Reiner and Michele gave a dinner party for the Mississippi cadre at a crowded restaurant owned by Wolfgang Puck. Zollo and Barbara Broccoli were there, and Lewis Colick and Elizabeth Lane, and the talk turned to the Untitled Mississippi Project and the film locales in Mississippi. There was some sort of uncouth celebratory dinner on the adjoining patio, and suddenly a woman from there descended on Reiner. "Hold it down!" she said. "We're trying to make toasts!" The host looked like a chastised child. On this night Puck himself helped serve.

"Why not open one of your restaurants in Mississippi?" someone asked him.

"Will you get me a passport?" he replied.

Bobby DeLaughter turned to his trusted cop Benny, sitting with his back to the door. "You carryin' any firearms, Benny?"

"Only knives," Benny replied. Everyone, Mississippians and Angelenos alike, stood and gave warm-hearted toasts to one another and to the film at hand. Reiner in his toast spoke of what he had learned from his time in Mississippi and the South, of the friendships he had made, of the feeling of its land, and of the importance and faith he placed in the movie. Bobby proposed an affectionate toast to Crisco and Bennett and what they had experienced together, when so often they had been unsure of the outcome. Zollo toasted Bobby: "This country was formed by common men acting uncommonly. Bobby DeLaughter is the uncommon common man." As we were leaving, someone asked Crisco, "Do you think it's dangerous outside in Malibu tonight, Charlie?" Crisco replied, "It's dangerous everywhere."

———

On the set one day Darrell Evers introduced us to his young son, Medgar Evers's grandson. Myrlie came in for a day. "All of us were very moved by her presence," Susanna Thompson recalled. James Woods had never met her. He was in his full Beckwith makeup. Reena Evers had gotten so accustomed to Woods's makeup, she said, "Mama, I want you to meet Jimmy." Myrlie turned around, extended her hand, and cringed.

Woods said, "Mrs. Evers, I'm here with you on this," but it took her a while to get over it. Her immediate urge, she said, was to put her hands around his throat. Myrlie asked Reiner if she could see some film footage of the re-created assassination. "Are you sure you want to see this?" he asked. "It's very graphic and very chilling."

"I've been living with this for thirty years," she said. "I can watch it." She, Darrell, Reena, and Yolanda King held hands while they watched. "If I start crying," Myrlie said, "I won't be able to quit." She did not cry.

Because everyone in the cast was in L.A. and they were filming at home in the studio, where there were no distractions and total control, the courtroom scenes of the 1994 trial were shot on Stages 14 and 15 in real sequence, which afforded yet another mystical déjà vu for those of us who had been there at the real happening. Benny Bennett said he would look around and shake his head to get his bearings: Was it real or unreal? Army Archerd, the veteran writer for *Variety* and long around the Hollywood circuit, led off his column: "I have rarely been as moved on a movie set as I was Wednesday." He noted that it was June 12, the thirty-third anniversary of Medgar's death, and he was struck by the past merging so astonishingly with the present.

The courtroom scenes required 175 extras representing Myrlie Evers supporters, Beckwith supporters, spectators, sketch artists, clerks, reporters, and deputies reproducing the tense, claustrophobic atmosphere of the original proceedings. Outside the windows was the re-created Jackson skyline, two prodigious gauze screens with blown-up color photographs and air currents behind them to simulate the breeze rustling the leaves of the trees in front of the City Hall directly across Pascagoula Street. Numerous setups and angles and considerable crowd movement were involved in these long days of courtroom shooting, hence a bizarre contrivance called "wild walls" was utilized. The walls of the courtroom were actually movable and removable to accommodate the cameras, lights, and other equipment. One afternoon after the filming of the scene in which the jury retires to deliberate and the cameras were shooting a few individuals tarrying in the chamber, I heard a strange murmurous sound that seemed to be originating from outside the windows. It took me a while to identify the noise. It was "rain," the same kind of light rainfall that had preceded the colossal storm that day twenty-eight months before.

There was pandemonium in the scene that duplicated the frantic rush back into the courtroom that Saturday morning of February 1994, when it was announced that the jury had reached its verdict. At the time, no one had anticipated such a swift decision, and people, including Myrlie and her children, had been scattered all over town. In an interminable series of shots that consumed an entire afternoon, the numerous extras and actors raced from the outside corridor to jam into the chamber before the actor playing Judge Breland Hilburn ordered the doors closed. People stumbled over one another. It was surprising to me that with the exception of Frank Capra III having been stung by a hornet in Mississippi there were no serious injuries in the filming of this movie. During a lull in this day's shooting, I found myself chatting with a middle-aged extra who said this was her first movie work in a long time because she had broken her arm on a studio set. During a scene like this? "No," she replied. "I fell down some stairs on my way to lunch."

During the scene in which James Woods was led away from the courtroom after the verdict was announced, I was sitting next to another extra on a courtroom pew. She was in camera range, but I was only inches outside of it. "That's a little much, don't you think?" she asked. "I mean, to have him led away by two *black* cops?" I had been there that very day, I said, and assured her that this was the way it happened. "You were *there*?" she said.

Judge Hilburn was played by an accomplished actor named Terry O'Quinn, and after the shooting one day he and Lewis Colick and I discussed the case. O'Quinn inquired about every aspect of the investigation and the trial itself and was particularly curious to know what the sentiments had been among Mississippians about going after Beckwith again after thirty years. He was also eager to know about my neighbor, the real Judge Hilburn. Suddenly I recognized O'Quinn as the mass murderer in the horror films *The Stepfather* and *The Stepfather II,* the fellow who always married divorced women with children and eventually hacked them into meticulous pieces before moving on to a new assignation. It would be interesting to tell Breland Hilburn on my return home that he was being portrayed by a homicidal psychopath.

One of the most troublesome scenes to shoot was the moment the jury was brought in for the lawyers' closing arguments. The members looked very much like the true-life jury of 1994, as if they could have been empaneled in Mississippi and transported en masse to Culver City. Reiner had advised Baldwin that this was his most important scene but that he should suppress being emotionally overwhelmed by what he was saying. Reena Evers was playing one of the jurors, sitting front and center only four or five feet from Baldwin. When he started the DeLaughter summation, Reena began sobbing uncontrollably. She continued doing so through the second take. Now Baldwin was getting choked up, as was just about everyone else in the room, including technicians and grips. He took Reiner aside and said, "You've got to get her to stop crying or I'm going to *start* crying because the woman is just killing me." Everyone consoled Reena, and she finally composed herself and they went on with it. There would be take after take from many angles, ending with Baldwin's closing words: "Is it ever too late to do the right thing?"

On the afternoon of the filming of the final courtroom scenes, after more than a week of shooting there, the director stood in front of the judge's bench and asked for attention. The chamber was still crowded with extras, crew, and actors. This concluded the courtroom scenes, he said. He thanked the extras and the crew. One by one he recognized by name the actors, the stars on down to the bit players, even the man who had played the bailiff. Each was applauded. Finally he recognized Reena Evers. She came down from the jury box and embraced Whoopi Goldberg, her brother Darrell, and Yolanda King. She was applauded for five minutes. For a long time no one left the room. The last to remain were the members of the jury, who were hugging and taking photographs of one another. Later, from outside, we could hear the jury that had convicted Byron De La Beckwith singing and clapping.

———

On Soundstage 7, where the interiors of Tara in *Gone With the Wind* had been filmed, they did the close-ups of Beckwith pulling the trigger of the gun. The honeysuckle and weeds and all the other components of the Jackson location actually looked more verdant on the soundstage because the real growth in Jackson was not planted but had been pulled and was half-dead by the time the scene was shot; here it was in pots, and fresh. James Woods was crouched down with his eye to the Golden Hawk scope. The rifle looked evil and menacing. They were using not the real gun, which had been ruled out as being in bad taste, but the exact model. "This is *heavy*," the actor said as he pulled the trigger.

Woods was irascible on the set, just as he had been in Mississippi, playing the Beckwith role to the limit even during breaks. There was a scene in which he and some of his supporters were dallying in the courtroom while the jury was deliberating. They were speculating on a hung jury. He approached me about his next line. "Please say to me in a Mississippi accent, 'All it takes is one of 'em. That's American justice.'" Just before another scene, he approached me again. "How do people in Mississippi pronounce 'Louisiana'?"

"Looz-iana."

"Looz-iana," he repeated. "Looz-iana."

Also on Soundstage 7 they reshot the close-ups of Myrlie's speech after the verdict had come in. This was the scene that had caused such problems when it was filmed in front of the court-

house in Jackson. The exterior of the courthouse steps and main
entrance had been reproduced here, down to the actual manufac-
turers' names on the fake doorknobs and locks. Even the two
round, metal, three-foot-high ashcans that had stood for years on
each side of the doors had been shipped in from Jackson by Shoeless Jack Stevens. Whoopi Goldberg was still having trouble with
this scene, which was crucial, since it would be the next-to-the-last
one of the movie. They did eighteen takes.

—

In both Mississippi and L.A., at the end of each day's filming, the
director, producers, and a few others, but never any of the actors,
went to a projection room to watch dailies—the various takes from
the previous day's shooting, which had just been received from the
laboratory. The most desirable takes would be chosen and turned
over to the film editor. These sessions had long been noted as exciting but intimidating moments: Had what they wanted ended up
on the screen? It was an elusive process. Reiner never knew
whether he had gotten the scene until the dailies came in, he said.
From there he still did not know whether the whole picture was
going to work until all the many scenes were strung together in the
larger context, but he did know that the scene itself was either
going to work or not work based on these screenings. Dailies were
really pieces-in-progress. "You can't see the forest for the trees.
You're in the midst of it. You can't tell until you put it all together."

In Culver City it was called the Cecil B. De Mille Projection
Room, where that director and Selznick and the others had viewed
what in those older days were called rushes. It consisted of seven
rows of seats resembling easy chairs, nine chairs to a row, on a
floor that sloped gradually upward. The director always sat just
under the projector on the top row. In front was a large screen. The
dailies never failed to fascinate me. The first ones I saw, of the
closing arguments of Alec Baldwin as Bobby DeLaughter and Bill
Smitrovich as Beckwith's lawyer Jim Kitchens, were a stunning
transmutation of what I had witnessed on the set—the people, the

courtroom setting, everyone, and everything suddenly physically larger than life. Elvis himself in his first Hollywood days was always amazed by how *imposing* he looked in dailies.

When the dailies from Goldberg's reenactment of Myrlie's closing lines on the courthouse steps came in, there was a tension in the projection room. The various takes consumed a long time on the screen. Often she cursed herself profusely, then said, "Let's do it again." The room was silent. Then the final take was finished and the lights came on. "She got it on the fourth take," Reiner said. "I was worried in Jackson, and I was worried here. This scene is a great opportunity for any actor or actress. It's like a pitcher serving up a seventy-five-mile-per-hour fastball straight down the middle of the plate. She got it on the fourth take. She whacked it out of the park. She whacked it out of the park into the upper deck."

———

The whole Castle Rock company moved out one day from the walled village of Culver City to the Los Angeles National Cemetery off Sepulveda Boulevard near Brentwood. This would represent Arlington National Cemetery in two scenes separated by twenty-seven actual years, Medgar Evers's funeral in 1963 and the 1991 exhumation of his body, which was taken to Dr. Baden's laboratory in Albany for the second autopsy.

The Los Angeles cemetery bore a striking resemblance to Arlington with its thousands of military tombstones of veterans of many wars stretching as far as the eye could see. It was a clear, smogless morning, and the birds were singing everywhere. All about were the flowering bougainvillea and the jacarandas and the eucalyptus trees, which looked a little like tall Southern weeping willows. The spot selected was on a rise that afforded a dominating view of the entire undulating terrain. The first of the two scenes to be shot was a montage of the exhumation, and since a coffin had to be dug out with a backhoe and lifted by a big hoist, the technicians had chosen a plot of ground where there were no graves. Medgar's tombstone and others nearby were contrived of plywood.

The names of the veterans on the other "stones" were the real ones close to his grave in Arlington. Tall pine trees had been nailed to wooden stands like Christmas trees and placed to block out the eucalyptus. Greens foreman Bobby Joe Garren explained that in the funeral scene tiny young pines would surround the grave site, but since the exhumation was twenty-seven years later, the trees would have grown to this size. Directly across the road from the Evers "grave" was a substantial plot of Civil War veterans, men who had migrated to California after that war: G. E. Aiken, Co. D, 41st Wisconsin Infantry; Lewis Trichler, Co. K, 1st New York Dragoons; D. H. Hunting, Co. A, 46th Illinois Infantry, and on and on. Nearby were veterans of the Spanish-American War, and beyond that, in vast endless rows, the World War I soldiers. It was a realistic, moving panorama.

Playing in the scene were Alec Baldwin as Bobby DeLaughter, Bill Macy as Charlie Crisco, Van Evers as himself, and two cemetery personnel, two grave diggers, a coroner, and a funeral director. The real Crisco had been recruited as one of the grave diggers. Bobby DeLaughter was also there that morning. During a break in the reenactment of the unearthing of the casket, I joined Bobby, Crisco, and Van Evers. They were remembering how solemn and sad they had felt that real day five years before when Van's father was exhumed. "It's like what Yogi Berra said," Crisco observed. "Déjà vu all over again." They all seemed a little shaken by how close this reenactment was to the true-life morning of 1991 in Arlington.

After this scene had been shot, there was a lull of a few hours before the duplication of the funeral, since Reiner had to attend his son Jake's graduation from preschool. At early lunch, under the enormous base-camp tent across Sepulveda Boulevard, it was beguiling to study the great mélange of extras in period costume for the funeral that afternoon as they dined at the long tables on Southern fried chicken, meat loaf, red snapper, and vegetable chili and mingled in unfunereal spirit, another collective vignette of a tragic moment out of the beleaguered 1960s. There were 140 of them in all, as noted on the roster for that day's shooting schedule: 100 ND mourners ("ND" meaning nondescript, or general), as well as government officials, reporters, film cameramen, children, veterans, military officers, news photographers, soldiers, NAACP dignitaries, a minister, and six male and one female Elk officers.

At the cemetery shooting, the tiny pine trees were in place. The actor playing Roy Wilkins, president then of the NAACP, rehearsed his eulogy. As the family and mourners gathered around the grave, with the coffin draped in the American flag, Reiner and others stood with Whoopi Goldberg and examined for details a June 28, 1963, *Life* magazine, which featured a photograph of the funeral. Whoopi's black suit and velvet-and-lace hat were the exact matches of Myrlie Evers's on that day.

The last scene to be shot reverted again to 1991. Medgar's exhumed coffin was in the back of the hearse, with Van Evers seated next to it. Behind the hearse in their rental car were Alec Baldwin as Bobby and Bill Macy as Crisco. The two vehicles moved slowly toward the main gate as those cars occupied by the original participants had done in 1991 as they commenced the lengthy journey from Arlington to Dr. Baden's autopsy lab in Albany. "It was a *very* long drive," Crisco remembered of that day. "We were worn slap out. If you'd have told me what was ahead of us, we'd have slowed down a little bit."

Chapter 11

WINDING DOWN

The final days of the filming, both interiors and exteriors, were shot at various venues in the Valley and in San Pedro. The Untitled Mississippi Project at last had a title, *Ghosts of Mississippi.* The consensus became that this title was the most appropriate to the theme of the film. The directional signs with arrows along the freeways and boulevards to the sets, however, still displayed the abbreviation UMP.

Several days were spent in and around a sprawling private dwelling set amid trees and profuse vegetation in the little town of Sierra Madre not far from the San Gabriel Mountains. This would serve as Bobby DeLaughter's house in the woods several miles from Jackson. Scenes from 1991, '92, '93, and '94 would be shot there. To duplicate the Deep Southern locale the resourceful greens foreman had resodded the back lawn, shipped in Spanish moss, crepe myrtles, and mimosas, and disguised the palm trees with oak "skins" up to twelve feet high, which was all the height the cameras would need.

On this warm, languid morning of heavy smog they were filming an exterior scene that had its origins in the day we visited Money,

Mississippi, near the site of Emmett Till's "wolf-whistle." Lucas Black, the small-town Alabama boy with the deep-gullied Southern drawl who was playing young Burt, was having his nose bloodied in front of the house by a neighborhood kid. Bobby would come along and break up the fight.

During these shots, workers were already preparing for one of the next day's scenes, Peggy and Bobby's wedding ceremony. They brought in white roses in large water buckets and decorating a wooden wedding arch with Queen Anne's lace and roses. If the Spanish moss were not enough to transport me home, I encountered on these premises my first California mosquito; one of the flower bearers surmised that this one had obviously eluded L.A.'s Mosquito Abatement Program, which gets them at the source. Later in the day the stand-in for one of the child actors was attacked by a swarm of ants and had to be treated with ointment. The set was beginning to resemble Mississippi in more ways than Spanish moss.

Shooting continued throughout the day and into the evening. Since this would be a late night, the crafts service man, Willie Radcliff, put his spareribs on the barbecue grill at 6:00 P.M. They were distributed three hours later, and everyone took a break to eat. The final shots of the night would seem to be simple and uneventful ones, although this would soon prove otherwise. They included various angles of Alec Baldwin pulling his gray Jeep Cherokee into the driveway, getting out with his briefcase and a sack of groceries, and climbing the back stairs into the house. "That Cherokee's awfully clean to have been up in the Delta," someone shouted from the shadows. There was a long wait while dust was applied to it.

"We need some Delta bugs on the windshield," the director said. After a time someone finally arrived with dead bugs. "Alec," Reiner said, "walk up the steps slowly. You've been in the dust in the Delta. You're tired. You struck out with the alibi witnesses."

On the second or third take of the driveway scene, the Cherokee broke down. Several expert technicians took turns at the ignition. The vehicle refused to crank. It was examined inside and out.

Under the raised hood the crew experts were looking at the engine and the battery with flashlights. They couldn't find anything wrong.

"It's the vortex!" Reiner suddenly exclaimed. "The damned *vortex*. Every movie has one vortex. We're in the vortex. Grinding to a halt. The vortex is when you don't think it'll take long to repair, but it takes forever. I've been there. The vortex is like a bug in a toilet, swirling down, down, down, when you flush and then, there it is again. There's nothing you can do. Everybody relax. I've learned a long time ago you can't let the vortex get you down."

It was 10:30 P.M., and everyone was tired. The set was like a nocturnal campsite now, with the wounded Jeep Cherokee serving as the campfire. Someone began singing the old Beatles song "Tomorrow Never Knows," about relaxing and floating downstream. As the workers scurried about the stricken vehicle, someone asked Frankie Capra how many spareribs he had eaten so far. "Twenty-two," he said, "but some of 'em might've been stuck together."

While Jeff Stott's young Labrador, named Sidney Ellen Wade after the president's girlfriend in *The American President*, lay dozing behind the monitors, various people lounged in the tall black canvas chairs and tried to pass the time. Zollo said he was wary of driving around L.A. after 9:00 P.M. Lyn McKissick, the script coordinator, reported that she had lived in a house on the grounds of Mississippi's Parchman prison while shooting John Grisham's *The Chamber*. Would Clinton sign the welfare bill? someone asked. The talk turned to Beverly Hills real estate. Also, were the women Chinese swimmers taking steroids in the Olympics? How good was that Japanese restaurant in Jackson? What are the best computer systems? What actress won the Oscar in *All the King's Men*? Who cares about the bad remakes of great old movies, like *The Day of the Jackal, The Postman Always Rings Twice, Diabolique, Cape Fear*? What did the snail riding on the turtle's shell say? *"Whee!"* How are the Menendez brothers doing, do you think? Rank the best four Hitchcocks in order. A rough consensus: *Vertigo, Rear*

Window, Psycho, North by Northwest. What about *The Birds?* came a complaint from the shadows. The original *The 39 Steps? The Man Who Knew Too Much? Suspicion? Rebecca?*

"One of the big differences between here and Mississippi," the director declared, "is that we have very few bugs." Time passing late into the Hollywood night.

In the midst of all this, only three days before the final shooting, I was oddly struck with a sudden and stabbing anxiety, or was it just a silly, private little foreboding? Did the vortex mean bad luck? Was it a crazy presage?

"How many more setups we got tonight, Frankie?" Reiner asked.

"Three."

"How much time are we talking about here?"

"Maybe thirty minutes."

"I'm going back to my trailer. Let me know when you get it handled."

In the director's trailer, which was parked down the street at the curb in front of a small bungalow with a statue of a black jockey on the front lawn, Reiner and Zollo were bandying more baseball-trivia questions. Name the sixteen players to have hit more than fifty home runs in one season. Ruth. Maris. Mantle. Greenberg . . .

There was a knock on the door, and Frankie Capra came in. "Rob, we got a problem. We just can't get the backup cranked either."

"Well, you're working on it, aren't you?"

"Of course. But something's wrong." A logistical discussion ensued between director and assistant director. If they wrapped up at midnight, when could dailies be seen? There was much arcane technical talk, including Alec Baldwin's twelve-hour daily portal-to-portal contract and additional payment after such-and-such an hour. How long could the child actors work? Capra departed, to return twenty minutes later. The backup still would not crank.

"The vortex is now official," Reiner said.

"What are the odds of two Cherokees breaking down?" Zollo

asked. We could shut down for the night now, Capra suggested, and reschedule these shots for day after tomorrow. A 3:00 p.m. call would give enough time. And that is what they decided.

The footnote to this story is that the fellow the transportation coordinator put in charge of the two Cherokees had gotten the keys switched. The keys to the backup were in the first one, and vice versa. Both of the vehicles were Jeeps, and the ignitions would turn but the engines would not start. "Hell," someone said, "we were out there taking the sons of bitches apart almost, and all it was was the keys were switched."

—

The next day they filmed an outdoor Mississippi wedding, culminating in numerous takes of the groom warmly kissing the bride. Susanna Thompson, playing Peggy DeLaughter, was a beautiful young woman, and while three or four dozen extras watched from their folding chairs near the wedding arbor, Alec Baldwin declared, "And I get *paid* for this!"

"I hope neither of you had the tuna and onions for breakfast," the director said.

"I had sturgeon," Baldwin replied.

After the seventh or eighth take, Reiner shouted, "Cut! Put the hose on this guy. Forty more and we've got this, Alec."

They prepared to film what was projected to be the final scene in the finished movie, of Bobby DeLaughter and his little girl, Claire, replanting their bottle tree, which had been blown down in the storm that had descended on Jackson the night before the trial verdict. Shoeless Jack Stevens had just sent to L.A. by Federal Express seventy-five bottles of various sizes and colors to be chosen from. This was Day 58 of 61 days of shooting, and everyone, sadly almost, talked about the conclusion being near. Since everyone knew this was to be the film's last scene, there was a feeling of drama on the set.

"Every movie needs one crane shot," Reiner commented. A huge crane, called a Lenny arm, was stationed on the back lawn. Take after take of close-ups were done of Bobby and Claire planting the tree. One shot was ruined by the sound of a low-flying airplane, another by the other child actors' voices as they played in an adjoining lawn, a third by a loud flock of birds overhead. The last line was filmed several times in two versions: "You two can grow up together" and "The two of you can grow up together." Then the crane gradually moved back and up to show Bobby, Claire, the tree, the house, the lawn, the encompassing woods. As it did so, the director began to hum an impromptu gospel song, as if to accompany the concluding scene.

They would shoot until well after midnight on this day, a set of difficult scenes to follow involving Bobby and his family rushing from the house after receiving a bomb threat on the telephone. One scene would include extras as neighbors, policemen, firemen, and bomb-squad officers with HINDS COUNTY and CITY OF JACKSON on their uniforms, and fire trucks, police cars, and bomb-squad vans. In the long lull before the setting up, people talked about their next jobs. Some of the crew were sound asleep under the shade of the "oak" trees, others were throwing footballs and doing the Hula-Hoop with the child actors. A few of the extras were picnicking on chicken eggrolls and pizza from the snack truck.

"This is a true story, right?" a middle-aged extra asked someone. Yes, he was told, and the circumstances were explained. "Are the real DeLaughters still alive?" Yes, and still young. "Well, isn't this something?"

Some relatives of Lucas Black were visiting from Alabama, and in the San Gabriel Valley their small-town Dixie accents were incongruous yet oddly reassuring: "I'm just plum wore out," they'd say, and "Them chairs *was* over yonder." This was the last big outdoor scene remaining, with a great deal of movement and activity, but there were no more than a dozen or so spectators across the way. Were people in this town inured to filmmaking?

In the port town of San Pedro, a nearly two-hour drive from West Hollywood in strident freeway traffic, the crew would do scenes in a movie theater in which Peggy and Bobby are watching *Presumed Innocent.* Upset over a turn in the Beckwith investigation, in which black leaders in Jackson have accused the D.A.'s office of putting on a show for black voters and demanding a special black prosecutor, Alec Baldwin storms out into the lobby and calls Myrlie Evers on a pay telephone with a BELL SOUTH sign on it, Shoeless Jack Stevens's final export from Jackson.

San Pedro had the reputation of being an unsafe town with tough gangs. It seemed relaxed enough on this night. The street where the theater itself was located had tattoo shops, shadowy bars, halfway houses, coffeehouses where old men were playing chess, and nautical stores with windows displaying spyglasses, duffle bags, and sheath knives. Reiner and Lilly Kilvert had wanted a theater that looked old and Southern. It was a marvelous faded bauble of an edifice from the early 1930s, which had been out of use for twenty years. It featured a large lobby replete on this night with a reconstructed concession stand offering popcorn, candy, and soda; it had a raked floor, golden leather seats, Art Deco chandeliers, ornate multicolored ceilings and carvings, and gold engravings even on the box-office exteriors. Frank Capra, Sr., held his sneak preview of *Lost Horizon* in this theater, and the audience reactions were so negative that he cut the first five reels.

Two hundred extras were on hand as movie patrons. They were invited to help themselves at the concession stand. Before they were directed into the theater itself, however, there was a long, intricate process, inscrutable to me, of synchronizing the film footage of *Presumed Innocent* into the action. Someone behind the monitors ironically remarked that one of the prosecutors in the scene being used had the nickname DeLay. Viewing this scene on the real screen and on the monitors, Reiner commented that the wife in the film was pointedly meticulous about the details of the homicide and its cover-up yet did not even bother to get rid of the murder weapon. When the extras filed in, he explained to them the substance of the scene about to be shot and appointed three or four of their number sitting near Alec Baldwin and Susanna Thompson to say *"Shhh!"* when the two of them began talking to each other during the movie on the screen. There were numerous takes.

The filming of the phone call in the lobby did not begin until nearly midnight. It was an important scene, some thirty lines long, in which Bobby apologizes to Myrlie for lying to her about not having found the murder weapon and promises to see the case through. The company had worked at the DeLaughter house until four-thirty that morning, and everyone was plainly exhausted. Baldwin could not get his lines. "This is a damned nightmare," he said after the fifteenth or sixteenth take. After about the twentieth take, he knocked a wastebasket over with his fist.

The scene required thirty-two takes, just in time to do a final exterior scene in front of the theater, a conversation between Peggy and Bobby. This had to be a nocturnal scene and was a race against time, with countless thousands of dollars to be spent if they had to postpone until the following Monday. They finished it only minutes before dawn.

—

During a break in the final day of shooting I talked with Alec Baldwin about the making of *Ghosts of Mississippi*. A shy, tentative rain was beginning to fall on old Pasadena, the first rain I had ever seen in Southern California. It had been intriguing to observe a movie professional playing a person one knew so well, and Baldwin's DeLaughter had come across as decent, solid, honorable, and unflashy, which was the real Bobby.

"I'm going to share something with you that's a little personal," he said. "When I'd make movies lately I'd be sitting there on the set dreaming constantly of where else I could be and what else I could be doing. I've made some less than wonderful movies in the last couple of years. When you do the bogus movies, it makes you want to quit. That's the definition of hell to me, you know, wanting to be somewhere else and you can't change that. Rob made me want to make movies again. Rob made it fun for me.

"I've played villains who had a lot of resentment, were driven by resentment and envy. They were very, very bitter because there were things they wanted in their lives and they didn't get them. I can understand this on an emotional level, the idea of resentment. You really don't give a fuck about those people. Analyzing them gets to be a little tiresome. I've done movies where I don't care. This movie is the total opposite of what I'm used to. You not only agree with the person, it's a great challenge to play him.

"When we were doing the summation scene before the jury, I knew I was never again going to have another opportunity like that as an actor in a movie in my whole life. Rob has a musical ear. You have to have an ear for how the words should sound on every level, the timbre of how you say them, the pace at which you say them. Rob came up to me and put it in an even bigger context. He said, 'This is four and a half years of your life. When you get up and give this summation you're looking these people in the eye and saying, Please, I'm begging you to see it my way. I spent four and a half years dogging this guy, and I *know* he's a killer.' I watched Marcia Clark deliver her summation in the O. J. Simpson trial. I watched her looking at the jury and every line that she would say, her *eyes* were saying, 'You ain't buying this, are you?' And they *didn't* buy it."

The most difficult scene for him as an actor was this summation. The most difficult for the *character* of Bobby was the one in which he drives to the deserted Evers house alone at night and relives the details of the murder. "That's when his fate is sealed, that's when he knows what he has to do. He wants so badly to give this up. He's dying for somebody to give him an excuse to not have to do this. He's dying for there to be a knock at the door and someone say, 'Bob, your nightmare is over. You're off the case. There's no need for it.' He's dying for someone to say, 'Beckwith's just died of a heart attack. It's over, Bob. Go home.' That doesn't happen, and he has to face what he has to do. He sits there and says, 'For God's sake,' and there's the Medgar line that he thinks to himself; 'I don't know if I'm going to heaven or hell, but I'm going from Jackson.'"

The night after the exhumation scene in the military cemetery, the one in which Bobby and Van Evers and Charlie Crisco were there together just as they had been at Arlington for the real exhumation in 1991, Baldwin and his wife, Kim Basinger, took Bobby and Peggy to dinner. "I remember looking at Bob and thinking to myself, 'You know, I'm glad that you exist, what an honor for me to play you in a movie.' In making a movie you have to have this instant freeze-dried familiarity with people. You've really got to go from zero to sixty. Then you never see them again as long as you live. You have love scenes with women where you're putting your tongue down into their spinal column and the next thing you know you never see them for as long as you live. It's very odd. But I'll tell you one thing that I know about this movie deep in my heart, I know I'm always going to be friends with Bobby DeLaughter."

———

The magnet of this movie, of course, was the director himself. On the set that last day Rob Reiner talked about the problems involved, particularly the familiar one of being accurate and true to history and at the same time trying to make the film dramatic and entertaining. "If I were making this story up, I might not have Bobby find the gun in his father-in-law's house. Not because I don't think it's amazing. It *is* amazing, but it's not believable. The audience may sit there and say, 'They made this up. This can't have happened.' So in a made-up story I might have him find the gun but find it in a more believable way and still make it dramatic. But it *did* happen.

"There was another major problem I wouldn't have had if there were not historical constraints. If I were just going to start from scratch and make a story up about a white supremacist who murdered a civil rights leader thirty years ago, there's the young man who finally brought him to justice. Here I've got this devil incarnate represented by Byron De La Beckwith, and I've got this hero represented by Bobby DeLaughter. What I'd do in the courtroom setting, I'd have them face off there. I'd have fireworks in the traditional dramatic elements of making a movie. But we know that Byron De La Beckwith didn't take the witness stand in the third trial. He did in the first two, but not in the third. So now I'm hamstrung. The antagonist and the protagonist can't clash on cross-examination. In the middle of the third act I'm having to constantly try to find ways to make it interesting and dramatic and at the same time be responsible to the accuracy of the history. That's been the hardest thing for me. I feel I have to be as exacting as possible, so that when people talk about Medgar Evers, they know that this is what happened."

He would not attend the wrap party the next night, he said, because it would be too sad for him. "I've had more emotional moments in the making of this film than in all the films I've done put together. This has been the most valuable and worthwhile experience for me since I started making movies. I know I'll never have this experience again ever."

—

The final shot of a movie is called "the martini," going back to the silent-film era, when that event was appropriately celebrated. On the caterers' truck on July 25, Day 61 of 61 days, was a sign: MARTINI DAY CAFE. The site of this milestone was an attractive, affluent domicile with appurtenances of the South, crepe myrtles and a magnolia, set near a quiet street in Pasadena, one of the oldest neighborhoods in Southern California, seat of old turn-of-the-century money. In *Ghosts of Mississippi* this would represent the home of Caroline Moore, widow of Judge Russel Moore and Bobby DeLaughter's former mother-in-law. Bobby and his kids, played by the child actors Lucas Black, Alexa Vega, and Joseph Tello, would arrive unannounced during Mrs. Moore's weekly bridge game. Bobby had come to see if he could find Byron De La Beckwith's murder weapon. The scene of his actually locating it in an upstairs den had already been filmed on a soundstage in Culver City. Tonight's last scene would be of Bobby's arrival at the house and his confrontation with Caroline, played by Diane Ladd, and three other bridge ladies. In the screenplay this was Scene 70, and the additional angle shots were 70A, 70B, 70C, 70D, and 70E. 70E would be the wrap.

This was a 6:00 P.M. call, and at the base tent for "breakfast" people greeted one another with their Good mornings. As they were setting up in the house, it began to rain, and someone in the crew remembered that it had rained in Woodville, Mississippi, on the first day of shooting, with no rain since then in either Mississippi or California—until now, the last day. Since these were interior scenes, the weather didn't matter, and it wasn't much of a rain anyway. Later, inside the house, they had finished Take 6 of Scene 70. *"Okay! Good! We got this!"*

During the break before 70A, the director began circulating through the house with an empty plastic bucket marked INTERIOR SPACKLING PASTE. "Roll the drums!" he shouted. It was a Reiner tradition on the final shooting to persuade every member of the cast and crew to put in a twenty-dollar bill with his name on it for a drawing. On every Friday of filming there had been similar drawings, but with a lower ante of five-dollar bills. He returned to the monitor with a handful of twenties in the bucket. "Put in as many as you want. Increases your chance of winning. Increases your chance of losing. The last night. Twenty-dollar day. What's happening here? That's all anyone has is hundred-dollar bills? Everybody knew it was a twenty-dollar day."

Alec Baldwin threw in several twenty-dollar bills with Lyn McKissick's and the executive assistant Trish Gallaher's names on them, and there was more applause all round. "These are for Lyn and Trish," he said. (Both of them were several months pregnant, and it was they who would eventually take the pot.) One by one the others tossed twenties into the bucket—bridge ladies, grips, gaffers, electricians, teamsters, child actors, makeup and hair people, set dressers. The director of photography threw in a twenty.

"Ladies and gentlemen, John Seale just brought it to one thousand, eight hundred and sixty dollars. Keep it coming!" the director implored. George Bamber, the second assistant director, was a reluctant gambler, he reminded the crowd, and had to be persuaded to participate on five-dollar days. He won two Fridays in a row, and when he left the movie his replacement won the following Friday.

Scene 70B, Take 1. "Two thousand, five hundred twenty dollars! Frankie, pick it up with the kids running in. Let's widen this shot a little bit. Lucas, Lexie, Joseph—to your marks! I need to get a position for Joseph."

Scene 70B, Take 2. "At the point at which Diane says, 'Ladies, you know Bobby,' put the kids in their positions."

70B, Take 4. "And cut! Very good!"

70B, Take 5. "Joseph, move a little more to your right, little buddy. Two thousand, six hundred forty dollars. I'm going to match the pot. If I win the draw, I won't take the money."

70B, Take 7. "I need to see Burt in the foreground. You can lean as much as you want, but not when Diane's talking. Fifty-two hundred and eighty. Biggest pot ever!"

It was hot in the crowded house, and from outside there was the sound of thunder, and the whole set was illuminated by a bolt of lightning. After a break Alec Baldwin returned from his trailer. He had just heard of a bombing at Centennial Park in Atlanta. Several people went outside to the snack truck, which had a TV. The details were sketchy. Charles Newirth remembered the Oklahoma City bombing had occurred during the wrapping up of *The American President*. The mood of the set was more serious now.

Scene 70C, Take 5. "Cut. Good. Print that one. Let's move on." The director stood up. "Lucas, Joseph, and Alexa are finished in the movie. You did great, you little guys." Everyone clapped, and there were hugs and kisses as the children made their final departure. It was getting on to midnight as the work continued. "We're approaching the finish," Frankie Capra said. People kept coming in with news of Atlanta.

The concluding scenes, 70D and 70E, would be of Diane Ladd opening the front door to be greeted by Alec Baldwin. Scene 70E, Take 2. "Very good! Let's do one more and we've got this."

Scene 70E, Take 3. "Print that! Diane's last scene. Alec's last scene. Last scene!" There was applause in the darkness beyond the lights, then one by one people began to leave.

These people had been working together for five months, often fourteen hours a day or more, at a high level of skill on a difficult and emotional story. In these final days of the filming, a subdued yet palpable emotion seemed to have touched everyone. I had observed this sentiment in expressions, in words, in silences. I knew it was genuine and wondered how to explain it. And then I knew: Given all that it was and could be, this movie had been an uncommon and even passionate thing for them. They were affected by its history, and it was winding down. They did not want it to end. Would it be successful?

The wrap party the following evening left much to be desired. It was decidedly anticlimactic. It was held in the murky basement of a restaurant in three or four separate rooms, and people couldn't mingle. It was crowded and noisy. Also, it was very dark and no one could see each other. It reminded me of a University of Mississippi fraternity party. This was eventually rectified, however, by the Mississippi contingent, which on this occasion also included Medgar Evers's children and grandchildren. They got together around one long table, asked for candles so they could see one another, and partied into the Beverly Hills night.

Chapter 12

ON THE BIG SCREEN

The final dailies, of Friday night's concluding scenes in the house in Pasadena, were viewed in the Cecil B. De Mille Projection Room in Culver City on Monday. The director was the last to arrive. John Grisham's *A Time to Kill*, which was also set in 1990s Mississippi and was filmed in Canton, only twenty miles north of Jackson, and involved a murder and a courtroom drama, had recently been released, and Reiner had just been to see it in an L.A. theater. "It's got pyrotechnics!" he told the others. "And rape, pillage, burnings, sex, and Sandra Bullock tied to a tree." He paused, with a look of concern. "Ours doesn't have any of that," he said, sounding rueful, as if wishing for the moment it did. "And it grossed fourteen million dollars the first weekend." Then, with a touch of condescension, "It celebrates vigilante justice." And, from worry to anger: "Vigilante justice!"

Later that day we took a last stroll around the Culver City studio. It was strangely hushed. In a corner of the back lot a modest scene for a TV movie was being filmed. The soundstages, so full of frenetic activity when they were filming *Ghosts of Mississippi*, were dark and deserted. I expected at any moment to see the specter of the slain Thomas Ince in his bowler hat staring down from the rafters. The Hinds County courtroom was gone. The D.A.'s offices were gone. Hollywood had moved on.

—

The editing of a film is essential to its rhythm and tempo. In Hollywood in the thirties, forties, and early fifties directors almost never edited their own pictures. In the highly compartmentalized studio system the editing department performed that task, and the director quickly moved on to another movie. Now, of course, the director is central to the process. Movie editing has been revolutionized by computers. Before the advent of the Avid Film Composer in the late 1980s, it would have taken the chief editor, Bob Leighton (who would have been editing all along from the first day), a week or two to finish his rough assembly of the film, then Reiner would need five to eight weeks to get a cut he was happy with. It was difficult, unwieldy work, with celluloid cut and spliced by human hand, then viewed through rudimentary Moviola gadgets. With the new technique the film was digitized and every printed take fed into a computer. With this advanced editing system, the director had taken three days on the most recent film, *The American President*. *Ghosts of Mississippi* was a somewhat more complicated movie, and the editing would require two to three weeks. Many thousands of feet of disconnected pictures would have to be condensed to a fraction of that footage, depending on the running time decided on. Then Reiner would take a look at it with a selected audience, go back and make some changes, and start working on the music.

I had earlier gotten a telephone call from Jimmy Buffett, who had read Rick Bragg's article on *Ghosts* in *The New York Times*. I had known Buffett for years. He was a fellow Mississippian, he said, loved Medgar Evers, knew the story in his heart, and offered to compose and sing an original song for the beginning or ending of *Ghosts*. Other motifs were decided on, however. The musical score had already been assigned to Marc Shaiman, who had worked with the director on *Misery, A Few Good Men, North,* and *The American President,* receiving an Oscar nomination for the latter. Since the whole movie took place in Mississippi and there were references to Robert Johnson, and since Medgar worked as an insurance agent and later for the NAACP in the Mississippi Delta, Delta blues music would be essential, as would gospel.

A Time to Kill was on everyone's mind. And yet another John Grisham work, *The Chamber,* had recently been filmed in Mississippi and would be released in September. Counting *Ghosts,* there would be three movies set in that state, all with courtroom climaxes, coming out within six months of one another. Was there a saturation point? Would audiences confuse them? Would the national obsession with Mississippi simply dissipate overnight one of these days? Why weren't they doing movies about Arkansas?

One afternoon Reiner mused on the fate of such movies and the workings of modern Hollywood. The face of the industry changed forever in 1975, he judged, with *Jaws,* the first film that could be called a blockbuster, one of that breed that went out and tore up the box office. Then came the *Star Wars* pictures, and Indiana Jones. "With the blockbuster mentality in this town everybody was shooting to get that hundred-million-dollar movie in. Since then it's gone even further in that direction, and it's very disturbing to me and some others. Not that I haven't made pictures that turned out to be blockbusters. Yet *A Few Good Men* has people sitting in courtrooms and talking, and there are no explosions, no sex, no nudity, no special effects."

A more recent Hollywood phenomenon was being called "the first weekend," which had startling parallels in other creative businesses, including book publishing, in which the blockbuster books were squeezing the good books dry. Ticket sales go immediately into computers, and studio analysts on the basis of first-weekend numbers and how other new movies had performed could forecast with a decent accuracy a film's "legs," or future commercial durability. "If you don't get that first weekend, you're dead," Reiner said. "You're going to be thrown out of the theater. You don't even have a chance. I did a picture that came out ten years ago called *Stand by Me*. That picture cost seven-point-five million to make and wound up doing about fifty-five million in America. It's done much more overseas. But it never made more than three and a half million on any given weekend. In those days you could still play a picture for a while and it would play out and you could make money. Now, if you don't get a big share of the audience in the first weekend in these tenplexes and twelveplexes and eightplexes, you're gone.

"It used to be the studio was a big operation. Now they're owned by monstrous conglomerations, and the studio is like this tiny little speck in the portfolio. The mentality of making films is so far re-moved from the creative process that it's astounding anything of quality ever gets made. It's very rough out there, and it's getting worse. Joel Siegel asked me the other day on television, 'What do you think, will *Ghosts* make money?' I said, 'No, I don't think it will make a dime,' based on what I see out there—*Independence Day* and such."

—

The first showing of *Ghosts of Mississippi* was held in a United Artists theater in downtown Pasadena in September, only six weeks after the final shooting. The talk about the movie in the trade was already good, and this would be the equivalent of the old sneak previews, but organized by a firm of pollsters specializing in consumer-marketing research that laid claims, I was told, to being "demographically scientific." The press had not been informed of the showing. The audience that filled the theater contained quite a few young people; it was about 20 percent black, and many were casually dressed in shorts, blue jeans, and sneakers, a distinctly American scene. The research company had already selected twenty or so of their number as a "focus group" to answer specific questions after the screening. The entire audience had already been given questionnaires. The main value of such evenings, it was said, was to get a visceral "feel."

The mood was solemn. Indeed the men from the research company in charge of distributing and then collecting the questionnaires, or preview cards, reminded me in their earnest solicitude a little of undertakers overseeing a big funeral. Lewis Colick had arrived early and was uncommonly on edge. After a similar showing in this same theater of the movie *Bulletproof,* for which he had written the script, the director had decided to reshoot the entire last scene.

Rob and Michele took seats near the back. He also was uncharacteristically nervous. Myrlie Evers was there, and so were the Castle Rock executives, and Carl Reiner, Fred Zollo, and his producing partner, Nick Paleologos from Boston. Zollo was skeptical of these evenings: "When you write a book, do you send it to a lot of strangers to read for possible revisions?" A man from the research firm stood before the audience and explained that they were about to see a "work in progress" without credits and with temporary music, called a "temp track." The music would be a mélange drawn from *The Shawshank Redemption, The American President,* and *Little Women.*

In his book *Monster* John Gregory Dunne confesses to the uneasiness he always had watching for the first time a movie whose screenplay he wrote, "seeing all the flaws and none of the virtues, if there are any," and one could imagine that the director, the producers, and the screenwriter felt much the same that evening:

It is unlike reading the manuscript of a book one wrote; a book does not cost millions of dollars to write, it does not have a predetermined release date, a book one can toss out and begin over again, with no one the wiser. Given the choice, I would have preferred seeing the movie alone in a screening room. In a theater, I count the people who go to the bathroom or to the concession stand, and wait to see if they return; I listen for coughs, watch for signs of restlessness, try to read body language, look for the whisperers, my eye on the audience rather than the screen, my demeanor is that of a school monitor overseeing a study hall.

As the film began, the audience seemed to like what they saw. They laughed at many of the humorous lines, especially Bill Macy's rendition of Charlie Crisco, and at several points they vigorously applauded. When it was over, they handed in their questionnaires. The movie people circled around the director, everyone trying to get his ear. Myrlie Evers embraced him. His father shook his hand and said, "A movie to be remembered. I'm proud of you." Rob Reiner said he was worried about the ending, that the applause he expected there was not all that impressive.

"We'd better go hear these numbers," Carl Reiner said. The research-company man, the "lead debriefer," had seated the twenty or so people in the focus group in the first two rows. In response to his questions, nine of them rated what they had seen "excellent," ten "very good," three "fair." Sixteen said they would "definitely" recommend it to friends. Some of the replies were oracular, others concise. "You really believe James Woods was that guy." "The second wife was very good." "Whoopi didn't age." "Whoopi moved me to tears at the ending, but I really didn't like it." "There are no movies like this out there now—a very important and moving film about real people and a real American problem." And so on.

Later, outside the theater, a stretch limo waiting for them at the curb, the director and his executives conferred again. A junkie drifted down the sidewalk like a scruffy tumbleweed in the wind and shouted to the driver, "Chauffeur-man! Hey, Chauffeur-man, you *proud* of yourself, aincha, baby?" Jeff Stott focused on the good scores that night. But if people get invited free, someone asked him, and got free popcorn and drinks, won't they inevitably give such high ratings? Not at all, he replied. He had been to Castle Rock showings that were trashed.

"I guess I'll have to do something about the ending," Reiner said. "We'll get back to work."

—

There was a lunch the next day in a private corner of the Maple Drive restaurant, known as the Castle Rock Commissary, with its view outside of a lush Beverly Hills thoroughfare and its flourishing panoply of bougainvillea. Zollo and Paleologos were there, as well as Lewis Colick. "Let's talk about the movie," Reiner said. *The American President* and *A Few Good Men*, he said, got a 90 percent "definitely recommend" rating, and they were entertainments. "Ours got a 78 percent—a true story about race that starts with a man getting shot in the back." The best scene in the film, he thought, was Bobby's conversation with Charles Evers at the Jackson radio station. Alec Baldwin was excellent but would not get enough credit because of the James Woods performance.

Rob Reiner was known as a director who rarely filmed any major scene that would not be in a finished movie, but now all that would go out the window because, among other things, this was such a complex story to tell, and it was faithful to real facts that might be a little tame. The length of the film now was two hours and eighteen minutes, and cuts were discussed, particularly near the conclusion, to tighten the pace.

The entire opening scene, filmed in Woodville, Mississippi, of Senator Bilbo delivering his racist harangue as young Charles and Medgar Evers looked on, would be deleted; the only visible evidence of a movie ever having been shot in that milieu would be Bobby Joe Garren's twice transplanted crepe myrtles. The film now would open with Beckwith's Valiant coming south through the Delta the night of the murder and the JFK voice-over.

Because he thought it too expository, Lewis Colick wanted to cut an early scene of a lunch at the Jackson Country Club, the one filmed at the Natchez mansion after the manager of the first one backed out, but it was decided that this scene was important for setting up many subsequent situations.

Parts of Bobby's investigation and also a few brief courtroom sequences would be deleted. And I personally regretted the cutting of the scene in the state supreme court chamber in which I played a reporter. Because it was judged anticlimactic, the concluding scene in which Bobby and his daughter replanted the bottle tree had already been dropped. Now the final scene in the movie would be of Charles Evers walking away from the courthouse after learning of the verdict. Key deletions would be made from the moment the jury went into deliberation to Myrlie's speech after the announcement of the verdict, including the simulated rainstorm and Myrlie and her children praying in their hotel room. Her speech itself would be shortened for dramatic effect, but shots of the interracial celebration after the verdict would be extended to let the consequences adequately "sink in." After these changes another screening would be arranged the following week with an audience drawn from "different demographics."

Regarding historical accuracy there were several aspects to be considered: the script itself, the director, the actors' interpretations, the physical elements—sets, set decoration, props, landscapes, vehicles—and the instances of artistic license. Accuracy and truth are two different things. I would come to consider *Ghosts of Mississippi* 100 percent faithful to the spirit of the truth and 80 percent to the spirit of accuracy. For the record there were four principal instances of license. These would be brought up later by some influential reviewers and presaged a problem attendant to contemporary social movies rooted in fact.

• The window of Bobby's Cherokee was not smashed and painted with a swastika. It *could* have been smashed, of course, but not directly in front of the Hinds County Courthouse (a location in full view of the police) as in the film.

• The confrontation in the courthouse men's room between Bobby and Beckwith was an embellishment of the much briefer and less histrionic real encounter, although this too could have happened.

• There was no frantic flight from the DeLaughter house after the telephoned bomb scare, although there *had* been such a threat. (And Bobby himself always thought it came from Thelma Beckwith herself.)

• In the powerful courtroom denouement, as cited earlier, the penultimate cross-examination of the alibi witness, the former cop from Greenwood, was performed not by Bobby but by D.A. Peters.

Bobby DeLaughter was uncomfortable with a few other embell-ishments. The scene in which he has lunch at the country club with his parents, who expressed criticisms of blacks, concerned him, because he was never a member of a country club and his parents generally supported him in the Beckwith investigation. Also, he never sang the song "Dixie" to help his frightened daughter go to sleep as Alec Baldwin did in the film—"a broad stroke," a subsequent reviewer would comment, "some might trace to the hand of Hollywood."

Lewis Colick, whose screenplay called for a considerably longer movie than the one finally released, would later cite four major changes in the final draft of his script which were made before filming had begun.

• His had more flashbacks to Medgar. Colick contended these gave more of a sense of Medgar as both an activist and a family man. One such scene was deleted, in which Myrlie is looking out the window of their house, and at a strange sound outside Medgar pushes her to the floor. In another, Medgar, dressed as a share-cropper, watches as Emmett Till's mutilated body is dredged out of the Tallahatchie River.

• His script made it a little more Myrlie's movie. With her on the verge of closure after thirty years, this version went more into her personal life, character, and family relationships.

• An eight-page scene was cut involving the exhumation and autopsy in which Bobby talks with Van Evers. "Bobby realizes he's inadvertently become part of something really big. If Medgar had been Joe Schmo who had been murdered thirty years ago and someone had come to Bobby, he'd have gone the last mile on that too. However, with Medgar it was different. He was a truly great man. I don't think the finished movie gives an adequate sense of Bobby's gradual recognition of what he's getting involved in, some-thing of utmost importance to America and Mississippi and his-tory. All this was finally dealt with in a quick montage."

• There was more of Beckwith in the Colick script, including one long and vivid scene. "Rob loved that scene, but I know he didn't want to make a three-hour movie." This scene was a confrontation between Beckwith and his nephew-in-law, Reed Massengill in a restaurant. Beckwith thinks Massengill, a writer, is interviewing him to do a glowing biography but ascertains that he is going for the truth. "Beckwith reveals a side of himself that makes him more multidimensional—one of those marginal men from a lost legacy with sexual problems, drinking problems. In this scene Beckwith scares Massengill to death. It shows what makes Beckwith tick. It gets into the deep darkness of him. It shows why he *hated* Medgar so much."

—

The second screening, this one before an older and more middle-class audience, embodied the new editing. It was warmly received. The approval rating was considerably higher than at the first showing.

Three gala premieres were now scheduled, in New York City on December 8, Jackson on December 12, and Los Angeles on December 16. The movie would open in selected cities just before Christmas to be eligible for the 1996 Oscars, and the national release would be shortly after the first of the new year. It would receive a PG-13 rating.

In Jackson Bobby could be seen driving to work in the same Jeep Cherokee made famous in the vortex incident; he had bought it for three thousand dollars. Dr. Michael Baden invited him to give a presentation on the Beckwith case before an international conference of homicide detectives in New York, where he received standing applause despite the fact that the Russian translator could not understand his accent. In a television interview Thelma Beckwith reiterated that it was Lee Harvey Oswald and not her husband who had murdered Medgar Evers, and that DeLay considered himself a political prisoner, victim of a menacing conspiracy between blacks and the liberal news media seeking to control America. When Whoopi Goldberg, now rehearsing a play in New York, was told that Myrlie Evers liked the movie and Whoopi's portrayal of her, she gave a sigh of relief. "Wheew! That's one imposing woman!"

—

A knowledgeable Hollywood veteran explained to me the differences between movie premieres in Los Angeles and those held elsewhere. In L.A. everyone is jaded. Three types of people attend L.A. premieres: those connected in some way with the movie; the curious; and those who want it to fail. Even in New York City people got excited about a movie premiere. New York premieres are fun. And premieres in the provinces are exhilarating.

In New York City JoAnne and I took Peggy and Bobby DeLaughter, as long promised, to a dinner that I was calling the Last Supper, as this was the night before the first general screening of a movie that would in all likelihood change their lives, as Alec Baldwin had predicted. Given his mild persona, Bobby had always been apprehensive of the attention the movie was placing on him, and on this night he was jittery. By coincidence James Woods and his brother were at an adjoining table; it was odd to see Byron De La Beckwith on the Upper East Side. The DeLaughters had never before been to New York, and we discussed in detail its considerable whims. There was much talk about the reception of the movie, and a toast or two to the DeLaughters and their Last Supper.

The premiere the following evening was at the magnificent old Ziegfeld Theater on West Fifty-fourth Street, once the site of the Ziegfeld Follies, and there was the traditional phalanx of limousines as they approached the klieg lights and beacon lights and the red carpet running from the front curb to the lobby. More than one thousand people filled the theater to capacity. This was a benefit for People for the American Way and the National Resources Defense Council, and the audience was mostly rich white Eastern liberals. Very few black people were present, two of the most notable being Coretta Scott King and Maya Angelou. Rob Reiner made opening remarks and introduced some of the actors present and the real people they were playing—Alec and Bobby, Bill Macy and Crisco, Jerry Levine and Jerry Mitchell, Benny Bennett, Whoopi Goldberg. Then he introduced Myrlie Evers, and everyone stood to applaud. She praised the movie and the director. It was an enthusiastic audience, and *Ghosts* went over very well.

—

The Jackson premiere was four days later. In New York Myrlie Evers told Reiner she would not attend the Mississippi showing. She had a premonition there would be some kind of trouble. Would there be trouble? the director wanted to know. Should security be tightened?

There was no trouble. At a party beforehand attended by prominent white and black Mississippians James Meredith, who had integrated Ole Miss with the resulting infamous riots in 1962—the Last Battle of the Civil War, it was called—was asked what effect he thought *Ghosts of Mississippi* might have on the state. "It won't do any harm," he said. Charles Evers was wearing a PT 109 tie clasp President Kennedy had given him in the Oval Office on the day of his brother's funeral; this was the first time he had worn it since then. He was worried, he said, that his emotions would not allow him to sit through the entire movie. Jeff Stott of Castle Rock was wondering if the movie might rekindle the same kind of hostility that the 1994 trial did. Benny Bennett was telling companions of the impact the Evers murder scene had had on him when he saw the film for the first time in New York. "I was a cop for many years," he was saying. "I've seen a lot of murders. None has bothered me. But when I saw that murder on the screen, the hair on the back of my neck was standing up and shivers ran down my spine to the tip of my toes."

The showing was held in Thalia Mara Hall, the city auditorium, only two blocks from the courthouse where so many of the scenes had been shot—admission free but by invitation only. The premiere of *A Time to Kill* had taken place here not long before, and Jackson again beheld the cavalcade of limos "lined up nose to tail" as the

Clarion-Ledger described it, the beacon and klieg lights pointing to the sky, the long red carpet stretching from Pascagoula Street to the lobby. There was much excitement in the air. The auditorium was packed to capacity with twenty-five hundred people, roughly half white and half black, and comprised one of the most arresting gatherings in the state's history, the largest audience ever to watch a movie at one location in Mississippi. (The premiere of *A Time to Kill* had been conducted in four smaller showings.) It was a "complicated" audience, as someone described it: young and old black activists, Old Jackson white conservatives, veteran white liberals, politicians, academics, cops, industrialists, white and black professionals and pastors and teachers and high school and college students. The director received a spontaneous standing ovation as he came to the stage. He called the movie "the most extraordinary experience I've ever had," thanked Mississippians for their help on the film, and introduced various of the actors to further standing applause. Alec Baldwin, who had recently been in Canada filming a movie with Anthony Hopkins, introduced Bobby DeLaughter, who made a long speech. Many in the audience had come as early as two hours before and were restless.

As the movie ran, all was quiet and hushed at first, but gradually the response became even more enthusiastic than in New York, with a number of ovations during the screening. There was jubilance when the final credits came. As the members of the audience gradually filed out, they appeared emotionally touched. Medgar Evers's sister, Elizabeth Evers Jordan, was there from Chicago. "I'm feeling really, really happy," she said. About Myrlie: "She held that all those years. She would never give up. The movie shows it."

Rubye Bryant Brakefield of Jackson, whom Medgar had given a ride home from an NAACP meeting the night he was killed, said, "The Lord works things in mysterious ways. I felt the time would come. I've been waiting for it. We needed this."

Charles Holmes, a professor at Tougaloo College, said the movie was fairly faithful to the real trial that he and his classes had attended. "I think it might show some progress had been made in terms of justice or race relations. But I have mixed emotions about it. Some may say that things have not changed."

Bishop William Houck of the Catholic Diocese of Jackson said, "It could challenge us Mississippians to continue to improve our own, not just way of life, but caring for all people in the state. We have not yet solved all the problems." Restaurateur Malcolm White commented, "If everyone can leave the theater feeling better about being in Mississippi and moving toward better race relations," then the film will have been worth it.

Charles Evers, who sat in front of me, stayed for the whole screening and was visibly moved. He found the reenactment of his brother's murder acutely painful. "It was almost unbearable, but there comes a time when you've got to make up your mind to do what you have to do. And I just felt like maybe this is the time I had to sit there, regardless of how it hurts, with the rest of the two thousand–plus people and see it through." He appreciated, he said, how the movie portrayed Bobby DeLaughter. Race relations in Mississippi today "are not what they're supposed to be," he said. "But the mere fact that there were many whites at the viewing of the picture of Medgar says it all. And I want to thank all the white people and blacks who came, but especially the whites because they didn't have to come." During the trial it had gratified him to see "old whites and old blacks, young whites and young blacks sit on a jury and convict an old racist bigot white man for killing a black man who happened to be my brother." The most significant thing to Evers was that "Mississippi convicted him and no one race can take credit for it." *Ghosts of Mississippi* showed that, he said.

In the generally warm and laudatory—indeed, almost celebrative—spirit of the Mississippi showing there were problems, however, problems that could be traced back to the film's inception and that would soon surface publicly in various reviews and articles. First there was Myrlie Evers's glaring absence from the home-state premiere. Then, during the opening ceremonies in the theater before that showing, Bobby DeLaughter had turned what was expected to be a brief talk about the significance of the film into a long apology for its departures from fact and to his family and fellow members of the district attorney's office for the way they were depicted. The director was stunned and furious. "Bobby's ruined our Mississippi premiere," he said afterward. "I could've done an Oliver Stone on this movie, but I didn't. Did they want me to do an Oliver Stone, for God's sake?"

In the next morning's *Clarion-Ledger,* under the headline GHOSTS IS EPIC EVIDENCE OF GOOD OVERCOMING EVIL, Orley Hood, the state's most widely read journalist, called the movie "a monument to vision, to integrity, to righteous stubbornness" and applauded it as "a victory both real and artistic." He went on: "The film gripped the audience, wrapping the 2,500 viewers deep in their own emotions, their own personal histories, their recollections of the endless struggle against human rights abuses. This is Alec Baldwin's picture, a career role and career performance. James Woods's every gesture, every nuance as Beckwith, was a body punch, a terrible reminder of a past that cannot be ignored."

Chapter 13

TROUBLES

There had been two grand premieres, with one more still to come, and a vast media promotion campaign, especially in New York surrounding that premiere. Almost all the major television talk shows did interviews one-on-one or in combination with Rob Reiner, Alec Baldwin, James Woods, Whoopi Goldberg, Myrlie Evers, and Bobby DeLaughter. For some time the Castle Rock marketing department had been dotting prime-time national television with trailers featuring Baldwin, Goldberg, and Woods. In the New York media blitz, the press and TV were brought in at ten-minute intervals for interviews with the director, the actors, and Bobby DeLaughter. Reiner himself did dozens of interviews in two days. The mood was one of excitement and optimism. Castle Rock believed that reviews would be 75 percent positive, 25 percent negative, and that given the nature and substance of the story the movie would have a salubrious impact on the country in racially troubled times.

On the *Oprah Winfrey Show* there had been an especially poignant moment. On camera Myrlie withdrew the wallet Medgar had on him the night he died and displayed the five-dollar bill with blood caked on Abraham Lincoln's face, and Medgar's 1962 poll-tax voter-registration form, also streaked with blood. She presented the registration form to Reiner, she said, as a gesture of appreciation from her and her family. Never an unemotional man, the director choked up, as did Oprah Winfrey, and when the camera panned in on the studio audience it was hard to find a dry eye.

—

As the main players anxiously awaited the national reviews that would come with the movie's release in selected cities on December 20, suddenly many of the intrinsic tensions detailed earlier in this narrative that had been more or less resolved during the filming itself began to erupt in public, as if the very proximity of its release were the catalyst. It would soon be not unlike a train wreck, cars shattered or out of control. The threads of this denouement were in the circumstances of the story itself, of course, in Mississippi, in Hollywood, in the nation, in the real characters and events, in "historical accuracy," as if all was beginning to be caught in the clashing voices of the contemporary society. Soon Rob Reiner would be like Brer Rabbit getting stuck in the Tar Baby.

Shortly before the Mississippi premiere the *Clarion-Ledger* published a lengthy front-page story going into detail on various personal and dramatic elements and stresses in the drama as previously presaged. Not long after this, on the day before the L.A. premiere, the *Los Angeles Times* ran a prominent reportorial piece examining personal facets of the film. The import of these articles, the first of them widely read in Mississippi, the other in California and the nation, was that for the first time the interior strains among the principals in the story, which had remained quiescent for a long time, were beginning to spill out publicly.

Had filmmakers served history or drama—or both—with the movie? John Webb asked in the *Clarion-Ledger*. "When Castle Rock producers set out to make *Ghosts of Mississippi*, they faced a dilemma as old as Shakespeare's *Henry IV* and as recent as Oliver Stone's *JFK*: Either you tell a story exactly as it happened, with the possible loss of dramatic moments, or you fictionalize events to engross the audience—focusing, for instance, on a compelling protagonist like Bobby DeLaughter, portrayed by Alec Baldwin."

The simmering disaffections regarding the script among members of the district attorney's office now became public. In the days to come the film would almost never be mentioned in Bobby's presence by anyone in the office. D.A. Peters told the *Clarion-Ledger* he had no intention of seeing the movie. "This was a trial," he said. "It was not a cause." Peters again objected that in the film it was Bobby who performed the crucial cross-examination of the Greenwood alibi witness rather than himself. The movie had him driving a Lincoln Continental rather than his sports utility car, he commented. "There are a lot of accurate things, like getting the court reporter's pen right, or gold-rimmed glasses. But they played footloose and fancy-free with important events," including the scene that implied political motives for the trial. Bobby DeLaughter in the newspaper report praised Peters for his significant contributions to the case. The movie was 80 percent accurate, he judged. "And for the other 20 percent, they've taken actual events and expanded on them or assigned them to a different character." Americans may still think *Mississippi Burning* was an accurate portrayal of the recent history of the state, he said. "The upshot of *Mississippi Burning* was that Mississippi cannot be relied upon to handle the situation. This film shows just the opposite." Unlike *A Time to Kill* with its mass scenes of hooded Klansmen and black activists waving their fists at one another, *Ghosts of Mississippi*, Bobby said, portrays a case that was "investigated, prosecuted, and celebrated by white and black together."

Lewis Colick was interviewed. He said he assigned the alibi-witness cross-examination to the DeLaughter character reluctantly. "Rob Reiner is the guy who said, 'This is what we're going to do.' It's not a documentary, it's a work of art. And you give your hero *everything*. You have to be faithful to history and basically tell it the way it happened, but you also have to help the story. My original film had more scope. I would never have envisioned a movie version of those events that would come in under three hours. But to get this made at all—you have to be grateful."

Additional criticism, when it began to appear, came from all directions, and in Mississippi not just from traditional white conservatives, hostile to the dredging up of the catastrophic past—nothing that pristine in *this* state. The night after the Jackson premiere Fred Zollo was in the bar of Hal & Mal's with some friends, including Homer Best, attorney for the Sheriff's Department, Ward Emling of the film office, and location man Charlie Harrington, and they were talking about what could be done to foster the movie business in Jackson. The discussion turned to *Ghosts of Mississippi*. The group had been joined by a Midwest-educated Jackson lawyer in his early forties, a prominent white liberal who had migrated from Tennessee years before. He turned on the producer and began castigating him for making movies about white people and the civil rights movement. "You stupid asshole!" he exclaimed and, after further haranguing, concluded, "You're not only an asshole, but a stupid asshole *idiot!*"

—

There would be more in this spirit to come nationally, though considerably less pointed. Shortly before the L.A. premiere on December 16, the movie industry's advance trade reviews appeared, setting the theme for many of the general reviews to follow. Political correctness carried the day in these trade reviews: Rob Reiner made the wrong film. The hero is white.

"There is certainly an intriguing story to be told here," *The Hollywood Reporter* judged, "but unfortunately it isn't the one Reiner . . . and Colick have chosen to tell. By focusing almost entirely on the trials and tribulations of . . . the white D.A. . . . and the toll it took on Bobby's family, while relegating the Myrlie Evers angle to the sidelines, the film resonates a been-there, done-that familiarity, particularly in light of the summer's *A Time to Kill*." And *Variety*: "When future generations turn to this era's movies for an account of the struggles for racial justice in America, they'll learn the surprising lesson that such battles were fought and won by square-jawed white boys."

This criticism was by no means unexpected, of course, since *Mississippi Burning* had inflamed vehement protestations for many of the same reasons. In *A Time to Kill,* a roguish white-knight lawyer succeeded in getting an acquittal for his black client who had murdered a white man. Both these movies were fiction. *Ghosts of Mississippi* was a true story. But that did not matter. Neither *Variety* nor *The Hollywood Reporter* found the film "dramatically satisfying" or "vivid and exciting." For this, the *Reporter* faulted the script, "which opts for truth over dramatic license." *Variety,* on the other hand, blamed the film's problems on lack of truth and too much dramatic license. Its reviewer, Godfrey Cheshire, attacked what he judged to be the film's blatant inaccuracies. He erroneously claimed the following:

1. That JFK's landmark civil rights speech did not occur on the night of Medgar Evers's murder.

2. That Charles Evers was a prominent politician in 1994, when the film showed him as a disc jockey, playing white people's kind of blues music.

3. That for a long time Myrlie Evers inexplicably withheld from Bobby DeLaughter the official transcripts of the 1964 trials.

4. That in the film there were no blacks in Bobby DeLaughter's office and no black police.

5. That Myrlie Evers and Bobby DeLaughter were too good, unrealistically so.

Regarding accuracy, it has to be pointed out that JFK's speech *did* occur on the night of the Evers murder. Charles Evers had not held political office since 1989 and now managed, announced, and spun discs for WMPR, a radio station in Jackson that played authentic down-home blues music. Myrlie Evers did withhold her copies of the 1964 trial transcripts from Bobby for a long time until he had gained her trust, and Whoopi Goldberg's film dialogue explained why. There *were* blacks in the film in the D.A.'s office, and there were many black police. In real life both Myrlie Evers and Bobby

DeLaughter were, in fact, idealists who had an exceedingly strong sense of right and wrong, uncommon personal integrity, and incredible emotional restraint. Had they been otherwise, they could probably never have succeeded in getting the Beckwith case reopened, and Medgar Evers's assassin would now be drinking mint juleps on his front porch under his Confederate banner in Signal Mountain, Tennessee.

Variety has great power in the motion-picture industry. In the view of the moviemakers, Cheshire's advance review would prove to be extremely damaging.

The *Los Angeles Times* reportorial piece, prominently published in the Sunday Calendar section before the Monday L.A. premiere, ran under the banner headline:

> WAKING THE GHOSTS
> Once again, Hollywood attempts to tell a story
> stemming from the civil rights era, and once
> again controversy is surely ensuing.

Ghosts of Mississippi, reporter Sean Mitchell wrote, "paints only part of the picture in choosing to focus on the story of the white assistant district attorney in Jackson, Mississippi, Bobby DeLaughter (played by Alec Baldwin), who went the final mile to win a conviction against Beckwith. The film pays less attention to Evers' widow, Myrlie (Whoopi Goldberg), who hounded authorities for 30 years to retry Beckwith—not to mention Evers himself, who is seen only briefly in a flashback to the night of his killing."

The story quoted Myrlie Evers at length. This was the first time since her speech at the Natchez Literary Festival in May that she had gone public with her concerns, and those remarks had not been covered in the press. She indicated to the *Times* that "she is unhappy with the finished film despite being quoted in publicity material as calling the movie 'wonderful.' . . . Myrlie Evers, as she herself puts it, 'worked for 30 years to bring the case to the place where Bobby DeLaughter *picked it up.*" The piece continued:

That Myrlie Evers . . . voices ambivalence about the film is surprising, since she served officially as a consultant to Reiner. In a phone interview from her home in Oregon, she chooses her words carefully in expressing her disappointment that her own pain and suffering and that of her three children are not larger factors in what ended up on the screen. "I have often described myself and my children as damaged goods, and in a sense we are. The wound is so deep it never really healed. I *wish* that could have been shown in the movie, what *we* went through. It was living hell.

"I wanted to be involved, and Rob was very generous with his time in listening to my suggestions and recommendations. But I know he felt he had to do it this way. It is his film, and I think he's a brilliant director. And Bobby DeLaughter deserves a tremendous amount of credit. But I suspect people will ask, 'What about Medgar? And what about his family?' " . . .

Asked how she felt about Goldberg's portrayal of her in *Ghosts of Mississippi,* Evers answers, "Whoopi Goldberg is a superb actress." There is a long pause before she adds, "I'm being very tactful. I don't want to cast any aspersions." . . .

For her, the film's happy ending, however, is muted.

"Perhaps one day," she says, "Hollywood will not say it has already been done and will be open to doing a full story on Medgar's life. I truly hope so."

Both Reiner and Zollo defended the film in the article. Reporter Jerry Mitchell, who broke the 1989 jury-tampering stories, when interviewed by the *Times* before he saw the movie at the New York premiere and complimented it, said he had problems with accuracy from his reading of the screenplay. He was a minor character in the movie, the *Times* pointed out. "The case would never have been re-opened without persistent pressure from the media," Mitchell said. "I think you miss some of that. And in reality it was a triumvirate of Bobby, Myrlie, and me. After the articles appeared, Myrlie used them to call for re-opening the case. I dug. Myrlie pushed. Bobby prosecuted." And he found it ironic that in the film

Bobby had been given the crucial cross-examination scene. Rob Reiner and the Castle Rock men were not pleased with Myrlie's on-the-record hesitations, which served to raise their personal stress levels several notches. But one would not have known this from the aura of the L.A. premiere.

The day after the *Los Angeles Times* story, the L.A. showing took place at the Mann National Theater in Westwood. It was a benefit for the NAACP, for which $100,000 was raised, and the capacity audience was racially mixed. Nearly all of *Ghosts'* actors, large and small, were there. Among the guests attending were Michael Douglas, Jamie Lee Curtis, James Caan, Teri Garr, and Billy Crystal. Once again the film was warmly received, if less exuberantly than in New York and Jackson. The honored guest was Myrlie Evers. In the opening ceremony she did not refer to her quoted comments in the *L.A. Times* of the previous day, but rather she first asked for and received a long standing ovation for the director. It was painful for her and her family to relive their suffering, she said, but it was worth it, for it was a fine, honest, and deeply emotional movie. She praised the cast. Everyone, she suggested, should win an Oscar. She discussed the civil rights movement, the NAACP, and the Medgar Evers project. *Ghosts of Mississippi,* she said, suggested hope for the future and was important because "it brings to a larger audience the awareness of how things were." She ended by celebrating Bobby DeLaughter as a hero. Alec Baldwin added: "I'm proud that Rob put this together. This is a tough one. This is hard to dramatize."

—

The film was released four days later in New York, L.A., Atlanta, and Washington, D.C., with the national date scheduled for January 3, 1997.

When the national print reviews started coming out, the personal anxieties stirred up by the film would be overtaken by them. In fact, many of these reviews unwittingly seemed to mirror some of these tensions, which began to emerge yet again. The reviews would be decidedly mixed; there were a number of excellent ones, but most were critical. There seemed little neutral ground. The trade reviews set the tone, followed by the big newspapers and magazines. The reviews were highly contradictory, as reviews sometimes are. A few attacked the film for artistic liberties (three or four quoted *Variety*'s specific charges of inaccuracies), others for too much mundane realism, but the most caustic ones criticized it not for what it was but for what it was *not* and what the reviewers wished it had been—the story of Medgar Evers and/or Myrlie Evers rather than the treatment of a white hero. Most reviewers who accepted *Ghosts of Mississippi* on its own terms, however, praised and recommended it. In this regard the perception of the movie was not unlike a Rorschach test: You can see anything you want to see, and what you see is who you are. The reviews that appeared during the first ten days would be a fairly reliable reflection of those that followed.

Under the headline BLACK HERO MISSING IN MOVIE DeWayne Wickham wrote in *USA Today* that "*Ghosts of Mississippi* treats the life and death of Medgar Evers as a mere backdrop to the story it tells about Bobby DeLaughter . . . who successfully prosecuted the bigot who shot the civil rights leader in the back. By so doing, the film's producers trivialize their claim that the movie is a true story. DeLaughter's story is but a historical footnote to the campaign Evers led in Mississippi against racial bigotry and discrimination—and the efforts of his widow to put his killer in jail." Richard Corliss in *Time* likened the film to *Mississippi Burning, Cry Freedom,* and other well-meaning movies about race, but "*Ghosts of Mississippi* is not really about the black civil rights struggle. It's about the white liberal's burden."

Roger Ebert, under the headline MISSISSIPPI FOCUSES ON WRONG STORY, observed in the Chicago *Sun-Times* that the "emotional center" of the film should probably be Myrlie Evers, and that Whoopi Goldberg plays her "like the guest of honor at a testimonial banquet," which is mostly the fault of the filmmakers "who see their material through white eyes and use the Myrlie character as a convenient conscience. . . . what we get, really, is self-congratulation: 'Whites may have been responsible for segregation, but by golly, aren't we doing a wonderful job of making amends.' "

LaMonte Brown in *The Mississippi Link* applauded Reiner for bringing the story to life, "but this isn't the movie they should have made." Kenneth Turan in the *L.A. Times* assailed the film for many of the same reasons, especially the white-hero aspect and the fact that the film, he said, was unfaithful to the real events, which could not have happened as portrayed. This was a persistent theme in other national reviews, that the story was a Hollywood lie, a contrived tale for effect, that could never have occurred in real life.

Teresa Wiltz, in the *Chicago Tribune,* proclaimed the film "a revisionist whitewashing," the latest in a long line of films from *To Kill a Mockingbird* to *Mississippi Burning* about the blacks' struggle for justice told through the experience of white males. According to Spike Lee, she reported, "These films (are) about the moral dilemma of the white liberal, and black people are pushed to the side. . . . [Hollywood executives] feel like they have to have a white lead to bring the audience in. And everything gets corrupted right then and there." Bernard Beck, associate professor of sociology at Northwestern University, was also cited: "These films are about a certain kind of white person who came of age at a certain age. That's who makes movies. There's a crisis of conscience that liberal, white progressive people have. It's no longer clear in white America who the good guys are. Today, race relations . . . make them pessimistic, confused, always putting their foot in their mouths. They like to remember a time when things made sense, when we were the good guys."

John Petrakis, also in the *Chicago Tribune,* analyzed the motives of the moviemakers and came to a different conclusion: The filmmakers "have such reverence for the civil rights movement and the principals involved that they take all the bumps, bruises, and rough edges out of the tale."

"This film runs so true to the Hollywood view of Southern white racism," Janet Maslin wrote in *The New York Times,* "that its hero's wife is the fading blond belle who won't stay with her man when the going gets tough."

The reviews that took the film to task for more aesthetic reasons emphasized such aspects as predictability, slowness of pace, patness, excessive delineation, "too real to be true," too much "haloes vs. horns," and that the moviemakers had a great story but did not seem to know what to do with it.

—

The *Jackson Advocate,* Mississippi's most prominent black newspaper, however, in a laudatory full-page review, praised Bobby DeLaughter, "who had the courage to face not only Byron De La Beckwith but the public criticism and political grandstanding which had surrounded the trial since the case was re-opened in 1989." Harper Barnes in the *St. Louis Post-Dispatch,* observing that the film had been criticized as merely another story of white people doing right by black people, emphasized that *Ghosts* was based on a true story. "Should the filmmakers have made the prosecutor black? And, in this case, the heroism is shared by Myrlie Evers, by a mostly black jury, and ultimately by the courageous Medgar Evers himself." Reiner "takes plenty of time to make it clear . . . how much sin Mississippi whites have to atone for, and how much racism remains in the Deep South."

Jake Matthews in *Newsday* began by acknowledging the director's "courage, or his chutzpa. Though Reiner has been identified with liberal causes since gaining fame in *All in the Family* as 'Meathead,' he's bound to be raked over the coals by the same outraged voices when Alan Parker's *Mississippi Burning* came out in 1988." The big difference, he argued, was that *Ghosts* had been faithful to the essential facts. Alec Baldwin gave a powerful performance, and if *Ghosts* strikes a patronizing note now and again, "it's telling a terrific story, and given the distance we have to travel to close the gap between the races in this country, its justice is exhilarating."

Jami Bernard in the New York *Daily News* wrote, "By juxtaposing the past with the present, director Rob Reiner also makes a convincing case for why history weighs so heavily on the conscience of a white, country-clubbish lawyer. Making history palatable for a movie audience is no easy task. Fact and fiction collide with their separate agendas. *Ghosts* works so well because it is balanced enough for sticklers while delivering a satisfying detective story." Desson Howe in *The Washington Post* praised the film for its "surprisingly satisfying amalgam of drama and history," and as "a stirring courtroom drama spiced up with colorful Mississippi characters drawn from real life."

"This story is too important to be forgotten," wrote Jeff Strickler in the Minneapolis *Star-Tribune*. Others agreed. Tim Appelo in the *Portland Oregonian* urged viewers "to forgive Reiner's aesthetic sins and concentrate on the sheer importance of the story he commendably chose to make—and no mogul was urging him to risk his name and neck on such an uncommercial project."

Eleanor Ringel in *The Atlanta Journal Constitution* observed that the movie was interesting because Bobby DeLaughter was not a "white-knight crusader." It took an insider to crack the Beckwith case: "The sons are the only ones who can try to pay for the sins of their fathers, and their fathers' fathers." Despite its flaws, *Ghosts* is important "because it tells a story that stays with you—a story too few of us knew."

Susan Waugh in the *St. Louis Riverside Times* acclaimed Colick's script for deftly weaving the events of the 1960s into the story of the 1990s. Until now Medgar Evers had gone uncounted. "*Ghosts of Mississippi* should change that forever. . . . Rob Reiner uses everything he learned about courtroom drama from making *A Few Good Men* to maximum effect. Like that film, *Ghosts* is a story about conscience. Bobby DeLaughter and Myrlie Evers participated fully in the making of this film: two who grew in conscience, courage, and trust."

The comments about the acting of Goldberg and Baldwin were mostly favorable, and the supporting roles by William H. Macy (Crisco), Susanna Thompson (Peggy), Bill Cobbs (Charles), and

Benny Bennett got high marks. The nearly unqualified praise from all sides was reserved for James Woods. Ebert cited his "shifty, squirming hatefulness"; *The Christian Science Monitor* called it an Oscar-caliber performance. *The New York Times* singled out Woods for his "wily malevolence," and *The Washington Post* called him "the villain of the year" who "creates moments of almost uncomfortable perfection." *The Wall Street Journal* complimented Woods for his prickly verve: "Beckwith dramatizes, more concisely than anything else in the movie, the changes that time has worked in the South."

Homer Best, the sheriff's lawyer and an avid reader, subscribes to *The New Yorker* and *The New Republic*, both of which have important film columns. "Neither ever mentioned *Ghosts,* even in passing," Best said. "That was significant to me, and especially disheartening because I so admire Stanley Kauffmann's reviews in *The New Republic.* I wanted him at least to write about it, whatever his judgment, because his judgment on films always matters to me."

—

In the midst of the response to the film, Charles Evers observed: "I wish someone would do a story about Medgar. But this wasn't a film about Medgar. It was about Byron, and how he smirked around the country, saying he killed my brother. The movie is about justice finally coming to the South when a white man is convicted of killing a black man. I don't know why people are upset about it."

Ghosts of Mississippi was going to have a tough time at the box office. For its first weekend of general release, January 3–5, it was ranked seventh in the Associated Press's top-grossing movies at five million dollars, behind *Michael, Jerry Maguire, Scream, 101 Dalmatians, One Fine Day,* and *Beavis and Butt-head.* The following weekend *Ghosts* dropped to twelfth with a $2.3 million gross, the third weekend to seventeenth with a $1.4 million gross. By the weekend of February 14–17, only six weeks after its general release, *Ghosts* had dropped completely off of the top-sixty charts. At the start of its third week, a stranger approached me in a restaurant and said he and his wife had just seen the film in a Jackson theater and liked it very much but thought it sad that they were among only a handful of people there. The movie would not even be shown in Oxford, home of William Faulkner and the University of Mississippi. "The hostile reviews have killed it," Ward Emling, the state film office director, said. "They never gave it a chance to stand on its own." It would be nominated for two Academy Awards: James Woods as Best Supporting Actor and Matthew W. Mungle and Deborah La Mia Denaver for Woods's makeup.

Burt DeLaughter was attending the Jackson theaters showing the movie to observe the reactions of the audiences. He had been hearing around him "Nigger lover," "Why did they bring all that up again?" and similar remarks. When a nearby woman whispered to the man with her that Bobby DeLaughter was nothing but a traitor, her companion replied, "Don't worry, we've already run him out of town."

Beyond the location problems and other matters, there was a noticeable backlash in portions of the state's white community that was absolutely racist in origin and extended to the box office, and this amounted to something of a boycott. I myself was severely disappointed by this "boycott mentality" in my state but not surprised, for the current outcroppings of the pre-1960s white mentality are smug and tangible and ultimately sorrowful and will be with us here forever, little matter what is ever said or done or whoever conceivably says or does it. When a friend of mine asked a well-heeled Jackson businesswoman if she had seen *Ghosts,* the woman replied: "My husband and I are sick of nigger movies." And the editor of the *Jackson Business Journal,* under the banner headline KEEPING THE "GHOSTS" IN THE CLOSET, trashed it solely on that basis (though in slightly cleaner language), then admitted he had not seen the movie, nor for that matter did he intend to.

Peggy DeLaughter was amazed at the way her life had evolved since the release of the movie. "I do not say *changed* because I've picked up and gone on doing those things I always do." One afternoon while she was making house rounds at the hospital in Jackson where she is a nursing coordinator, a hospital orderly, a black man in his midthirties whom she did not know, got into a conversation with her. He said he had recently seen a movie called *Ghosts of Mississippi*. Thinking that he was aware of her connection with the movie, she asked him how he liked it. He had many good things to say about it. "You know," he said, "there was a nurse in the movie who reminded me of you."

"Really," Peggy replied. "In what way?"

"Well," he said, "she was such a nice person and she had some mannerisms, you know, teasing and kidding around like you do." Then the connection dawned on him. "It was you! What is your last name? I just gotta hug you!" Peggy said she came away from that chat with a warm feeling of gratitude for Susanna Thompson's having portrayed her as such a nice person.

The movie was eliciting unusual responses in people. One of them was Kim Goldman, sister of Ron Goldman, who had been murdered in Los Angeles along with Nicole Brown Simpson. On Christmas night Kim Goldman and a friend sat in a darkened theater in L.A. watching *Ghosts*. "The similarities to our situation are amazing," she whispered to her friend, as quoted in Fred Goldman's book, *His Name Is Ron*. "His family—the trials—it's eerie to watch." At one point, when the camera panned in on Medgar's tombstone during the exhumation scene, Kim Goldman gasped: Medgar was born on July 2, Ron's birthday, and was killed on June 12, the date of her brother's death. Norma Fields, a highly respected journalist who had covered Mississippi in all its facets for the *Tupelo Daily Journal* for more than a quarter of a century, during which she was known for her no-holds-barred toughness, honesty, and directness, not to mention her knowledge of the state and its people, had recently retired to California and went to see *Ghosts* there with a friend. In letters back to Mississippi she said she had been "thunderstruck." She had never seen a movie that "stuck as closely to the facts as I knew them to be as a reporter there. Scene after scene I kept interfering with my friend's concentration by grabbing her arm and saying, 'Incredible—that's the exact way it happened!'" She got her other California friends to go see it also. "I've seen the movie twice more since then—a rarity since I normally avoid reruns—and each time it's become more and more impressive to me not only for its factual verities but its essential truths as well. This is a great and honest work, and you have to have covered Mississippi for many years to say so. Whoever says it's not a true work has real problems about things as they truly were. In other words, they simply don't *know*."

Other reactions among faceless moviegoers apparently ran deep, and in the days after *Ghosts* came out Bobby DeLaughter himself began to get complimentary letters from strangers, including children, most of them addressed merely to the District Attorney's Office, Jackson, Mississippi. Here is a small sampling:

From a woman in Traverse City, Minnesota: "I want to thank you for restoring my faith in humanity and for giving me hope that someday the world will be color-blind."

From a woman in California: "I am a full-time college student in Los Angeles. I recently viewed *Ghosts of Mississippi*, which is the actual reenactment of your pursuit for justice during the Medgar Evers trials during the 1980s. Although this film *attempts* to depict the true essence of your courage, character, and sincere determination, I am certain that it does not do you justice for the things you and your family have endured. As an African-American female planning to pursue a career in law, I would like to take this opportunity to express my extreme gratitude for your fight for justice. Great African-American leaders such as Medgar Evers paved the way for myself and all African-Americans. I now consider you, Mr. DeLaughter, to be one of my national heros of all time."

From a man in Albany, New York: "I just saw the movie *Ghosts of Mississippi*. I was 11 when Medgar Evers was killed. I really had no recollection of it. I want to express to you my sincerest admiration to you for what you accomplished for our country, and the South in particular, by diligently working on the Medgar Evers murder case. In many respects what you did for justice and equality took the same amount of courage as that displayed by the freedom riders, the protesters, and the civil rights marchers of the early 1960s. In many respects you took just as big a chance as Medgar Evers did. I guess it is true that 'it is never too late to do the right thing.' "

From a young man in Conroe, Texas: "I am writing to you on behalf of the movie *Ghosts of Mississippi*. . . . I know you're not Alec Baldwin, and I know that not everything in the movie was verbatim. It was the spirit of bravery in your character that made me write this letter. . . . Maybe hope is lost for those from the past, but not for my generation or those of the future. I sincerely hope that others are as inspired as I am by this movie. You are truly a light at the end of the dark tunnel we call racism. You acted 'boldly' sir. In time, I hope we as a country can too."

From a seventh-grade civics teacher in Leawood, Kansas, who took fifty of her students to see the film, each of whom wrote him a letter: "I felt that the movie was very powerful. This movie had such a powerful impact on my students. We have spent days studying the trial and my students are eager to learn more."

From a woman in Santa Monica, California: "My daughters (ages 11 and 12) and I saw the *Ghosts of Mississippi* film last night. I wish that words could adequately explain what that movie meant to us. For me, as an adult who was born in 1951 in Ohio and educated there, the message was different from the message received by my children (who were born in Los Angeles in 1984 and 1985). My children have not been able to stop talking about the movie. . . .

"You might be interested in knowing that we saw the film in

Santa Monica (which is where we live and where the O. J. Simpson trial is being held; with regard to the O. J. Simpson case, CNN routinely describes Santa Monica as an upscale community that is integrated, but is 65–70% 'white'). The audience in the movie theater last night was typical of our community. At the end of the movie, when the verdict was announced, the entire theater stood and applauded."

From a twelve-year-old seventh-grade girl in Jackson: "On Saturday I saw *Ghosts of Mississippi*! Before the movie I didn't know what I was getting myself into. Your part of the movie inspired me so greatly I was *speechless*. You are a truly brave man of Mississippi, or at least in my book! To stand up for what you believed and to draw the line even if your family wasn't with you all of the time, is a big thing to do. To stand up and show what you believe is a true leader. Thank you! Thank you!"

Bobby was getting telephone calls from black people in Jackson. One in particular from a woman moved him deeply. Her husband was the manager of a prominent chain grocery store and had been hearing his employees talking about how good *Ghosts of Mississippi* was. The couple had just seen it. The woman went on and on over the telephone about how great she thought the film was and of the importance of Bobby's prosecution. As a black raised in the South she was so touched, she said, she wanted to thank Bobby personally, and all her friends felt the same way. Then, later that afternoon, the woman arrived unannounced at the D.A.'s office with her three little boys to meet Bobby. She said she wanted her sons to be able to say in later years that they had shaken his hand. After they left, she telephoned yet again to invite the DeLaughters to her family's house for dinner the next night, where the movie and the call were further discussed. Bobby gave them a *Ghosts* movie poster with the inscription, "To Joe, Renita, and the boys, our new friends and Mississippians."

—

The most central and complicated issue surrounding *Ghosts of Mississippi* was whether it was nothing more than a white man's fantasy that should never have been made. The movie evoked serious questions regarding the quality of heroism, and what we *make* of heroism in the contemporary popular culture. Those who admired the movie credited it with increasing its viewers' awareness of true American heroes: Medgar Evers, who gave his life for civilized values; Myrlie Evers, who suffered and did not give up; and Bobby DeLaughter—"one man can make a difference." Many of the harshest critics and skeptical viewers were bothered because they saw the hero as Bobby and distrusted his white heroism for being too good, too decent, too saintly, too unreal.

Very shortly after the two critical articles by Kenneth Turan and Sean Mitchell in the *Los Angeles Times* questioned *Ghosts* for focusing on a heroic white person getting his eyes opened about his and society's racism, the *Times* ran a conspicuous piece by Michael Levin. This article made no reference to *Ghosts* but instead specifically addressed itself to the movie *The People vs. Larry Flynt:* "I miss decency. I miss the time in our culture when movies were about heroes. . . . Isn't there anyone else they could make a movie about? Someone out there displaying some courage, someone to emulate?" And in a letter to the editor in the *Times* after its critical pieces, the actor Wayne Rogers, well known for his role in the *M*A*S*H* television series, who in *Ghosts* played the Southern white liberal lawyer Morris Dees, wrote:

> Mitchell says that Reiner's film "paints only part of the picture" in choosing to focus on the story of the white assistant district attorney in Jackson, Mississippi, Bobby DeLaughter, who "went the final mile" to win a conviction against Medgar Evers' killer, Byron De La Beckwith. . . .
> Yes, it is discouraging that the story of Evers, his brave life and

tragic death and enduring legacy, has not been told as the subject of its own film. That notwithstanding, it would appear that Turan's opinion ("even if the facts skew toward accurate, the nuances in *Ghosts of Mississippi* are all wrong") is founded in some personal argument that facts should be used to make a different film, one whose "nuances" agree with his vision. To accuse Hollywood—and, by implication, *Ghosts*—of not telling the truth or "anything close to it" is a distortion of the facts. And to review the film you wanted it to be instead of the film that was made is to miss the point. . . .

Of course, the march to racial equality was led primarily by blacks, but why obliterate the history of the whites who encouraged and even joined in the trek? The view of the filmmakers that your writers seem to have missed is not the celebration of Medgar Evers' life and the idealization of him after his death but that in spite of the horrible injustices inflicted on blacks by a white-dominated community, progress has been made.

White people who had not been willing previously to stand against the tide were doing so, and, in this case, had prevailed. That was the point of the film.

Matters having to do with *heroes*—these are admittedly questions rather than answers. Why do we so often suspect them and not accept them? We *say* we want heroes, but what do we really want? Why do we distrust someone who is "too good"—*disbelieve*, in fact, his heroic qualities? Since this was about redemption and the righting of a grievous wrong, why are these not honorable themes? Should the other perspective negate the honor and legitimacy of such things? Can a white man do a legitimate movie with a black man as its hero? Among those who could not accept a white hero although he had real heroic qualities, why does Bobby's fortitude negate the heroism of Medgar and Myrlie? Did he not add to the *recognition* of their heroism? If he had been black with the same saintly qualities, would we have accepted the saintliness? Why does producing a work with a white hero mean that one cannot passionately believe in the heroism of black Americans? Does a work about the personal struggles of a white man mean, automatically and by the same token, that one must deny the struggle and rage and pain and bravery of black people?*

I am no arbiter on such matters, but I do know that in the years to come the country will need all the heroes and heroines it can get, no matter what their color.

———

I will not easily forget how eager and committed everyone was during the making of *Ghosts*. This feeling seemed to have gone beyond the call of Hollywood duty. For Rob Reiner, James Woods observed, the film was "a sacred mission. He maintained the tidal wave of passion that he incited every day." I had watched the director during this project. I had seldom seen someone so invested in something. Beneath his garrulous ebullience lay a steadfast talent, a generous heart, and a profound regard for his fellow human beings. He turned out to be one of the best people I ever knew.

On the last day of shooting Woods's driver had asked, "Jimmy, is this the only picture you've ever worked on where not one unkind word was said by anyone for the entire duration?" And Woods said, "Yes, it was." This sentiment had been expressed almost universally on the set and was patently no public relations gambit; it was too genuine and spontaneous for that. Susanna Thompson had spoken of "the *heart* that went into this movie, the feeling of community, the wonderful people." An individual in an important nonacting, nonexecutive position had said to me: "I've worked on about thirty-five movies. I'm freelance. On many of them I've encountered some of the most uncivil people I've ever known in my life. Maybe it's the big-money aspect of this business. I've never worked with

---

* In this period a black writer, Gene Cartwright, was being castigated by black talk show hosts and bookstore owners because the characters in his first novel, *I Never Played Catch with My Father*, were white people. The author complained that black bookstores would have nothing to do with him.

such *good* people as I have on this movie. So much of this is Reiner. And they all believe in what they're doing." The roundly critical reception of *Ghosts* would be an emotional blow to many.

Six months or so after the release of the film, Rob Reiner reflected on it: "I've long felt the only way you can judge the artistic value of a film, or for that matter any artistic endeavor," he mused to me, "is through the passage of time. Contemporaneous criticism is by nature subject to the social and political conventional wisdom of the times. The preponderance of negative criticism of *Ghosts of Mississippi* focused on the notion that to make a film that had civil rights and race relations as a backdrop, one shouldn't have a white protagonist. If that's indeed something to be concerned with, then the criticism should have gone further to advocate not making the film at all. The film is not the story of the civil rights movement, nor is it the Medgar Evers story, both valid subjects about which to make movies. Rather, it's about the reinvestigation and reprosecution of Byron De La Beckwith. And Bobby DeLaughter, the white assistant D.A., was the central figure in that reinvestigation and reprosecution.

"We're living in racially divisive times, and too often we can be drowned in political correctness," he said. "I believe racial harmony between blacks and whites can be achieved only through the continued efforts of blacks and whites. I hope that time will view *Ghosts* as one of those efforts. I'm proud of this movie."

And Lewis Colick: "After all is said and done, this was one of the most enriching experiences I've ever had as a human being and as a writer." He cited the deep friendships he made, especially with the DeLaughters. "Certain elements didn't approve of the movie, but I've heard from moviegoers all over the country, who've told me they were moved, perhaps even changed by it. Most gratifying of all was the positive response of the Evers children, Van, Darrell, and Reena. Despite the presumptuous and dangerous implication of some critics that all self-respecting black people should be offended by this film, the Evers children embraced it. They love Bobby DeLaughter and consider him a hero for incarcerating the man who murdered their father. They are the only people whose opinion ever really meant a damn to me. *Ghosts of Mississippi* is not a perfect film, but its heart is in the right place, and after thirty years, people once again know who Medgar Evers was. I'll always be proud to have been a part of that.

"Though we didn't always agree, Rob's fine heart, commitment to excellence, and abundant talent are evident throughout the picture. It was a pleasure to work with him."

Months later Alec Baldwin also pondered the meaning of the film to him as an actor and a person, and its aftermath. "When Rob approached me with this opportunity," he recalled to me, "I immediately signed on. I knew Rob was the ideal director to tell such a story because of his moviemaking skills and his political courage. As we moved toward shooting, the cast and other creative elements who joined on assured me that we'd make a memorable film.

"The actual shooting of the picture was a joy," he said. "I think few opportunities to tell the story in the best possible way got by us. When we were done, Bobby and Peggy had become my friends. At the New York premiere, I responded in a way I've rarely, if ever, felt from watching one of my own pictures. I believed we'd done a good job. The subsequent reaction from the mainstream media, and particularly the New York–L.A. axis, puzzled me. It seemed we were handed the bill for all of the other civil-rights-oriented films that featured a white protagonist. *Cry Freedom* with Kevin Kline, *A World Apart* with Barbara Hershey, and *Mississippi Burning* all had offended many people's sensibilities as to what a civil rights drama should be.

"On top of that, some prominent black figures in our society either withheld their support or bashed us outright, as did Spike Lee. It seems many black political leaders today shudder at the notion that real progress in the civil rights movement, or what's left of it, might depend on the role played by whites. They believe maybe that real progress shouldn't hold out for whites, any whites, to do the right thing, and I guess one can't argue with that. Spike

Lee, on the other hand, is a Hollywood filmmaker and therefore a businessman. As such, making money is his primary concern. As the sine qua non of black anger toward whites in the culture today, Lee had no choice but to condemn the film. Racial harmony would put Lee out of a job."

In the days after *Ghosts'* release Reiner addressed the National Governors' Conference in Washington, D.C., on the early human brain, teenage pregnancy, and drug abuse among the young, advocating major resources to be allocated to problems of childhood. He directed for ABC-TV a prime-time special on brain development, which featured Hillary and Bill Clinton, Colin Powell, Tom Hanks, Robin Williams, Billy Crystal, Oprah Winfrey, Charlton Heston, Roseanne, Carl Reiner, Mel Brooks, and others, and he succeeded in getting the Clintons to host a Washington summit on early childhood development, "to raise awareness about how the first three years critically impact the way a child later deals with society." Shortly after that, on a CBS television special he was presented with a People's Choice tribute, selected by voters around the country.

At the Academy Award ceremonies in March 1997, James Woods lost the Oscar for Best Supporting Actor to Cuba Gooding, Jr., in *Jerry Maguire*. Mungle and Denaver lost the Oscar for Makeup to Rick Baker and David Leroy for *The Nutty Professor*. John Seale, director of photography for *Ghosts*, won the Oscar in that category for his work on *The English Patient*, a wonderful film that also took Best Picture.

By mid-March *Ghosts* was ranked twenty-ninth in accumulated United States box-office grosses among 1997 films still playing in theaters; the figure was $13 million. This stood in contrast with the top earners, the reissues of the *Star Wars* trilogy, which had earned over $1 billion. *Jerry Maguire* was fourth at $141 million, and *101 Dalmations* fifth at $134 million. *That Darn Cat*, the film just above *Ghosts* in twenty-eighth place, had outgrossed it by nearly $3.5 million. *Ghosts* was destined to lose substantial millions. By the summer of 1997 John Grisham's *A Time to Kill* had grossed $109 million in the United States and was still making money.

—

What, then, is the legacy left? Was it worth it? Had it mattered at all? And what is still here in the nation after this movie leaves the screen?

I became involved in this movie because I believed the story said something important about the possibilities of people, their dark side and their hopeful side. I believed that the country needed this message and that it was ready-made for Hollywood—a gift to Hollywood from Mississippi. A lover of movies since earliest childhood, I became engrossed in learning about how movies are made, the inner workings of which I knew little and probably will never come remotely close to again. And it was fun. Everything was going along well as an accolade to moviemaking: a good and meaningful story, good actors, good food, good friendship and camaraderie. There was nothing remotely cynical or sinister here about key decisions that led to certain unforeseen results. I had expected Hollywood to instruct me about *Hollywood,* its mores and fantasies and illusions. I had not expected Hollywood to teach me something about my own state and country and its citizens. Yet in the whole experience and its aftermath, that is what happened—and it somehow had to do, quite simply, with the depths to which things go, with the shadow behind the act, with the *elusiveness* of our reluctant civilization, and that everything in it pertains to race. I knew this beforehand but neglected its complete dimensions. *Ghosts of Mississippi* —its making and its reception—moved me to stark realizations.

The comments of many, including the unsolicited and anonymous responses to Bobby, would suggest that numbers of national viewers who knew little or nothing of Medgar Evers did come away with a feeling for the importance of him and his life and example, for the perseverance and suffering of his widow and children, for what one man with the help of two tough cops came to do to

achieve justice, and for what the long-postponed guilty verdict signified in the most tortured state of the Great Republic. My own in-
tuition, rightly or wrongly, is that "average" audiences cared for the
film much more than the critical reception might suggest. At its
best the movie was uplifting and educational; and in the long run
that is more significant than Academy Awards. Most people nowa-
days see movies through video rentals or as reruns on television, so
there would be a big and uncommitted audience waiting, including
children, and as Whoopi Goldberg suggested, the children would
be the most important of all. I personally consider *Ghosts* a responsible work, a deeply contemporary one that, as with a number
of fine movies caught over time in the passions, snares, and toils of
their own years, will likely outlive those conflicts and gradually settle into the American consciousness, for a movie, as a book, lives
or dies on its inherent life-giving truth and passion. *Ghosts of Mississippi,* I believe, will endure.

I may be wrong, of course, but of one thing I am sure: It is the
ghost of Medgar Evers that reigns over this tale. His ghost reigns
over the collective memory of the 1950s and 1960s. It reigns over
everything that has happened in the state of Mississippi since
1963, having planted the seeds from which emerged the changing
perspectives of its beleaguered modern-day society. It reigns over
his widow and children, having given meaning to their lives and
strengthening their assurance and resolve to reopen the case. It
reigns over his brother Charles, who reveres his memory. It reigns
over Bobby DeLaughter, whose diligence culminated in justice,
and who in his opening argument in the 1994 trial called Medgar's
ghost "the focal point" of everything Beckwith and others like him
hated. It reigns over the black and white jurors in the 1994 trial. It
reigns over the assassin himself, who boasted once too often of
having murdered him, languishing now in his lifetime cell. It
reigns over the producer Zollo and the director Reiner, who would
never have made the movie were it not for his ghost. It reigns over
the screenwriter Colick and the actors Baldwin, Goldberg, and
Woods, all drawn to the movie because of it. It reigns over Charlie

Harrington of Cape Cod, who had his location problems and learned something from them. It reigns over the making of the movie itself, because even though he was not a major part of it, his ghost resides indwellingly in its heart, spirit, and soul. And, finally, it reigns irrevocably over the nation today, giving Americans a reason to be less despondent and more reason to be hopeful.

—

March 1997 saw the death of the old-guard Democrat who resoundingly defeated Bobby DeLaughter for the judgeship of the appellate court after the Beckwith trial. The vacancy would be filled by gubernatorial appointment. Matt Friedman, conservative columnist for the *Clarion-Ledger,* wrote that "naming DeLaughter, the man touted for finally putting the murderer of Medgar Evers behind bars and who was subsequently celebrated in the movie *Ghosts of Mississippi,* would make for some great poetry for this state." Bobby's selection "would serve to rub Hollywood's nose in the misguided notion that he is destined to forever endure persecution in this state for prosecuting Byron De La Beckwith." A few days later Governor Kirk Fordice appointed his own staff attorney, a personage who had represented him in his blustery political and court warfares. The governor said he hoped to shape a more conservative judiciary. "This may be one of the most important things we have done as governor," Fordice declared.

That June, Jackson elected its first black mayor in history, Harvey Johnson, Jr., an urban planner, former state tax commissioner, and former college professor whose reasoned analyses of both local and state problems had characterized his campaign. With considerable white support he defeated a field of five others in the Democratic primary without a runoff, including the incumbent mayor of eight years, Kane Ditto, a highly qualified and respected white progressive, and then the Republican nominee in the general election with a 70 percent majority. The transfer of power was accomplished with remarkable friendliness on both sides. The

Clarion-Ledger covered Johnson's July inauguration under the page-one banner WITH OATH, NEW ERA LAUNCHED. I was there, across the street from the courthouse where DeLay was finally convicted, with blacks and whites, including many young people of both races, sweltering under the hot sun. The vista reminded me a little of the interracial scene outside the courthouse just over three years before when the guilty verdict was announced, and the "stadium wave" effect, as Bobby DeLaughter described it, that it had then on the outside throngs. Before this larger biracial audience at city hall Johnson spoke particularly of the legacy of Medgar Evers, and of the other "long-distance runners, the brave souls who spilled their blood for equality under the law. Lord, just think how far we've come. I don't ever want to go back." Amos Brown, the black San Francisco supervisor who was a guest for the occasion, declared, "We are the beneficiaries of Medgar Evers."

Bill Minor, the longtime journalist covering the inaugural, was awash in memories, recalling as he did the countless instances in the 1960s when this antebellum city hall of Jackson was an unshakable bastion of racial supremacy. His most vivid memory was of the day a group of respected black clergymen came here with hats in hand to ask Mayor Allen Thompson for such concessions as black school crossing guards, a black on the city police force, and the creation of biracial committees. "The affable Thompson," Bill Minor remembered, "performed like a plantation squire, patronizing the ministers as though they were his faithful sharecroppers, listening to their niggling complaints. Then with a big smile, he sent them away empty-handed. However, before they left, the ministers, without recrimination, warned Thompson that the mood of the black community had reached the point that there would likely be demonstrations if the city made no concessions." The date was May 27, 1963. A day or so later, for the first time, blacks took to the streets on behalf of voting rights, lunch-counter sit-ins, and department store boycotts. Hundreds of them, including many black schoolchildren, were arrested and hauled away in city garbage trucks to stockades on the state fairgrounds. Less than two weeks later Medgar was murdered.

In a front-page *Clarion-Ledger* column Orley Hood noted that this mayor's inaugural was thirty-four years and twenty-five days after Medgar was "shot in the back in the dark of the night." He wrote:

> The first scene of Rob Reiner's movie *Ghosts of Mississippi* was shot on the courthouse square in Woodville, a depiction of a Theodore Bilbo speech decades ago that actually took place in Decatur. The scene ended up on the cutting room floor, but older Mississippians can picture it in their minds. Charles Evers and his little brother Medgar were children then, the only dark faces in the crowd, shaded by tall trees and warmed by fiery rhetoric. If you don't watch out, said Bilbo, pointing at the kids, if you don't stand firm, then one day you might find these little boys running things.
>
> On Monday morning, a most historic day for Jackson and Mississippi, the background was strikingly similar, the old majestic white-columned government building. The spectators fanning themselves beneath the tall trees. Folks in suits and overalls, kids in their shorts, women in their shimmering summer dresses, all gathered to listen. Except this time it was Harvey Johnson, not Theodore Bilbo, who was doing the talking. . . . This time the message was togetherness, not separation; participation, not exclusion; love, not war.

EPILOGUE

On a wintry January forenoon I took a long drive alone. On this day I had just learned that my friend James Dickey, the poet, had died; another, younger friend had just been inaugurated president of the United States for a second time. I listened to his inaugural speech on the car radio. He was addressing himself to racial reconciliation in America.

Something compelled me to drive out to Medgar's old street in Jackson. I wanted to inspect the state of the imposing live oak tree that the motion-picture people had dug up from the front lawn of the Evers house and transplanted to an open vicinity down the way, near the intended site of the parking lot for the Medgar Evers Museum. The tree, I was happy to note, was flourishing.

I drove north, toward the Delta. I wished to return to the cotton fields out from Satartia where they had constructed the gas station across from the little black church half a year before, the Gas and God set Shoeless Jack Stevens and the other set dressers had called it, built for the scene in which Bobby, Crisco, and Benny had stopped to fill up and to allow Bobby to telephone Myrlie

Evers in Oregon. I had the urge to see if anything at all, after the enthusiastic contrivance and activity of that day, remained there of Hollywood.

It was bitterly cold, so cold that small shards of ice were floating in the Yazoo River. Under the petulant skies in the seared fields the cotton stubble lay intractably somber and gray. Both Jim Dickey and Bill Clinton had always been intrigued by this relentless Delta land, by the powerful and impenetrable sway it always holds on you. Farther on, black kids with socks on their hands against the cold were shooting baskets. Not far from here was a large plantation owned by the father of a comrade of mine, and when we were boys one long-ago summer the father had gotten us to pick cotton for a day, bending low with our burlap bags to our backs, scratching our fingers on the prickly stuff under the devastating August sun. Negro people of all ages, including many children, surrounded us there. At the end of our exertions, near dusk, we weighed in and found we had earned about $1.25 apiece. I believe to this day my friend's father wished to provide us a lesson: Behave yourselves and make good grades, because labor is exceedingly hard.

Here, in the field off to the right of this road, had been the Untitled Mississippi Project base camp with its colorful commissary tent, trailers, and technicians' trucks, the vista all empty and quiet now. As I approached the locale of the set I noticed a funeral was in progress in the cemetery next to the church, and I parked the car an honorable distance away. The pallbearers were carrying the coffin across an incline. I waited a long time, until one by one the hearse and cars and pickup trucks drove away. Then I went down there. In the cemetery two grave diggers were shoveling dirt onto the grave, their shovels struggling hard against the icy pile of earth, in such contrast to that movie day when it was so hot the dirt had seemed like cement.

The service station and its trappings had vanished altogether. Even the fabricated driveway had faded into the encompassing land. It was as if Hollywood had never set foot here at all, neither palpable memory nor dream to show for it, and the eternal Delta earth was all that really mattered. Everything representative of the 90210 zip code was about as far away from here as any place could be. I took a long stroll around the spot where the set had been, and then on the lawn of the church itself, and near the base of an old chinaberry tree I discovered a solitary granola-bar wrapper, disintegrated and half hidden in the soil, the only item left of Hollywood to commemorate this terrain, that and the sixty seconds or so that were appearing on a screen.

I remembered the old black man at the church that day: his talk of this earth, of its being his too, and of his progeny dwelling now in Detroit and Chicago and Gary.

What is it that would still be here after Hollywood departed? Black and white people trying to live together on this common soil. Heroes and villains. Suffering and pain. Human history and memory.

I gazed about me on this solitary return, the bereft sweep of the fields and the meandering Yazoo at the farthest distance and the gaunt ashen remnants of the primeval Delta forests beyond. "The ruined woods we used to know," Faulkner wrote, in a metaphor for the human beings who once inhabited them, "don't cry for retribution. The men who have destroyed it will accomplish its revenge." Storm clouds were gathering, and I felt a few drops of rain. The only sound from all around me was the grave diggers' shovels at the church. I recalled not only my Faulkner, but my Tennyson:

> *The woods decay, the woods decay and fall,*
> *The vapors weep their burthens to the ground,*
> *Man comes and tills the field and lies beneath,*
> *And after many a summer dies the swan.*

Medgar Evers had known this ground in his deepest being, how crucified it had been by slavery, peonage, and affliction, how tragic and ineluctable and abiding it was. He had fought with all he had in him against the cruelties of this land, yet a part of him had passionately loved it. It was his final and supreme contradiction, the contradiction that made him real. This was *his* land, and it was mine also. His ghost still envelops this land, too, just as it does all the people and places and happenings in this story—including, of course, the man who wrote it.

ACKNOWLEDGMENTS

I am grateful to JoAnne Prichard, Claudette Murphree, Anne Stascavage, David Rae Morris, Ruth Tuttle Williams, and Jack Bales for their indispensable help on this book. Thanks also to Curtis Wilkie of *The Boston Globe* and to the following writers for the Jackson *Clarion-Ledger:* Jerry Mitchell, Orley Hood, John Webb, Billy Watkins, Grace Simmons Fisher, and Sherry Lucas. Ward Emling, director of the Mississippi film office, Homer Best of the Hinds County Sheriff's Department, and Clarence Hunter of the Tougaloo College Library provided valuable insights, as did the writings of Myrlie Evers, Charles Evers, Adam Nossiter, Maryanne Vollers, and Reed Massengill. All the principals in my narrative, both the "real" people of the true story and the movie ones, were generous with their assistance. Finally, my warm gratitude as always to my friend and agent, Theron Raines, and to my comrade and editor at Random House, Bob Loomis.

W.M.
November 1997
Jackson, Mississippi

A MEDGAR EVERS READING LIST

Evers, Charles. *Evers*. New York: World Publishing Company, 1971.

———. *Have No Fear: The Charles Evers Story*. New York: John Wiley and Sons, 1996.

Evers, Myrlie. *For Us, the Living*. Jackson: University Press of Mississippi, 1994.

Massengill, Reed. *Portrait of a Racist*. New York: St. Martin's Press, 1994.

Nossiter, Adam. *Of Long Memory: Mississippi and the Murder of Medgar Evers*. New York: Addison-Wesley, 1994.

Vollers, Maryanne. *Ghosts of Mississippi: The Murder of Medgar Evers, the Trials of Byron De La Beckwith and the Haunting of the New South*. New York: Little, Brown, 1995.

In addition:

For Us, the Living: The Medgar Evers Story was a 1983 Public Broadcasting System (PBS) American Playhouse production, which is available in some video-rental stores and libraries.

Castle Rock Entertainment, Inc., has produced an educational civil rights CD-ROM for schools on *Ghosts of Mississippi* and Medgar Evers. Write Castle Rock Entertainment, 335 North Maple Drive, Beverly Hills, California, 90210.

INDEX

ABOUT THE AUTHOR

WILLIE MORRIS's mastery at melding autobiography and significant history has been demonstrated in *North Toward Home, New York Days,* and *The Courting of Marcus Dupree.* In 1996, he was the recipient of the Richard Wright Medal for Literary Excellence. He has written sixteen books, including two novels and the memorable *My Dog Skip.* He lives in Jackson, Mississippi.

ABOUT THE TYPE

This book was set in Fairfield, the first typeface from the hand of the distinguished American artist and engraver Rudolph Ruzicka (1883–1978). Rudolph Ruzicka was born in Bohemia and came to America in 1894. He set up his own shop, devoted to wood engraving and printing, in New York in 1913 after a varied career working as a wood engraver, in photoengraving and banknote printing plants, and as an art director and freelance artist. He designed and illustrated many books, and was the creator of a considerable list of individual prints—wood engravings, line engravings on copper, and aquatints.